Kaplan Publishing are constantly finding new ways to make a difference to your studies and our exciting online resources really do offer something different to students looking for exam success.

This book comes with free MyKaplan online resources so that you can study anytime, anywhere. This free online resource is not sold separately and is included in the price of the book.

Having purchased this book, you have access to the following online study materials:

CONTENT	ACCA (including FFA,FAB,FMA)		FIA (excluding FFA,FAB,FMA)	
	Text	Kit	Text	Kit
Electronic version of the book	✓			
Check Your Understanding Test with instant answers	✓			
Material updates	✓			
Latest official ACCA exam questions*				
Extra question assistance using the signpost icon**		✓		
Timed questions with an online tutor debrief using clock icon***		✓		
Interim assessment including questions and answers	✓		✓	
Technical answers	✓	✓	✓	✓

*   Excludes F1, F2, F3, F4, FAB, FMA and FFA; for all other papers includes a selection of questions, as released by ACCA
**   For ACCA P1-P7 only
*** Excludes F1, F2, F3, F4, FAB, FMA and FFA

How to access your online resources

Kaplan Financial students will already have a MyKaplan account and these extra resources will be available to you online. You do not need to register again, as this process was completed when you enrolled. If you are having problems accessing online materials, please ask your course administrator.

If you are not studying with Kaplan and did not purchase your book via a Kaplan website, to unlock your extra online resources please go to www.mykaplan.co.uk/addabook (even if you have set up an account and registered books previously). You will then need to enter the ISBN number (on the title page and back cover) and the unique pass key number contained in the scratch panel below to gain access.

You will also be required to enter additional information during this process to set up or confirm your account details.

If you purchased through Kaplan Flexible Learning or via the Kaplan Publishing website you will automatically receive an e-mail invitation to MyKaplan. Please register your details using this email to gain access to your content. If you do not receive the e-mail or book content, please contact Kaplan Publishing.

Your Code and Information

This code can only be used once for the registration of one book online. This registration and your online content will expire when the final sittings for the examinations covered by this book have taken place. Please allow one hour from the time you submit your book details for us to process your request.

Please scratch the film to access your MyKaplan code.

Please be aware that this code is case-sensitive and you wi
within the passcode, but not when entering the ISBN. For f
please visit www.MyKaplan.co.uk

ACCA

Applied Skills

Corporate and Business Law (LW ENG)

Study Text

British library cataloguing-in-publication data

A catalogue record for this book is available from the British Library.

Published by:

Kaplan Publishing UK
Unit 2 The Business Centre
Molly Millars Lane
Wokingham
Berkshire
RG41 2QZ

ISBN 978-1-78740-393-2

Acknowledgements

These materials are reviewed by the ACCA examining team. The objective of the review is to ensure that the material properly covers the syllabus and study guide outcomes, used by the examining team in setting the exams, in the appropriate breadth and depth. The review does not ensure that every eventuality, combination or application of examinable topics is addressed by the ACCA Approved Content. Nor does the review comprise a detailed technical check of the content as the Approved Content Provider has its own quality assurance processes in place in this respect.

We are grateful to the Association of Chartered Certified Accountants and the Chartered Institute of Management Accountants for permission to reproduce past examination questions. The answers have been prepared by Kaplan Publishing.

Contents

Introduction

How to use the Materials

These Kaplan Publishing learning materials have been carefully designed to make your learning experience as easy as possible and to give you the best chances of success in your examinations.

The product range contains a number of features to help you in the study process. They include:

1   Detailed study guide and syllabus objectives

2   Description of the examination

3   Study skills and revision guidance

4   Study text

5   Question practice

The sections on the study guide, the syllabus objectives, the examination and study skills should all be read before you commence your studies. They are designed to familiarise you with the nature and content of the examination and give you tips on how to best to approach your learning.

The **study text** comprises the main learning materials and gives guidance as to the importance of topics and where other related resources can be found. Each chapter includes:

- The **learning objectives** contained in each chapter, which have been carefully mapped to the examining body's own syllabus learning objectives or outcomes. You should use these to check you have a clear understanding of all the topics on which you might be assessed in the examination.

- The **chapter diagram** provides a visual reference for the content in the chapter, giving an overview of the topics and how they link together.

- The **content** for each topic area commences with a brief explanation or definition to put the topic into context before covering the topic in detail. You should follow your studying of the content with a review of the illustration/s. These are worked examples which will help you to understand better how to apply the content for the topic.

- **Test your understanding** sections provide an opportunity to assess your understanding of the key topics by applying what you have learned to short questions. Answers can be found at the back of each chapter.

- **Summary diagrams** complete each chapter to show the important links between topics and the overall content of the paper. These diagrams should be used to check that you have covered and understood the core topics before moving on.

- **Question practice** is provided at the back of each text.

Quality and accuracy are of the utmost importance to us so if you spot an error in any of our products, please send an email to mykaplanreporting@kaplan.com with full details, or follow the link to the feedback form in MyKaplan.

Our Quality Co-ordinator will work with our technical team to verify the error and take action to ensure it is corrected in future editions.

Icon Explanations

 Definition – Key definitions that you will need to learn from the core content.

 Supplementary reading – These sections will help to provide a deeper understanding of core areas. The supplementary reading is **NOT** optional reading. It is vital to provide you with the breadth of knowledge you will need to address the wide range of topics within your syllabus that could feature in an exam question. **Reference to this text is vital when self studying.**

 Test your understanding – Exercises for you to complete to ensure that you have understood the topics just learned.

 Illustration – Worked examples help you understand the core content better.

On-line subscribers

Our on-line resources are designed to increase the flexibility of your learning materials and provide you with immediate feedback on how your studies are progressing.

If you are subscribed to our on-line resources you will find:

1   On-line referenceware: reproduces your Study Text on-line, giving you anytime, anywhere access.

2   On-line testing: provides you with additional on-line objective testing so you can practice what you have learned further.

3   On-line performance management: immediate access to your on-line testing results. Review your performance by key topics and chart your achievement through the course relative to your peer group.

Ask your local customer services staff if you are not already a subscriber and wish to join.

ACCA Support

For additional support with your studies please also refer to the ACCA Global website.

Study skills and revision guidance

This section aims to give guidance on how to study for your ACCA exams and to give ideas on how to improve your existing study techniques.

Preparing to study

Set your objectives

Before starting to study decide what you want to achieve – the type of pass you wish to obtain. This will decide the level of commitment and time you need to dedicate to your studies.

Devise a study plan

Determine which times of the week you will study.

Split these times into sessions of at least one hour for study of new material. Any shorter periods could be used for revision or practice.

Put the times you plan to study onto a study plan for the weeks from now until the exam and set yourself targets for each period of study – in your sessions make sure you cover the course, course assignments and revision.

If you are studying for more than one paper at a time, try to vary your subjects as this can help you to keep interested and see subjects as part of wider knowledge.

When working through your course, compare your progress with your plan and, if necessary, re-plan your work (perhaps including extra sessions) or, if you are ahead, do some extra revision/practice questions.

Effective studying

Active reading

You are not expected to learn the text by rote, rather, you must understand what you are reading and be able to use it to pass the exam and develop good practice. A good technique to use is SQ3Rs – Survey, Question, Read, Recall, Review:

1   **Survey the chapter** – look at the headings and read the introduction, summary and objectives, so as to get an overview of what the chapter deals with.

2   **Question** – whilst undertaking the survey, ask yourself the questions that you hope the chapter will answer for you.

3   **Read** through the chapter thoroughly, answering the questions and making sure you can meet the objectives. Attempt the exercises and activities in the text, and work through all the examples.

4   **Recall** – at the end of each section and at the end of the chapter, try to recall the main ideas of the section/chapter without referring to the text. This is best done after a short break of a couple of minutes after the reading stage.

5   **Review** – check that your recall notes are correct.

You may also find it helpful to re-read the chapter to try to see the topic(s) it deals with as a whole.

Note-taking

Taking notes is a useful way of learning, but do not simply copy out the text. The notes must:

- be in your own words
- be concise
- cover the key points
- be well-organised
- be modified as you study further chapters in this text or in related ones.

Trying to summarise a chapter without referring to the text can be a useful way of determining which areas you know and which you don't.

Three ways of taking notes:

Summarise the key points of a chapter.

Make linear notes – a list of headings, divided up with subheadings listing the key points. If you use linear notes, you can use different colours to highlight key points and keep topic areas together. Use plenty of space to make your notes easy to use.

Try a diagrammatic form – the most common of which is a mind-map. To make a mind-map, put the main heading in the centre of the paper and put a circle around it. Then draw short lines radiating from this to the main sub-headings, which again have circles around them. Then continue the process from the sub-headings to sub-sub-headings, advantages, disadvantages, etc.

Highlighting and underlining

You may find it useful to underline or highlight key points in your study text – but do be selective. You may also wish to make notes in the margins.

Revision

The best approach to revision is to revise the course as you work through it. Also try to leave four to six weeks before the exam for final revision. Make sure you cover the whole syllabus and pay special attention to those areas where your knowledge is weak. Here are some recommendations:

Read through the text and your notes again and condense your notes into key phrases. It may help to put key revision points onto index cards to look at when you have a few minutes to spare.

Review any assignments you have completed and look at where you lost marks – put more work into those areas where you were weak.

Practise exam standard questions under timed conditions. If you are short of time, list the points that you would cover in your answer and then read the model answer, but do try to complete at least a few questions under exam conditions.

Also practise producing answer plans and comparing them to the model answer.

If you are stuck on a topic find somebody (a tutor) to explain it to you.

Read good newspapers and professional journals, especially ACCA's Student Accountant – this can give you an advantage in the exam.

Ensure you know the structure of the exam – how many questions and of what type you will be expected to answer. During your revision attempt all the different styles of questions you may be asked.

Further reading

You can find further reading and technical articles under the student section of ACCA's website.

Paper introduction

Paper background

The aim of ACCA **Corporate and Business Law**, is to develop knowledge and skills in the understanding of the general legal framework, and of specific legal areas relating to business, recognising the need to seek further specialist legal advice where necessary.

Objectives of the syllabus

- Identify the essential elements of the legal system including the main sources of law.

- Recognise and apply the appropriate legal rules relating to the law of obligations.

- Explain and apply the law relating to employment relationships.

- Distinguish between alternative forms and constitutions of business organisations.

- Recognise and compare types of capital and the financing of companies.

- Describe and explain how companies are managed, administered and regulated.

- Recognise the legal implications relating to insolvency law.

- Demonstrate an understanding of corporate and fraudulent behaviour.

Core areas of the syllabus

- Essential elements of the legal system.

- The law of obligations.

- Employment law.

- The formation and constitution of business organisations.

- Capital and the financing of companies.

- Management, administration and the regulation of companies.

- Insolvency law.

- Corporate and fraudulent behaviour.

ACCA Performance Objectives

In order to become a member of the ACCA, as a trainee accountant you will need to demonstrate that you have achieved nine performance objectives. Performance objectives are indicators of effective performance and set the minimum standard of work that trainees are expected to achieve and demonstrate in the workplace. They are divided into key areas of knowledge which are closely linked to the exam syllabus.

There are five Essential performance objectives and a choice of fifteen Technical performance objectives which are divided into five areas.

The performance objectives which link to this exam are:

1   Ethics and professionalism (Essential)

2   Governance risk and control (Essential)

The following link provides an in depth insight into all of the performance objectives:

https://www.accaglobal.com/content/dam/ACCA_Global/Students/per/PER-Performance-objectives-achieve.pdf

Progression

There are two elements of progression that we can measure: first how quickly students move through individual topics within a subject; and second how quickly they move from one course to the next. We know that there is an optimum for both, but it can vary from subject to subject and from student to student. However, using data and our experience of student performance over many years, we can make some generalisations.

A fixed period of study set out at the start of a course with key milestones is important. This can be within a subject, for example 'I will finish this topic by 30 June', or for overall achievement, such as 'I want to be qualified by the end of next year'.

Your qualification is cumulative, as earlier papers provide a foundation for your subsequent studies, so do not allow there to be too big a gap between one subject and another. We know that exams encourage techniques that lead to some degree of short term retention, the result being that you will simply forget much of what you have already learned unless it is refreshed (look up Ebbinghaus Forgetting Curve for more details on this). This makes it more difficult as you move from one subject to another: not only will you have to learn the new subject, you will also have to relearn all the underpinning knowledge as well. This is very inefficient and slows down your overall progression which makes it more likely you may not succeed at all.

In addition, delaying your studies slows your path to qualification which can have negative impacts on your career, postponing the opportunity to apply for higher level positions and therefore higher pay.

You can use the following diagram showing the whole structure of your qualification to help you keep track of your progress.

Syllabus objectives

1   We have reproduced the ACCA's syllabus below, showing where the objectives are explored within this book. Within the chapters, we have broken down the extensive information found in the syllabus into easily digestible and relevant sections, called **Content Objectives**. These correspond to the objectives at the beginning of each chapter.

Syllabus learning objective	Chapter reference

A   ESSENTIAL ELEMENTS OF THE LEGAL SYSTEM

1   Law and the legal system

(a)	Define law and distinguish types of law.[1]	1
(b)	Explain the structure and operation of the courts.[1]	1

2   Sources of law

(a)	Explain what is meant by case law and precedent.[1]	1
(b)	Explain legislation and evaluate delegated legislation.[1]	1
(c)	Illustrate the rules and presumptions used by the courts in interpreting statutes.[1]	1
(d)	Identify the concept and impact of human rights law.[1]	1

B   THE LAW OF OBLIGATIONS

1   Formation of contract

(a)	Analyse the nature of a simple contract.[2]	2
(b)	Explain the meaning of an offer and distinguish it from an invitation to treat.[2]	2
(c)	Explain the termination of an offer.[2]	2
(d)	Explain the meaning and consequence of acceptance.[2]	2
(e)	Explain the need for consideration.[2]	2
(f)	Explain adequacy and sufficiency of consideration.[2]	2
(g)	Analyse the doctrine of privity.[2]	2
(h)	Distinguish the presumptions relating to intention to create legal relations.[2]	2

2   Content of contracts

(a)	Distinguish terms from mere representations.[1]	2
(b)	Define the various contractual terms.[1]	2
(c)	Explain the control over terms in consumer contracts and the operation of exclusion clauses in non-consumer contracts.[2]	2

Syllabus learning objective	Chapter reference
D THE FORMATION AND CONSTITUTION OF BUSINESS ORGANISATIONS	
1 Agency law	
(a) Define the role of the agent and give examples of such relationships paying particular regard to partners and company directors.[2]	5
(b) Explain the formation of the agency relationship.[2]	5
(c) Define the authority of the agent.[2]	5
(d) Explain the potential liability of both principal and agent.[2]	5
2 Partnerships	
(a) Demonstrate a knowledge of the legislation governing the partnership, both unlimited and limited.[1]	6
(b) Discuss the formation of a partnership.[2]	6
(c) Explain the authority of partners in relation to partnership activity.[2]	6
(d) Analyse the liability of various partners for partnership debts.[2]	6
(e) Explain the termination of a partnership, and partners' subsequent rights and liabilities.[2]	6
3 Corporations and legal personality	
(a) Distinguish between sole traders, partnerships and companies.[2]	7
(b) Explain the meaning and effect of limited liability.[2]	7
(c) Analyse different types of companies, especially private and public companies.[2]	7
(d) Illustrate the effect of separate personality and the veil of incorporation.[2]	7
(e) Recognise instances where separate personality will be ignored (lifting the veil of incorporation).[2]	7
4 The formation and constitution of a company	
(a) Explain the role and duties of company promoters, and the breach of those duties and remedies available to the company.[2]	7
(b) Explain the meaning of, and the rules relating to, pre-incorporation contracts.[2]	7

Syllabus learning objective	Chapter reference
(c) Describe the procedure for registering companies, both public and private, including the system of streamlined company registration. [1]	7
(d) Describe the statutory books, records and returns, including the confirmation statement and the register of people with significant control, that companies must keep or make. [1]	7
(e) Analyse the effect of a company's constitutional documents. [2]	7
(f) Describe the contents of model articles of association. [1]	7
(g) Explain how articles of association can be changed. [2]	7
(h) Explain the controls over the names that companies may or may not use. [2]	7

E CAPITAL AND FINANCING OF COMPANIES

1 Share capital

(a) Examine the different types of capital. [2]	8
(b) Illustrate the difference between various classes of shares, including treasury shares, and the procedure for altering class rights. [2]	8
(c) Explain allotment of shares, and distinguish between rights issue and bonus issue of shares. [2]	8
(d) Examine the effect of issuing shares at either a discount, or at a premium. [2]	8

2 Loan capital

(a) Define companies' borrowing powers. [1]	8
(b) Explain the meaning of loan capital and debenture. [2]	8
(c) Distinguish loan capital from share capital and explain the different rights held by shareholders and debenture holders. [2]	8
(d) Explain the concept of a company charge and distinguish between fixed and floating charges. [2]	8
(e) Describe the need and the procedure for registering company charges. [2]	8

3 Capital maintenance and dividend law

(a) Explain the doctrine of capital maintenance and capital reduction. [2]   8

(b) Explain the rules governing the distribution of dividends in both private and public companies. [2]   8

F MANAGEMENT, ADMINISTRATION AND REGULATION OF COMPANIES

1 Company directors

(a) Explain the role of directors in the operation of a company, and the different types of directors, such as executive/non-executive directors or de jure and de facto directors, and shadow directors. [2]   9

(b) Discuss the ways in which directors are appointed, can lose their office and the disqualification of directors. [2]   9

(c) Distinguish between the powers of the board of directors, the managing director/chief executive and individual directors to bind their company. [2]   9

(d) Explain the duties that directors owe to their companies, and the controls imposed by statute over dealings between directors and their companies, including loans. [2]   9

2 Other company officers

(a) Discuss the appointment procedure relating to, and the duties and powers of, a company secretary. [2]   10

(b) Discuss the appointment procedure relating to, and the duties and rights of a company auditor, and their subsequent removal or resignation. [2]   10

3 Company meetings and resolutions

(a) Distinguish between types of meetings: general meetings and annual general meetings. [1]   10

(b) Distinguish between types of resolutions: ordinary, special, and written. [2]   10

(c) Explain the procedure for calling and conducting company meetings. [2]   10

G   INSOLVENCY LAW

1   Insolvency and administration

**H   CORPORATE FRAUDULENT AND CRIMINAL
       BEHAVIOUR**

1   Fraudulent and criminal behaviour

                                    KAPLAN PUBLISHING

The superscript numbers in square brackets indicate the intellectual depth at which the subject area could be assessed within the examination. Level 1 (knowledge and comprehension) broadly equates with the Knowledge module, Level 2 (application and analysis) with the Skills module and Level 3 (synthesis and evaluation) with the Professional level. However, lower level skills can continue to be assessed as you progress through each module and level.

The examination

Examination format

	Number of marks
Section A	
–25 × 2 mark objective test questions	50
–20 × 1 mark objective test questions	20
Section B	30
	——
–5 × 6 mark multi-task questions	100

Total time allowed: 2 hours

English legal system

Chapter learning objectives

Upon completion of this chapter you will be able to:

- explain the difference between civil and criminal law

- explain the structure and operation of the civil courts and tribunal systems

- explain the meaning of judicial precedent, ratio decidendi and obiter dicta

- illustrate how the doctrine of judicial precedent works in relation to the civil courts

- explain how legislation is made and the doctrine of sovereignty

- set out the rules and presumptions used by the courts in interpreting statutes

- identify the concept of human rights as expressed in the Human Rights Act 1998 (HRA 1998).

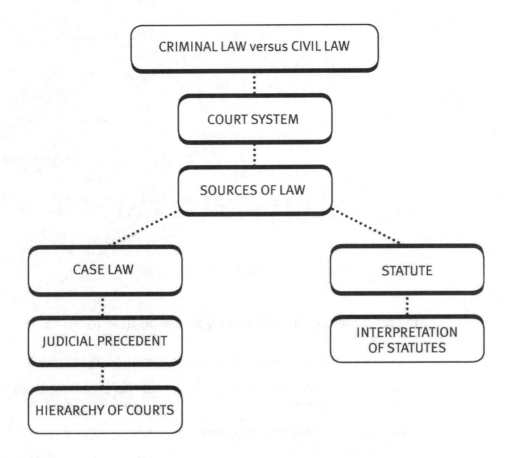

1 Definition of Law

The principles and regulations established in a community by some authority and applicable to its people whether in the form of legislation or of custom and policies recognised and enforced by judicial decision.

2 Types of Law

The English legal system distinguishes several types of law. The ones we will look at are:

- Common law and equity
- Private law and public law
- Criminal law and civil law.

Common law and equity

Following the Norman conquest, English law has been described as a common law system. This was a system whereby a number of legal concepts from Norman law were incorporated into the English system.

Common law:

- developed from local customs
- introduced the system of precedent (see **section 4**)
- the only remedy is damages
- may be rigid and inflexible.

Judges would travel around the country and apply a mixture of precedent and common sense to build up a body of internally consistent law. However, this would sometimes result in harsh consequences.

To deal with the issue that damages are not always a suitable remedy, equity was developed two or three hundred years later after common law and introduced fairness into the English legal system.

Equity:

- developed as a petition by a party who felt the common law had led to injustice
- it is more flexible than the common law
- it introduced new discretionary remedies, e.g. injunctions and specific performance
- it is concerned with fairness and therefore will not be granted if there is undue delay in bringing the case or if the petitioner has himself acted unfairly, or where there is no mutuality (both parties should be able to bring a case).

Private and public law

Within the English legal system, two distinct areas of law operate: private and public law. They both aim to create social order, but have a number of distinct differences.

Within public law, different categories exist. These include criminal law, constitutional law, administrative law, social welfare law and all deal with matters relating to the whole country.

Private law is concerned with the law enforced between individuals. This can include contract law, family law and other areas which deal with intellectual property rights (copyrights, designs and patents), land law (and the way in which it is transferred), probate (dealing with wills and how property is distributed after someone dies) and company law (which deals with the ways in which companies are created and rules regulating how they operate their business).

Criminal law versus civil law

Criminal law	Civil law
Criminal law relates to conduct of which the State disapproves and which it seeks to control. It is a form of public law.	Civil law is a form of private law and involves the relationships between individual citizens.
Purpose – the enforcement of particular forms of behaviour by the State, which acts to ensure compliance.	**Purpose** – to settle disputes between individuals and to provide remedies.
In criminal law the case is brought by the **State** in the name of the Crown. A criminal case will be reported as Regina v ..., where Regina means the Latin for 'queen'.	In civil law the case is brought by the **claimant**, who is seeking a remedy. The case will be referred to by the names of the parties involved in the dispute, such as Brown v Smith.
Burden of proof – on the prosecution.	**Burden of proof** – on the claimant.
Standard of proof – guilt must be shown **beyond reasonable doubt** (high standard of proof).	**Standard of proof** – liability must be shown on the **balance of probabilities** (lower standard of proof).
Object – to regulate society by the threat of punishment.	**Object** – usually financial compensation to put the claimant in the position he would have been in had the wrong not occurred.
If found guilty the criminal court will sentence the accused and it may fine him or impose a period of imprisonment. If innocent the accused will be acquitted.	The civil court will order the defendant to pay damages or it may order some other remedy, e.g. specific performance or injunction.

Test your understanding 1

Which one of the following statements is correct?

A   The aim of the criminal law is to regulate behaviour within society by the threat of punishment.

B   The aim of the criminal law is to punish offenders.

C   The aim of the criminal law is to provide a means whereby injured persons may obtain compensation.

D   The aim of the criminal law is to ensure that the will of the majority is imposed upon the minority.

3 The court system

The main English civil courts

The following diagram shows the main civil courts. The term 'first instance' refers to the court in which the case is first heard. Appeals are heard in a different court. The arrows show the way a case will progress through the court system.

Supreme Court (previously House of Lords)
Five Justices of Supreme Court hear appeals from the Court of Appeal and exceptionally from the High Court

↑

Court of Appeal (civil division)
Three Lords Justices of Appeal hear appeals from the High Court and County courts

↑

High Court of Justice
One High Court judge in first instance.
Queen's Bench Division (QBD) hears first instance cases of contract and tort.
Chancery Division (ChD) deals with land law, trusts, company law, partnership law, insolvency, etc. It hears appeals from County courts on probate and insolvency.
Family Division hears matrimonial cases.
Each Division of the High Court also has a Divisional Court which hears appeals from other courts.

↑ ↑

Magistrates' court	**County court**
Jurisdiction is mainly criminal (see section on criminal courts) but does have civil jurisdiction in family matters such as contact orders, adoption, and maintenance. There are also powers of recovery of council tax arrears and charges for water, gas and electricity.	First instance civil claims in contract, tort, landlord and tenant, probate and insolvency. One district judge hears small claims. The hearing is informal and no costs are awarded. One circuit judge hears most fast-track, and some multitrack, cases.

The House of Lords was replaced by the Supreme Court on 1 October 2009. This new court has assumed the judicial functions of the House of Lords. The Law Lords that used to sit in the House of Lords now sit as twelve Justices of the Supreme Court, with a President at its head.

The Supreme Court was established by the Constitutional Reform Act 2005. It was felt that there needed to be a separation of powers between the judicial functions of the House of Lords (to decide issues in relation to the law) and the legislative functions of the House of Lords (to make the law) to give assurance of the independence of the judges.

The Supreme Court is now in a separate building from the House of Lords and has its own appointment system, staff and budget.

The three-track system

When a claim is received, it will be allocated to one of three tracks for the hearing.

1   The small claims track – deals with simple claims valued at no more than £10,000, an informal court.

2   The fast-track – deals with moderately valued claims of between £10,000 and £25,000, expected to last no more than one day.

3   The multitrack – deals with claims of over £25,000 and/or complex claims.

Note: the County court deals with all cases allocated to the small claims track, the majority of fast track and some multi track cases. All other claims are dealt with by the High Court.

The main English criminal courts

SUPREME COURT
Five Lord Justices of Supreme Court hear appeals from the Court of Appeal and exceptionally from High Court.

COURT OF APPEAL (Criminal division)
Three Lord Justices of Appeal hear appeals from the Crown Court.

CROWN COURT
Presided over by a judge whose role is to decide questions of law and impose the punishment.

Case will be heard before a jury whose role is to decide questions of fact i.e. whether defendant is guilty of the offence.

Divisional Court of the Queen's Bench Division
Three judges preside.
Hears case stated appeals from Magistrates Court on points of law
Appeals go directly to the Supreme Court.

MAGISTRATES COURT
Court of first instance. Deals with criminal cases in various ways:
- Summary offences – decides whether defendant is guilty of the offence and imposes the penalty. Penalties are less in the Magistrates court.
- Indictable offences where there is to be trial by jury. Magistrates will conduct committal proceedings to make sure the defendant has a case to answer.

- Offences triable either way – the defendant can choose whether to be tried in the Magistrates court, or to be tried in the Crown court.

Presided over by either:
- Lay Magistrates. The bench usually consists of three.
- District judge sitting alone.
Appeals on questions of fact go to the Crown Court.

Case stated appeals on questions of law go the High Court. Can be made by the prosecution and the defence

Other courts

Court of Justice of the European Union (CJEU)	European Court of Human Rights (ECtHR)	Judicial Committee of the Privy Council (JPC)
The CJEU deals with actions between the EU institutions and the member states. It is the ultimate authority on the interpretation of European law. The CJEU is therefore superior to the Supreme Court. Cases are referred to the CJEU by national courts.	The final court of appeal in relation to matters concerning HRA 1998. Proceedings in the English courts must have been exhausted before ECtHR will hear a case.	The highest court of appeal for a number of Commonwealth countries, crown dependencies and UK overseas territories. Hears both civil and criminal appeals. The right to appeal to the JPC is regulated by the constitution and legislation of the particular country. Proceedings take place in the Supreme Court of the UK.
No appeal.	No appeal.	No appeal.

Tribunals

Tribunals are also an important part of the English legal system and are an alternative to using the court system to settle a dispute.

Employment tribunals are established to hear disputes between an employee and their employer on certain statutory employment matters, such as unfair dismissal (see **Chapter 4**).

Employment tribunals are composed of one employment judge, plus two expert laymen who are drawn from panels representing both sides of the industry.

Appeals are to the employment appeal tribunal (EAT) and can only be made on a point of law.

The EAT is composed of one High Court judge, plus two or four expert laymen.

KAPLAN PUBLISHING

Court v Tribunal

	Court	**Tribunal**
Expertise	Case may not be heard by a specialist in that particular area of law.	Case will be heard by someone who has expertise in that arear.
Speed	A slower process.	A much quicker process.
Cost	Legal aid maybe available but if not can be an expensive process.	Legal aid is not available (except for land tribunals and EAT's) but can be a much cheaper procedure.
Proceedings	Strict rules relating to evidence, pleading and procedure.	Much less formal and can be less intimidating.
Decisions	Are bound by the doctrine of judicial precedent, therefore make consistent decisions.	Not bound by the doctrine of judicial precedent, therefore risk of making inconsistent decisions.

4 Sources of law

Overview

European Union law takes precedence over all other sources.

Legislation takes precedence over case law.

Equity prevails over common law.

Case law

Throughout this text you will find examples of cases which have come before the courts. These cases are not simply examples of the way in which the law is applied; they also illustrate the way in which the law is made.

Case law can be subdivided into common law and equity (covered earlier).

Doctrine of judicial precedent

The system, adopted by the judges, of following the decisions in previous cases is called the doctrine of judicial precedent.

- Some precedents are **binding** (meaning they **must** be followed in later cases).

- Others are merely **persuasive** (meaning that a judge in a later case **may** choose to follow it but he is not bound to do so).

There are three factors to be considered in deciding whether a precedent is binding or persuasive:

- the hierarchy of the courts

- ratio decidendi and obiter dicta

- the material facts of the case.

The hierarchy of the courts

As a general rule, the precedents of higher courts bind lower courts, but not vice versa.

Supreme Court – binds all lower courts. From 1966 does not bind itself.

Court of Appeal – binds all lower courts and itself in civil cases unless earlier decision overruled or is inconsistent with European law.

High Court – not bound by its own decisions, but strong persuasive authority.

The 1966 Practice Statement was made on behalf of himself and the House of Lords (now the Supreme Court) by Lord Gardiner. Lord Gardiner proposed that they could depart from a previous decision if it appeared right to do so. This would allow the law to develop in line with changes in society.

Although there have been a number of cases where the House of Lords (now the Supreme Court) has overruled or amended its own earlier decisions, it is also reluctant to exercise these powers too frequently.

Ratio decidendi and obiter dicta

The ratio decidendi is the legal reason for the decision. It is capable of forming the binding precedent. It is a statement of law which is carried down to later decisions.

Obiter dicta are statements which are not part of the ratio, they are other statements made by the judges such as hypothetical situations or wide legal principles. They are persuasive rather than binding. This means that the judge can take the statement into account (and usually will) when reaching his decision, but he does not have to follow it.

Facts of the case

In order for a precedent to be binding on a judge in a later case, the material facts of the two cases must be the same. If they are significantly different, the precedent will be persuasive rather than binding.

When is a precedent not binding?

A precedent is not binding where it:

- has been overruled by a higher court.

- has been overruled by statute.

- was made without proper care (per incuriam). This is where a decision of a court is held to be wrongly decided because the judge was misinformed of the law. A judgment per incuriam is not binding and has no authority.

- can be distinguished from the earlier case, i.e. the material facts differ. A previous case is only binding in a later case if the legal principle involved is the same and the facts are similar. Where the facts are materially different then a previous decision does not need to be followed.

Advantages and disadvantages of judicial precedent

Advantages

- Reaching decisions as a result of the doctrine of precedent makes the system consistent. It becomes easier to predict the result of litigation.

- It allows the English legal system to be flexible. Decisions can be adapted and extended to reflect changes in society.

- The law is clear. As it is only the ratio decidendi that is followed it is easy to see what law is being applied.

- Decisions arise from actual events, therefore the system is practical.

Disadvantages

- The law is very complex because there is a vast number of cases, and inconsistencies can arise. The same judgement may contain differing, and even conflicting, arguments making the precedent hard to understand and even harder to apply.

- The law can become rigid, leading to inflexibility and loss of development.

- Case law is reactive rather than proactive. Rather than dealing with issues in advance and stating the law, a case is considered and a decision made once a particular situation has arisen.

> **Test your understanding 2**
>
> **Which one of the following statements is untrue?**
>
> A   Decisions of the Supreme Court (formerly the House of Lords) bind all lower courts.
>
> B   The Supreme Court (formerly the House of Lords) is not bound by its own decisions.
>
> C   Decisions of the Supreme Court (formerly the House of Lords) override statute.
>
> D   Appeals can be made from the Supreme Court (formerly the House of Lords) to the CJEU.

5   Legislation

Types of legislation

Legislation falls into two categories:

- Acts of Parliament
- delegated legislation.

Acts of Parliament

Parliament consists of:

- the House of Commons
- the House of Lords
- the Monarch.

In order to become an Act of Parliament, a Bill must go through the following stages in both Houses:

- first reading – the name of the Bill and the its proposer is read out
- second reading – debate takes place on the principles of the Bill and it is then voted upon
- committee stage – a smaller number of MP's consider the wording of the Bill. This stage can last several months depending on the contentiousness of the Bill
- report stage – the Bill as amended by the Committee is reported back to the full House
- third reading – the Bill is read for the final time.

At the end of this process in both Houses, the Bill must receive the Royal Assent.

Note that an Act does not necessarily come into force immediately. Its provisions may take effect on a piece-meal basis. An example is the Companies Act 2006.

Doctrine of sovereignty of Parliament

Parliament is sovereign. This means that, in theory, it is only Parliament that can make new law and it can make any law it wishes. However it cannot pass an Act which can never be repealed.

The courts cannot question the validity of an Act. However, they must refuse to apply an Act that contravenes EU law.

Delegated legislation

For many reasons, Parliament has delegated some of its legislative powers to other bodies. Usually, Parliament passes an 'enabling' Act setting out the policy involved and the objectives it wishes to achieve. The Act then delegates the task of filling in the details to some other body.

Rules enacted under such powers are called delegated legislation, and the following are examples:

- statutory instruments: made by Government Ministers
- bye-laws: made by local authorities
- Orders in Council: made by the Privy Council in the name of the Monarch on the advice of the Prime Minister.

Delegated legislation has a number of advantages:

- It saves Parliamentary time.
- It may benefit from access to technical expertise, thus leaving Parliament free to consider and debate the underlying principles.
- Flexibility – it is quick and easy to make and to change.

However, it also has a number of disadvantages:

- Its volume and lack of publicity means that it can be difficult to keep up with the changes introduced.
- It is criticised as being undemocratic as it is made without recourse to the elected House of Commons.

There are a number of means of controlling delegated legislation:

- **Parliamentary** – Since 1973 there has been a Joint Select Committee on Statutory Instruments, whose function it is to scrutinise all statutory instruments. They have the power to draw the instrument to the attention of both Houses on any number of grounds, but cannot do so on a ground which relates to the actual merits of the instrument or the policy it is pursuing.
- **Judicial** – The courts can challenge the validity of delegated legislation through the process of judicial review. It can be challenged on the grounds that the person making it has acted 'ultra vires', by exceeding their powers outside of the authority granted to them.

Ultra vires

There are two types of 'ultra vires':

- Procedural ultra vires: when a piece of delegated legislation is deemed to have not followed the correct procedure which was required by the enabling act. In **Agricultural Training Board v Aylesbury Mushrooms Ltd (1972)** the appropriate government Minister failed to observe the prescribed procedure for introducing regulations. The procedure allowed for consultations with appropriate organisations but this procedure was not followed. In particular the Minister failed to consult the Mushroom Growers' Association and therefore proposals requiring the establishment of a training board were held to be ultra vires and ineffective.

- Substantive ultra vires: when a piece of delegated legislation is deemed to be void because it places provisions on an area beyond the powers given to the decision-maker by the Enabling Act. In **Strickland v Hayes Borough Council (1986)** a local authority had introduced a bye-law prohibiting the singing or reciting of obscene songs or use of obscene language. This was held to be ultra vires, on the basis that the bye-law was too widely drafted because it covered acts carried out on private property as well as public land.

- **Human Rights Act 1998** – Delegated legislation is secondary legislation, therefore it can be declared invalid by the courts if it is incompatible with HRA 1998.

Test your understanding 3

1 **Which of the following statements is correct?**

   (I)   In the event of a conflict between equity and the common law, the common law prevails.

   (II) An Act of Parliament can overrule any common law or equitable rule.

   A (I) only

   B (II) only

   C Neither (I) nor (II)

   D Both (I) and (II)

2 **Which of the following is NOT a form of delegated legislation?**

   A Orders in Council

   B Statutory instruments

   C Local authority bye-laws

   D Acts of Parliament

6 Rules of statutory interpretation

Introduction

The process by which judges assign meanings to ambiguous words or phrases in statutes is called the interpretation of statutes.

Judges can use certain aids, rules and presumptions to help them assign a meaning to a word.

Aids to interpretation

The courts can use the following aids to help them interpret a statute:

- the legislation itself (i.e. its definition section).

- judicial precedents.

- the Interpretation Act 1978 – the Act defines certain terms frequently found in legislation. The Act also states that 'unless a specific intention to the contrary exists, the use in a statute of masculine gender terminology also includes the feminine, and vice versa'.

- the Oxford English Dictionary.

- Hansard (to see what was said in Parliament when the Bill was being debated). In **Pepper v Hart (1992)** the House of Lords established the principle that when primary legislation is ambiguous then, under certain circumstances, the court may refer to statements made in the House of Commons or House of Lords in an attempt to interpret the meaning of the legislation.

- sources of EU law. Since the United Kingdom joined the EU in 1972 they agreed to conform with existing and future EU law. One of the many sources of EU law is a Directive which generally addresses the member states and requires that the states take action within an identified time period to change their own law. When in doubt courts may look to the Directive for guidance on interpretation.

- Human Rights Act 1998 (see later).

Literal rule

Words must be given their ordinary dictionary meaning, even if this produces an undesirable outcome.

Fisher v Bell (1961)

Facts: The court had to consider the meaning of the wording 'offer for sale'. It was an offence to 'offer for sale' offensive weapons. A shopkeeper had flick-knives with price tags attached on display in his shop window.

Held: The court applied the fundamental principles of contract law in a literal fashion, accepting that the display of flick-knives was an invitation to treat. It was the customer who made an offer to buy. In consequence, the shopkeeper was found not to be acting illegally. The aim of Parliament, however, had been to prevent sales of offensive weapons.

Golden rule

Where the literal rule gives more than one meaning or provides an absurd result, the golden rule is used to ensure that preference is given to the meaning that does not result in the provision being an absurdity.

Adler v George (1964)

Facts: A conviction was challenged on the basis of what appeared to be a miswording in the Official Secrets Act (1920). This Act made it an offence to obstruct a member of the armed forces `in the vicinity of' particular locations, but not actually `in' those locations. The defendant was actually inside an Air Force base at the time of the incident, which he claimed was beyond the literal scope of the Act.

Held: The words 'in the vicinity of' a prohibited place in the Official Secrets Act were held to cover the acts of the defendant which took place 'within' a prohibited place.

Mischief rule

Used to interpret a statute in a way which provides a remedy for the mischief the statute was enacted to prevent.

Gorris v Scott (1874)

Facts: The Contagious Diseases (Animals) Act 1869 provided that any ship carrying animals should contain them in pens. The defendant neglected his duty, and some of the claimant's sheep were washed overboard and lost.

Held: Since the purpose of the statute was to prevent the spread of contagious disease, and not to guard against the danger of the property being washed overboard, the claim failed.

Purposive rule

This is a more modern approach. Here the court is not just looking to see what the gap was in the old law, it is making a decision as to what they felt Parliament meant to achieve.

Gardiner v Sevenoaks RDC (1950)

Facts: The purpose of an Act was to provide for the safe storage of film wherever it might be stored on 'premises'. The claimant argued that 'premises' did not include a cave and so the Act had no application to this case.

Held: The purpose of the Act was to protect the safety of persons working in all places where film was stored. If film was stored in a cave, the word 'premises' included the cave.

Eiusdem generis

General words mean the same kind of thing as the specific words they follow.

Powell v Kempton Park Racecourse Co (1899)

Facts: Section 1 of the Betting Act 1853 prohibited betting in a 'house, office, room or other place'. The issue was whether a ring at a racecourse was an 'other place' for the purposes of this statute.

Held: The Lords decided that if the eiusdem generis rule was applied, the specific words such as 'room' and 'office' that preceded the general phrase 'or other place' created a class of indoor places. As a ring on a racecourse was outside it would not fall within this category. Therefore the Act did not apply to restrict gambling here.

Expressio unius exclusio alterius

Where a statute seeks to establish a list of what is covered by its provisions, then anything not expressly included in that list is specifically excluded.

Presumptions

There are presumptions which will generally apply unless the legislation specifically states otherwise, for example:

- A statute cannot conflict with international law. An Act should therefore be interpreted as giving effect to international obligations.
- A statute does not have any retrospective effect.
- A statute does not alter the common law.
- A statute does not exclude the jurisdiction of the court.
- Legislation does not extend beyond the territorial jurisdiction of the UK.

7   Human Right Act 1998

What is its purpose?	HRA 1998 incorporates the European Convention for the Protection of Human Rights and Fundamental Freedoms 1950 into UK domestic law.
What is Convention law?	Convention law means the Convention and the decisions of the ECtHR.
How does it affect judicial interpretation?	UK courts must take Convention law into account when deciding a question that has arisen in connection with a Convention right.
Any impact on the doctrine of precedent?	Judges will not be bound by a previous interpretation of existing legislation where it did not take into account Convention rights. Note that the ECtHR is free to depart from its own previous decisions. In **Stafford v UK (2002)** the court overruled its previous decision in **Wynne v UK (1994)**. It held that the Home Secretary's role in fixing the minimum tariff for a person convicted of murder was a sentencing exercise and not merely an administrative implementation of the sentence. It was therefore incompatible with the convention.
What if legislation is incompatible with the Convention?	Any existing legislation must be interpreted so it is compatible with the rights under the Convention. If a court feels that legislation is incompatible with the Convention and it cannot interpret it in such a way to make it compatible, then it may make a **declaration of incompatibility**. However, the declaration does not make the legislation invalid. It is left to Parliament to remedy the situation through new legislation. However, the courts do have the power to declare delegated legislation (e.g. statutory instruments) to be invalid.
What is derogation?	A derogation is a provision which allows for all or part of a legal measure to be applied differently, or not at all by public authorities. However, where rights have been derogated the public authority can mitigate its actions by demonstrating a legitimate need to derogate and that the derogation was proportionate to the need. For example, the UK may choose not to enforce a specific provision in the HRA due to circumstances such as the threat of terrorism.

KAPLAN PUBLISHING

Bellinger v Bellinger (2003)

Facts: The House of Lords had to consider whether or not a male to female transsexual could be treated as a female under the Matrimonial Causes Act 1973.

Held: The court was unable to interpret the Act to allow the transsexual to be considered female. It did however issue a declaration of incompatibility.

The **Gender Recognition Act 2004** addressed the issue in **Bellinger v Bellinger (2003)**. The purpose of the Act is to provide transsexual people with legal recognition in their acquired gender. This is an example of the passing of a statute to put right a perceived unfair outcome of a case.

Mendoza v Ghaidan (2003)

Facts: The Rent Act 1977 allows a spouse to inherit a statutory tenancy. In **Fitzpatrick v Sterling Housing Association Limited (1999)**, the House of Lords had declined to allow same-sex partners to inherit statutory tenancies on the grounds that they could not be considered to be the wife or husband of the deceased.

Held: The Court of Appeal held that the Rent Act, as the House of Lords had construed it in the **Fitzpatrick** case, was incompatible with the Convention on the grounds of its discriminatory treatment of surviving same-sex partners. The Court held that the incompatibility could be remedied by reading the words 'as his or her wife or husband' as meaning 'as if they were his or her wife or husband'.

The above case is an example of how the judges used the Golden Rule to interpret statute.

8   Chapter summary

Criminal
- aims to regulate society
- prove beyond reasonable doubt.

CRIMINAL LAW versus CIVIL LAW

Civil
- compensates
- proves on balance of probabilities.

Court system
- Supreme Court
- Court of Appeal
- High Court.

Tribunals
- types of tribunals
- compared to court

SOURCES OF LAW

Case law
- common law
- equity.

Statute
- Acts of Parliament
- Delegated legislation.

Judicial precedent
- ratio decidendi
- obiter dicta.

Interpretation of statutes
- literal rule
- golden rule
- mischief rule.
- purposive rule

HIERARCHY OF COURTS

Test your understanding answers

Test your understanding 1

A

The aim of the criminal law is not to punish offenders. The criminal law threatens punishment to offenders, and therefore aims to deter individuals from breaking the law, i.e. it seeks to regulate behaviour by the threat of punishment.

Test your understanding 2

C

Decisions of the Supreme Court are binding on all lower courts. However, the Supreme Court is not bound by its own decisions. Statute overrides decisions of the Supreme Court. Appeals can be made from the Supreme Court to the CJEU.

Test your understanding 3

1   **B**

Equity is a body of discretionary rules devised by the court on the basis of fairness to remedy defects in the common law. It is therefore incorrect to say that common law prevails over equity. However, statement (ii) is correct. The effect of a new statute is to overrule any common law or equity rule that is inconsistent with the provisions of the new statute.

2   **D**

Orders in Council, statutory instruments and local authority bye-laws are all examples of delegated legislation. Acts of Parliament are not.

Contract law

Chapter learning objectives

Upon completion of this chapter you will be able to:

- explain the essential elements of a contract

- explain what is and is not an offer

- explain the meaning and consequence of acceptance

- explain the meaning of consideration

- explain the doctrine of privity and the main exceptions

- distinguish the presumptions relating to the intention to create legal relations

- distinguish terms from mere representations

- define the various contractual terms

- explain the effect of exclusions and evaluate their control

- explain the meaning and effect of breach of contract

- explain the rules relating to the award of damages

- analyse the equitable remedies for breach of contract.

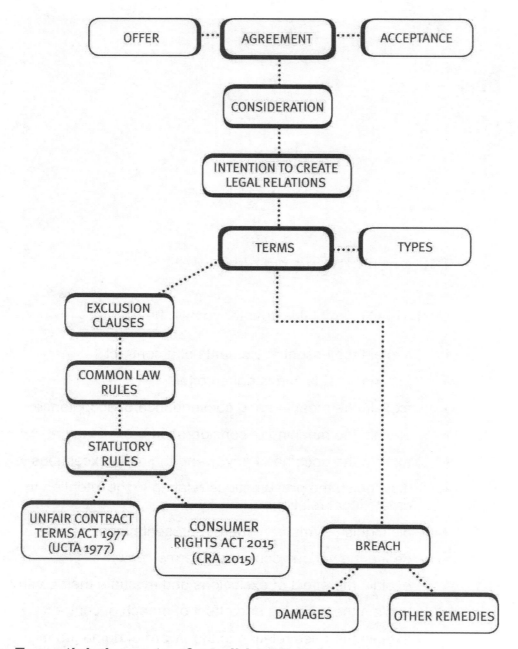

1 Essential elements of a valid contract

The following elements are needed to form a valid contract:

- **Agreement**, i.e. offer and acceptance.

- **Consideration.**

- **Intention to create legal relations.**

- **Capacity** – each party must have the legal power to bind itself contractually. For example persons under the age of eighteen (minors) and persons of unsound mind or under the influence of alcohol have limitations on their power to contract.

- **Legality** – the courts will not enforce a contract which is deemed to be illegal.

Form of the contract

General rule

A contract can be in any form – **simple contract**. It may be written, or oral, or inferred from the conduct of the parties. Most contracts are simple contracts.

Exceptions

Some contracts must be made in a particular form such as in writing or they will be void. These include bills of exchange, cheques and the transfer of shares in a company. Contracts for the sale of land must also be in writing.

Specialty contracts

Conveyances of land and leases for three years or more must be by deed – these are known as specialty contracts. Such contracts must be in writing, signed, witnessed and delivered (i.e. intended to take effect).

The limitation period for a contract made by deed is 12 years. For all other contracts, the limitation period is six years.

Subject to contract

Where the words 'subject to contract' are used this means the parties to an agreement are not legally bound until a contract has been executed. Even though the parties have agreed terms, the matter effectively remains in a state of negotiation. Furthermore, either party can withdraw from the transaction without liability.

Test your understanding 1
The vast majority of contracts are 'simple'. What is the meaning of the word 'simple' in this context?
A   The terms of the contract are set out in writing.
B   The contract does not need to be in any particular form to be binding.
C   The contract contains fewer than ten provisions.
D   The contract is not supported by consideration.

2 Offer

 What is an offer?

An offer is a definite and unequivocal statement of willingness to be bound on specified terms without further negotiations.

An offer can be in any form – oral, written or by conduct. However, it is not effective until it has been communicated to the offeree. For example, if a reward is offered for the return of a lost item, it cannot be claimed by someone who did not know of the reward before they returned the item.

An offer can be made to a particular person, to a class of persons or even to the whole world – **Carlill v Carbolic Smoke Ball Co (1893)**.

What is not an offer?

(1)   An invitation to treat is not an offer.

 An invitation to treat means an invitation to the other party to make an offer; e.g. 'we may be prepared to sell' – **Gibson v Manchester City Council (1979)**. An invitation to treat cannot be accepted to form a valid contract.

Examples of invitations to treat:

Most advertisements

General rule – an advertisement is an invitation to treat, not an offer, as shown in:

Partridge v Crittenden (1968)

Facts: The defendant put the following advertisement in a magazine: 'Bramblefinch cocks and hens, 25s each'. The Protection of Birds Act 1954 made it an offence to offer such birds for sale.

Held: This was an invitation to treat and not an offer. The advertisement stated that the birds were for sale, not that the seller would sell to all comers. The defendant was therefore not in contravention of the Act.

Exception to an advertisement not being an offer

Note, however, that it would be an offer if no further negotiations were intended or expected. This is the position in **Carlill v Carbolic Smoke Ball Co (1893)**, where the advertisers made it clear that they would pay money to anyone complying with the terms of the advertisement.

KAPLAN PUBLISHING

Carlill v Carbolic Smoke Ball Co (1893)

Facts: The manufacturers of a medicinal 'smoke ball' advertised in a newspaper that anyone who bought and used the ball properly and nevertheless contracted influenza would be paid a £100 reward. Mrs Carlill used the ball as directed and did catch influenza. The defendant claimed that there was no enforceable contract because Mrs Carlill had never notified the company that she accepted its offer.

Held: The court rejected the defendant's argument on the basis that the wording of the advert was such that Mrs Carlill needed only to comply with the terms of the offer and there was no further negotiations intended. Once Mrs Carlill had satisfied the conditions she was entitled to enforcement of the contract. Furthermore, weight was placed on the £1000 bank deposit that claimed to 'show their sincerity in the matter' in showing that the advertisement was not just a mere 'puff'.

Shop window displays

Fisher v Bell (1961)

Facts: The Restriction of Offensive Weapons Act 1959 created a criminal offence of 'offering for sale' certain offensive weapons. A shopkeeper was prosecuted under this statute for displaying a flick knife in his shop window, and thus 'offering it for sale'.

Held: A window display was not an offer of sale, but only an invitation to treat. So the display did not infringe the law.

Goods on shop shelves

Pharmaceutical Society of Great Britain v Boots Cash Chemists (1953)

Facts: Statute requires that the sale of certain pharmaceuticals must be carried out under the supervision of a qualified pharmacist. Boots operated a store where the drugs were displayed on a self-service basis and the customers paid at a cash desk for the goods they had selected. A pharmacist was present at the cash desk but not at the shelves where the goods were displayed with a price tag. The Pharmaceutical Society claimed that the statute was being contravened.

Held: The display of goods in a shop was not an offer, but an invitation to treat. It was the customer who made the offer and Boots could either accept or reject this offer at the cash desk (in the presence of the qualified pharmacist). The act constituting the acceptance is the ringing up of the price on the till by the cashier and at that moment a binding contract of sale is made.

Tenders

A **tender** arises where one party issues a statement asking interested parties to submit the terms on which they are willing to carry out work or supply goods. The person inviting the tender is simply making an invitation to treat. The person submitting a tender is the offeror and the other party is free to accept or reject the offer as they please.

The effect of acceptance depends upon the wording of the invitation to tender. If the invitation states that the potential purchaser **will require** a certain quantity of goods, acceptance of a tender will form a contract and they will be in breach if they fail to order the stated quantity from the person submitting the tender.

If, on the other hand, the invitation states only that the potential purchaser **may require** goods, acceptance gives rise only to a standing offer. In this situation there is no compulsion on the purchaser to take any goods, but they must not deal with any other supplier. Each order forms a separate contract and the supplier must deliver any goods required within the time stated in the tender. The supplier can revoke the standing offer, but they must supply any goods already ordered **(Great Northern Railway v Witham (1873))**.

(2)   **A mere statement of selling price** in response to a request for information is not an offer.

Harvey v Facey (1893)

Facts: The defendant (F) was in negotiations with the regarding the sale of his store. The claimant (H) sent the defendant a telegram stating: "Will you sell us Bumper Hall Pen? Telegraph lowest cash price-answer paid." On the same day, F sent H a reply by telegram stating: "Lowest price for Bumper Hall Pen £900." H sent F another telegram agreeing to purchase the property at the asking price. F refused to sell and H sued for specific performance and an injunction to prevent the new buyer from taking the property.

Held: The court held that by replying to H's question regarding the lowest price of the property, F did not make an affirmative answer to the first question regarding his willingness to sell. The defendant's response to the query was simply a statement of information. It was not an offer capable of being accepted by the claimant.

(3)   A **mere statement of intention to sell** is not an offer.

Harris v Nickerson (1873)

Facts: The defendant placed an advertisement in London papers that certain items, including some office furniture would be placed up for auction over three days. The claimant obtained a commission to buy the office furniture and expended time and expense to travel to bid for the office furniture. On the third day, the lots for the office furniture were withdrawn. The claimant sued for loss of time and expense.

Held: An advertisement that goods will be put up for auction does not constitute an offer to any person that the goods will actually be put up, and that the advertiser is therefore free to withdraw the goods from the auction at any time prior to the auction.

Auction

As we have just discussed the original advertising of the auction is not an offer. When the auctioneer asks for bids that constitutes an invitation to treat. When a bid is made that is deemed to be an offer. When the auctioneer's hammer falls the winning offer has been accepted and there is a legally binding contract.

Cross offers

Sometime two parties make identical or similar offers to each other without knowing that the other has made an offer. These are known as cross offers. In such a case, no binding contract will be created as no one has accepted the offer made by the other.

Termination of an offer

Once an offer has been terminated, it cannot be accepted. An offer can be terminated by:

- revocation
- rejection
- lapse.

Revocation

Revocation by the offeror can be made at any time before acceptance, even if the offeror has agreed to keep the offer open.

Routledge v Grant (1828)

Facts: G offered to buy R's horse and stated that the offer would remain open for six weeks. However, before the six-week period had elapsed, G withdrew the offer.

Held: G was entitled to withdraw the offer at any time before acceptance.

The revocation must be communicated to the offeree, i.e. it must be brought to his actual notice.

Byme v Leon Van Tienhoven (1880)

Facts: An offer was posted on 1 October. It reached the claimant on 11 October. The claimant immediately cabled his acceptance. In the meantime, the defendant had changed his mind and posted a letter of revocation on 8 October. The revocation was received by the claimant after he had cabled his acceptance.

Held: The revocation did not take effect as it was not communicated to the claimant prior to his acceptance. The contract was therefore binding.

The revocation can be communicated by the offeror or a reliable third party.

Dickinson v Dodds (1876)

Facts: The defendant agreed to keep an offer open for two days. However, in the meantime the defendant sold the property to a third party. The offeree was told of the sale by a third party, but then attempted to accept the original offer.

Held: This was a reasonable way of communicating revocation. The offer was therefore properly revoked and could not be accepted.

There are two exceptions to the above rules on revocation:

- If the offeree pays the offeror to keep the offer open, any revocation will amount to a breach of that collateral contract. The offeree could claim damages for the loss of the opportunity to accept the offer, although he could not accept the offer itself.

- In the case of a unilateral/option contract, the offeror cannot revoke his offer once the offeree has begun to perform the acts which would amount to acceptance.

Errington v Errington (1952)

Facts: A father offered to transfer his house to his son if the son paid the mortgage. The son began to pay the mortgage but, when the father died, his personal representatives wanted to withdraw the offer.

Held: The offer could not be withdrawn because the son, by paying some of the instalments, had started acceptance.

Rejection

Rejection by the offeree may be outright or by means of a counter-offer.
A counter-offer is an offer made in response to an offer.

Hyde v Wrench (1840)

Facts: Wrench offered to sell Hyde a farm for £1,000. Hyde made a counter-offer, by offering £950. Wrench rejected this. Later Hyde came back and said that he now accepted the original offer of £1,000. Wrench rejected it.

Held: Hyde could no longer accept the original offer. It had been terminated by the counter-offer and was no longer capable of acceptance. His 'acceptance' was merely a fresh offer which Wrench was free to turn down.

Note that a mere request for further details does not constitute a counteroffer.

Stevenson v McLean (1880)

Facts: M offered, in writing, to sell a quantity of iron to S at a given price. S replied querying delivery times, but before receiving a reply sent a further letter accepting the offer. This acceptance crossed in the post with a letter of revocation from M to S. M refused to supply the iron to S, arguing that S's query was a counter-offer.

Held: M could not treat the query as a counter-offer. S had not intended to prejudice M's position, just to establish the boundaries of the deal. Therefore M's offer was still open when S wrote accepting it.

Lapse

An offer will lapse on:

- the death of the offeror (unless the offeree accepts in ignorance of the death)

- the death of the offeree

- the failure of a condition. If the offer was made subject to a condition, it will lapse on failure of that condition

- after the expiry of a fixed time (if any) or after a reasonable time. What is a reasonable time may depend on the subject matter of the contract.

Ramsgate Victoria Hotel Co v Montefiore (1866)

Facts: The defendant applied to the company to buy some shares in June and paid a deposit. He didn't hear anything until November when the company sent him a letter of allotment as acceptance and a request for the balance. By this time the defendant had changed his mind and no longer wanted the shares.

Held: The offer was for a reasonable time only and since five months had passed since the offer had been made the offer was deemed to have lapsed. The defendant was not bound to buy the shares. Their value could have changed dramatically in such a long period.

If the goods are perishable the time for lapse will be very short.

Test your understanding 2

1   **What is the legal effect of the following statement in a newspaper?**

'For sale. Computer, monitor and laser printer. Good condition. £500.'

A   The statement is an offer for sale

B   The statement is a 'mere puff or boast'

C   The statement has no legal effect

D   The statement is an invitation to treat

> 2 Simon offers to sell his car to Tony for £600. Tony is unsure but, as he is leaving the pub, asks Simon if he can tell him by 9am the next day. Simon agrees. Later that night Tony meets Rick, a reliable mutual friend, who tells him that Simon has decided to keep the car. Tony visits Simon at 8.30am and accepts the offer.
>
> **Is there a contract?**
>
> A Yes, because the revocation has not been communicated.
>
> B No, because revocation can be communicated by a reliable third party.
>
> C Yes, because Simon has agreed to keep the offer open.
>
> D No, because the promise to keep the offer open was gratuitous.

3 Acceptance

 What is acceptance?

Acceptance is the unqualified and unconditional assent to all the terms of the offer.

It can be oral, written or by conduct – **Carlill v Carbolic Smoke Ball (1893)**.

The offeror can stipulate a particular mode of acceptance. However, if he merely requests a mode, the offeree is not limited to that mode.

Communication

As a general rule, acceptance is not effective until it is communicated to the offeror.

Entores v Miles Far Eastern (1955)

Facts: The claimants, who were based in London, made an offer by telex to the defendants in Amsterdam. The defendants accepted by telex. The point at issue was where the acceptance had taken place, i.e. in Amsterdam at the time the defendants sent the telex or in London when it was received. It can be important to know which country the contract was concluded in as different countries have different legal rules.

Held: Acceptance is not effective until it is communicated. Therefore the contract was made in London.

The following conclusions can be drawn from the **Entores** case:

- If a fax, telex or telephone message is received during normal business hours, that is when it is communicated even though it might not be read until later.

- If a fax, telex or telephone message is received outside normal business hours, it is deemed to be communicated when the business next opens.

Note, in addition, that the offeror can expressly or impliedly dispense with the need for communication – **Carlill v Carbolic Smoke Ball (1893)**. However, he cannot stipulate that silence is acceptance.

Felthouse v Bindley (1863)

Facts: The claimant was interested in buying a horse and had discussed with his nephew the purchase of a horse belonging to him. The claimant wrote to his nephew and stated in this letter that he assumed the horse was his for £30.15 if he did not receive a response from his nephew. The nephew did not reply, and instructed the defendant, an auctioneer he had engaged to conduct a sale of his farming stock, to withhold the horse from the auction. By mistake, the defendant allowed the horse to be put up and sold. The claimant sued the defendant for damages.

Held: An acceptance of offer will not give rise to a binding agreement unless it is expressly communicated to the individual who makes the offer. Although the nephew had the intent to sell his horse to the claimant at the offered price, he did not communicate this intention to his uncle, or do anything to bind himself. Since property was not vested in the claimant, he had no right to bring action against the defendant.

The postal rule

The postal rule is an exception to the rule that acceptance must be communicated.

The postal rule states that acceptance is complete as soon as the letter is posted.

Adams v Lindsell (1818)

Facts: The case involved two parties in the sale of wool. On 2 September, the defendants wrote to the claimants offering to sell them certain fleeces of wool and requiring an answer in the course of post. The defendants, misdirected the letter so that the claimants didn't receive it until 5 September. The claimants posted their acceptance on the same day but it was not received until 9 September. Meanwhile, on 8 September, the defendants, not having received an answer by 7 September as they had expected, sold the wool to someone else.

Held: The question for the court was whether a contract of sale had been entered into before 8 September when the wool was sold to the third party. If the acceptance was effective when it arrived at the address or when the defendant saw it, then no contract would have been made and the sale to the third party would amount to revocation of the offer. However, the court held that the offer had been accepted as soon as the letter had been posted. The defendant was therefore liable in breach of contract.

However, the postal rule only applies if:

- the letter is properly stamped, addressed and posted, and
- post is a reasonable method of communication.

It applies even if the letter is never received by the offeror.

Household Fire Insurance v Grant (1879)

Facts: G applied for shares in HFI. HFI posted a share allotment letter to G, accepting his offer. The letter was not received.

Held: Once the letter was posted, HFI could not recall it. They had accepted G's offer to take shares.

However, the postal rule does not apply if the offeror states that he must actually receive the acceptance – **Holwell Securities v Hughes (1974)**.

Test your understanding 3

1   On 1 September, Seller Ltd sent a fax to Buyer Ltd offering to sell a machine at a price of £10,000, and stating that Buyer Ltd must accept by 10 September. On 3 September, Buyer Ltd sent a fax to Seller Ltd asking 'Will you accept payment over three months?'.

On 5 September, Seller Ltd sold the machine to New Ltd, and on 6 September received a second fax from Buyer Ltd accepting the offer and offering to make immediate payment.

Which one of the following is correct?

A   There is no contract between Seller Ltd and Buyer Ltd because the offer was withdrawn on 5 September when the machine was sold to New Ltd.

B   There is no contract between Seller Ltd and Buyer Ltd because Buyer Ltd's fax of 3 September amounted to a counteroffer which destroyed Seller Ltd's original offer.

C   Seller Ltd and Buyer Ltd contracted on 3 September.

D   Seller Ltd and Buyer Ltd contracted on 6 September.

2   A Ltd placed the following advertisement in a local newspaper:

'We are able to offer for sale a number of portable colour television sets at the specially reduced price of £5.90. Order now while stocks last.'

The advertisement contained a mistake in that the television sets should have been priced at £59.00. B Ltd immediately placed an order for 100 television sets.

Which one of the following statements is correct?

A   B Ltd has accepted an offer and is contractually entitled to the 100 television sets.

B   A Ltd can refuse to supply B Ltd as the advertisement is not an offer, but an invitation to treat.

C   A Ltd can only refuse to sell the television sets to B Ltd if it has sold all its stock.

D   As B Ltd has not yet paid for the television sets, the company has no contractual right to them.

3   Alf sends a letter to Bert on 1 January offering to buy Bert's antique Ming vase for £1,000. On the same day Bert sends a letter to Alf offering to sell to Alf the same antique Ming vase for £1,000.

Alf now changes his mind and wishes to know the likely legal position.

A   There is a valid contract; Alf and Bert have reached agreement and waived the need for acceptance.

B   Both have made offers on the same terms and no acceptance is necessary.

C   There is agreement, but no contract since neither Alf nor Bert knew that their offers had been accepted.

D   There is a contract but is lacks consideration since neither Alf nor Bert has paid a price for the other's promise.

4   Consideration

The basic rule

Every simple contract must be supported by consideration from each party. However, contracts made by deed (specialty contracts) do not require consideration unless the terms of the agreement require it.

 Definition

'Consideration is an act or forbearance (or the promise of it) on the part of one party to a contract as the price of the promise made to him by the other party to the contract': **Dunlop Pneumatic Tyre Co v Selfridge & Co Ltd (1915)**.

'Some right, interest, profit or benefit accruing to one party, or some forbearance, detriment, loss or responsibility given, suffered or undertaken by the other': **Currie v Misa (1875)**.

 Types of consideration

Executory consideration is given where there is an exchange of promises to do something in the future.

For example, when a person agrees to pay for some goods 'cash on delivery'. Both the payment and the delivery are 'executory', i.e. to be completed at a later date.

Executed consideration means that the consideration is in the form of an act carried out at the time the contract is made.

For example, handing over 60p and receiving a newspaper. Both the payment and the handing over of the paper are executed at the time of the contract.

Sufficient consideration

Consideration must be sufficient but need not be adequate.

Sufficient means that:

* there must be some monetary value to the consideration

* it must be capable in law of amounting to consideration.

The words 'need not be adequate' mean that there is no need for each party's consideration to be equal in value.

Chappell v Nestle Co Ltd (1959)

Facts: Records were sold for 1s 6d plus three chocolate wrappers.

Held: The wrappers were part of the consideration even though they had minimal value.

Thomas v Thomas (1842)

Facts: A promise to lease a house to a widow for rent of £1 a year was binding.

Held: The consideration had some value, and so was sufficient at law, even though it was inadequate as a years rent.

White v Bluett (1853)

A son's promise to stop complaining did not amount to consideration as it had no monetary value.

Past consideration

Past consideration is insufficient and therefore is **not valid**.

Consideration is past if the consideration is an act which has been wholly performed before the other party gives his promise.

Re McArdle (1951)

Facts: A mother and her three grown-up children lived together in a house. One of the sons and his wife did some decorating in the house and later the other two children promised to pay towards the decorating costs and signed a document to this effect.

Held: It was held that the promise was unenforceable as all the work had been done before the promise was made and was therefore past consideration.

However, the situation in **Re McArdle (1951)** can be contrasted with that in **Re Casey's Patent (1892)**.

Facts: A and B owned a patent and C was the manager who had worked on it for two years. A and B then promised C a one-third share in the invention for his help in developing it. The patents were transferred to C but A and B then claimed their return.

Held: C could rely on the agreement. Even though C's consideration was in the past, it had been done in a business situation, at the request of A and B and it was understood by both sides that C would be paid and the subsequent promise to pay merely fixed the amount. There was an implied promise to pay as the development of the patent had been requested by A and B.

Performance of an existing duty

As a general rule, performance of an existing statutory duty is not sufficient consideration.

Collins v Godefroy (1831)

Facts: A witness was promised payment if he would attend court and give evidence.

Held: This did not amount to consideration as he was legally required to attend court.

Similarly, performance of an existing contractual duty is not consideration.

Stilk v Myrick (1809)

Facts: A captain promised to share the wages of the deserting seamen with the rest of the crew who had contracted to sail the ship home.

Held: The promise was not binding as there was no extra consideration from the seamen, they were merely doing what they had contracted to do.

However, there are three exceptions:

1   If the existing contractual or statutory duty is exceeded, there is sufficient consideration.

Glasbrook Bros Ltd v Glamorgan County Council (1925)

Facts: Glasbrook Bros Ltd requested the police to provide protection in excess of the statutory requirement.

Held: The police had provided sufficient consideration to give entitlement to remuneration by providing the extra officers over and above the statutory requirement.

Hartley v Ponsonby (1857)

Facts: A high number of desertions from a merchant ship rendered the vessel unseaworthy since it was now undermanned. Extra pay was offered to the crew if they remained loyal and sailed the ship home.

Held: The promise of extra money was recoverable by the seamen who remained loyal, since they were now working in a dangerous situation not contemplated by their original contractual undertaking (i.e. they were doing more than required by their original contract).

2   The performance of an existing contractual duty may be sufficient if it confers some benefit of a practical nature on the other party.

Williams v Roffey Bros (1990)

Facts: W agreed to do some carpentry in a block of flats for R at a fixed price of £20,000, by an agreed date. The contract contained a 'time penalty' clause and R agreed to pay an extra £10,000 to ensure that the work was completed on time. If the work had not been completed on time, R would have suffered a penalty in his own contract with the owner of the flats.

Held: The Court of Appeal decided that, even though W was in effect doing nothing over and above the original agreement to complete the work by an agreed time, there was a new contract here for the £10,000. The court decided that both W and R benefited from the new contract. Two reasons were given:

- Even though W merely did what he was already contracted to do, this nevertheless conferred a practical benefit on R in that R not only avoided penalties under the head contract, but also the cost and aggravation of employing substitute contractors.

- R's promise to pay the extra £10,000 had not been extracted by fraud or pressure. (It was R who had approached W and had volunteered the extra money.) It would be inequitable to go back on his promise.

3   The performance of an existing contractual obligation is sufficient consideration to support a promise from a third party.

Shadwell v Shadwell (1860)

Facts: The claimant was engaged to E (at this time an engagement was an enforceable contract). The claimant's uncle wrote him a letter saying "I will pay you £150 per year during my life until your income as a barrister shall reach 600 guineas per annum if you marry E". When the uncle died the claimant sought to recover outstanding amounts. The deceased's personal representatives argued that the claimant was already under a contractual obligation to marry when the uncle made the offer, and therefore the claimant supplied no consideration.

Held: There was sufficient consideration as the uncle had promised the claimant a reward and in return the uncle had received a promise to which he previously had no right. The contract was between the claimant and E. The uncle was a third party and the claimant promised to marry E in consideration of the payments.

Illegal acts

An illegal act is insufficient to amount to consideration.

Test your understanding 4

1   **The law enforces bargains not bare promises. The presence of which of the following indicates the former?**

    A   Intention to create legal relations

    B   Consideration

    C   Capacity

    D   Legality

2   **Consideration need not be adequate but must be:**

    A   Money

    B   Sufficient

    C   Of equivalent value to the goods

    D   Accepted

The part-payment problem

The problem – if A accepts £400 from B in full and final settlement of a debt of £500, can A sue for the remaining £100?

General rule – the rule in **Pinnel's case (1602)** states that payment of a smaller sum does not discharge a debt of a greater amount. This has been affirmed in **Foakes v Beer (1884)**.

Exceptions

There are four exceptions to the rule in **Pinnel's case**:

* where the part payment is made by a third party

* composition with creditors (i.e. the creditors all agree to accept a sum which is less than they are owed)

* accord and satisfaction

    – accord means that both the parties agree freely to the part payment.

    – satisfaction (i.e. consideration) might be payment at an earlier date, payment at a different place, payment in a different currency, etc.

D & C Builders v Rees (1966)

Facts: R owed money to D & C and knew that D & C were in financial difficulties. R offered to pay a smaller sum to be accepted in full and final payment of whole amount. R stated that it was not accepted , the claimant would get nothing. The claimant reluctantly accepted the smaller sum but later sued for the balance.

Held: The claimant could successfully sue for the balance. Several reasons contributed to the court's decision, amongst them were:

- In view of the pressure put on the claimant and the claimant's reluctance there was no true accord

- payment by cheque and cash are, in these circumstances, no different. Therefore the payment by cheque did not amount to consideration: it conferred no benefit over and above payment in cash

- the equitable doctrine of promissory estoppel.

Promissory estoppel

The doctrine of promissory estoppel is based on the principles of fairness and justice. It prevents a person going back on his promise to accept a lesser amount.

The principle was established in **Central London Property Trust v High Trees House (1947)**.

Central London Property Trust v High Trees House (1947)

Facts: Claimants let a block of flats to the defendants in 1937 at an annual rent of £2,500 pa. The defendants were then going to sublet the flats. Owing to World War II and London being bombed, some of the flats became empty and it was impossible to re-let them. In addition the existing tenants had their rent reduced. The claimants agreed to accept half the rent for the rest of the war.

Held: The full rent was payable from the end of the war. The doctrine of promissory estoppel would stop the claimants from recovering the full rent foregone during the war years. High Trees House were expected to reduce their rent as a result of the rent reduction by Central London Property Trust, which they did thereby proving their reliance on the waiver.

The principle is subject to the following conditions:

- There must be an existing contract between the parties.

- The claimants must voluntarily waive their rights under the contract.

- There must be an intention that the defendants should rely on the waiver.

- The defendants must alter their legal position because of the waiver.

The doctrine has a number of limitations:

- It is a shield not a sword, i.e. it is a defence not a cause of action.
- It may only have a suspensory effect, as shown in the **High Trees case**. (The claimant's rights were suspended during World War II, but reinstated for the future once the war had finished.)
- The party seeking to use it as an equitable defence must also have acted fairly in their dealings with the claimants.

In **D & C Builders v Rees** (above) Mrs Rees attempted to rely on promissory estoppel, but it was held that she could not do so as she had attempted to force the claimant to accept less and thus had not acted fairly herself i.e. she did not 'come to equity with clean hands'.

5 Privity of contract

The general rule

Only the parties to a contract:

- acquire rights and obligations under it
- can sue and be sued on it.

Exceptions

There are a number of exceptions to the general rule regarding privity of contract:

- The Contracts (Rights of Third Parties) Act 1999 allows a person who is not a party to a contract to enforce it so long as the contract was for his benefit and he was expressly identified, by name or description.
- A contract between two parties may be accompanied by a collateral contract between one of the parties and a third person relating to the same subject matter.

Shanklin Pier v Detel Products (1951)

Facts: The claimant owned a pier and wanted it repainting. They contacted Detel, a paint manufacturer to enquire about the qualities of the paint and were told it lasted 7–10 years. The claimant employed contractors to do the painting and specified that Detel paint be used. The contractors completed the painting but the paint began to flake after only 3 months. The claimant sued Detel, who argued that there was no contract between them.

Held: There was a collateral contract between Detel and the claimant. Detel had promised that the paint would last between 7–10 years and claimant's request for the contractors to use Detel paint was consideration for that promise.

- Under the rules of land law, restrictive covenants run with the land to which they relate i.e. that a future owner will be subject to restrictions made in previous contracts.

Tulk v Moxhay (1848)

Facts: The owner of several pieces of land sold a plot to another party, making a covenant to keep a particular area "uncovered with buildings" such that it could remain a pleasure ground. Over the following years the land was sold several times over to new parties, eventually to the defendant. The defendant, who was aware of the covenant at the time of purchase, refused to abide by the covenant as he claimed he was not in privity of contract and so was not bound by it.

Held: An injunction was granted against the defendant to restrain a breach of the covenant.

- Insurance law allows a third party to take the benefit of a contract of insurance for example where the policy is for life insurance which will pay out to a third party in the event of the policy holder's death.

- Trust law allows a beneficiary to enforce a trust.

- Agency law allows an agent to make a contract between his principal and a third party, even though the third party may be unaware that he is acting as an agent. Agency is covered later in **chapter 5**.

- An executor can enforce contracts made by the deceased for whom he is acting.

Beswick v Beswick (1967)

Facts: A coal merchant sold his business to his nephew in return for a pension during his lifetime and the payment of a smaller pension to his widow, on his death. After the uncle died, the nephew stopped paying the widow. She sued the nephew in her own personal capacity and in her capacity as the administrator of her husband's estate.

Held: Although she was not a party to the contract and could not sue in her own personal capacity, she could sue in her capacity as the administrator of her husband's estate.

6 Intention to create legal relations

Introduction

In order to create a contract, both parties must intend to enter into a legal relationship. If it is not clear from the contract that the parties intended legal consequences then the law presumes the intention of the parties based on the type of agreement.

Domestic or social agreements

It is presumed that there is no intention to be legally bound, unless it can be shown otherwise.

Balfour v Balfour (1919)

Facts: The defendant, who was about to go abroad, promised to pay his wife £30 per month in consideration of her agreeing to support herself without calling on him for any further maintenance. The wife contended that the defendant was bound by his promise.

Held: There was no legally binding contract between the parties. As it was a domestic agreement it was presumed the parties did not intend to be legally bound.

The usual presumption that agreements between spouses living happily together are not legally enforceable does not apply when they are about to separate, or have already separated. In such instances the circumstances of the case can be shown to rebut the presumption.

Merritt v Merritt (1970)

Facts: A husband, separated from his wife, wrote and signed a document stating that, in consideration of the wife paying off the outstanding mortgage debt of £180 on their matrimonial home, he would transfer the house standing in their joint names into her sole ownership. The wife paid off the outstanding mortgage debt, but the husband refused to transfer title in the house to her, alleging that his promise was a domestic arrangement and did not give rise to legal relations.

Held: The husband's promise was enforceable, the agreement having been made when the parties were not living together amicably. A legal relationship is contemplated where a husband deserts his wife and an agreement is concluded on ownership of the matrimonial home occupied by the wife and children. The circumstances of their separation was enough to rebut the presumption.

The presumption that there is no intention to be legally bound will also be rebutted where the evidence shows that the parties made formal and/or detailed financial arrangements.

Simpkins v Pays (1955)

Facts: Pays and her granddaughter, together with Simpkins, a paying lodger, submitted an entry each week in a fashion competition appearing in the Sunday Empire News. All three devised a separate solution to the competition, but they were submitted on one coupon only, in Pays' name. The entry fees and postage were shared equally. The granddaughter made a correct forecast and Pays received a prize of £750. Simpkins claimed a one-third share of the prize money.

Held: Although this was an arrangement in a domestic context the presumption was rebutted: it was a legally enforceable joint enterprise and the parties clearly intended to share any prize money. 'There was mutuality in the arrangements between the parties and an intention to create legal relations'. It was decided that on the facts this went beyond a mere friendly agreement and became a joint enterprise.

Jones v Vernon's Pools Ltd (1938)

Facts: Jones contended that he had forwarded a winning entry to the defendant company of football pools promoters, but they denied having received it. In order to deal with this type of eventuality, a clause was printed on the pools coupon which Jones had signed, stating that 'any agreement ... entered into ... shall not ... give rise to any legal relationship ... but ... is binding in honour only'.

Held: A contract did not exist between the parties, since the wording of the agreement clearly negated any such intention. Jones could not, therefore, sue the pools company for breach of contract.

Commercial agreements

It is presumed that there is an intention to be legally bound, unless it can be shown otherwise.

This is a strong presumption that can only be rebutted by clear evidence to the contrary.

Test your understanding 5

Which of the following statements is/are correct?

(I) If an agreement is stated to be 'binding in honour only', the parties have decided that the agreement should not have contractual force.

(II) If an agreement is not in writing, the parties are presumed to have intended that it should not be legally enforceable.

A   (I) only

B   (II) only

C   Neither (I) nor (II)

Letter of comfort

Often in international contracts a letter of comfort is used to assure a contracting party that a parent company will provide its subsidiary with the necessary resources to fulfil the contract. However, legally a letter of comfort does not require the parent company to fulfil the obligations incurred by its subsidiary and therefore has no legal effect.

7 Contractual terms

Terms versus representations

A statement, written or oral, made during the negotiations leading to a contract, may be a term of the contract or merely a representation inducing the contract.

A representation is something that is said by the offeror in order to induce the offeree to enter into the contract. It may or may not become a term of that contract.

The distinction between terms and representations is important because, if a statement is untrue, the remedies available to the innocent party differ:

- if the representation becomes a term of the contract, the innocent party has remedies for breach of the term as well as for misrepresentation

- if, however, the representation does not become a term of the contract, the innocent party will have remedies only for misrepresentation which are based on equitable remedies (see **section 11**).

Sources of terms

Terms may be express or implied.

Express terms are those specifically inserted into the contract by one or both of the parties. They must be clear for them to be enforceable.

Scammell v Ouston (1941)

Facts: An agreement provided for the balance of the price to be paid ....`on hire purchase terms over a period of two years'....

Held: The words 'hire purchase terms' were considered too imprecise as the seller had a range of such terms.

Implied terms are not expressly included in the contract, but they are nevertheless still part of the contract. They may be implied by statute or by the courts, or rarely by custom. An example of this is a contract of employment which has implied terms such as an employee's duty to obey lawful and reasonable orders (see **Chapter 4**).

Express terms will generally override implied terms. However, some statutory terms cannot be overridden by express agreement.

The sources of terms are summarised in the following diagram:

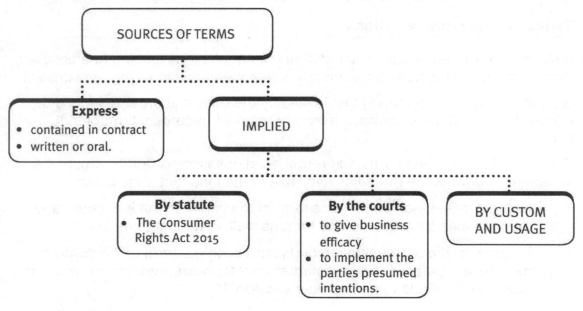

The Consumer Rights Act 2015

The Consumer Rights Act 2015 came into force on 1 October 2015 making consumer rights clearer and easier to understand. The legislation covers:

- what should happen when goods are faulty;

- what should happen when digital content is faulty;

- how services should match up to what has been agreed, and what should happen when they do not, or when they are not provided with reasonable care and skill;

- unfair terms in a contract (more coverage in Section 8: Exclusion Clauses, which also explains which types of contracts are classed as "consumer contracts").

Sale of goods

When a product is sold it must be of satisfactory quality, fit for purpose and as described.

Goods shouldn't be faulty or damaged when you receive them. The test would be what a reasonable person would consider satisfactory for the goods in question. For example, bargain-bucket products won't be held to as high standards as luxury goods.

The goods should be fit for the purpose they are supplied for, as well as any specific purpose you made known to the retailer before you agreed to buy the goods.

The goods supplied must match any description given to you, or any models or samples shown to you at the time of purchase.

If goods which are purchased are faulty the following remedies are available:

- Up to thirty days – an immediate refund.

- Up to six months – the right to have the item repaired or replaced. If the attempt to repair or replace the item is unsuccessful the consumer has the right to a refund or a price reduction if they wish to keep the product. The goods are presumed to have the fault when they were purchased and the onus is on the seller to prove that the fault was not present at the time of purchase.

- Up to six years – if the goods do not last a reasonable length of time the consumer may be entitled to some money back. The burden is on the consumer to prove that the product was faulty at the point of purchase.

Sale of services

A service must be carried out with reasonable care and skill. In practice this means that a service must be carried out to the same or similar standard to that which is considered acceptable within their trade or profession. Industry standards within a particular service sector, relevant codes of practice and even the law (such as building regulations and credit legislation) are useful benchmarks to consider when deciding whether a service has been carried out with reasonable care and skill.

If a service has not been provided with reasonable care and skill the following remedies are available:

- Right to repeat performance – where a service is not carried out with reasonable care and skill then the service must be performed again so that it conforms with the contract. The repeat performance should be carried out within a reasonable time, without significant inconvenience and at no cost to the consumer.

- Right to a price reduction – if repeat performance of a service is impossible or it cannot be carried out within a reasonable time or without causing significant inconvenience, then the consumer is entitled to a price reduction. This can be a full refund, for example, where the consumer has had no benefit from the service and it will need to be started again. A price reduction can be calculated by comparing the difference between the contract price and the value of the service actually performed.

Sale of digital content

Digital content refers to data which are produced and supplied in digital form such as software, e-books, music, films and 'apps'.

As with goods there is a requirement that the digital content must be of satisfactory quality, fit for purpose and as described.

The remedies available under the Act are:

- Right to repair or replacement – this must take place within a reasonable time and without significant inconvenience to the consumer

- Reduction in price – this is only triggered if the remedies of repair and replacement are not possible or the seller has not complied with the right to a repair or replacement within a reasonable time.

- Repair of damage – the consumer has a right to compensation or repair in respect of any damage caused by the faulty content to a device or to other digital content.

Implied by the courts

The Moorcock (1889)

Facts: There was an agreement by a wharf owner to permit a ship owner to unload his ship at the wharf. The ship was damaged when, at low tide, it was grounded on the bottom of the river on a hard ridge.

Held: It was an implied term, though not expressed, that the ground alongside the wharf was safe at low tide since both parties knew that the ship must rest on it.

Types of terms

There are three types of terms:

- conditions
- warranties
- innominate terms.

The distinction between the types of term is important because it determines the remedies that may be available in the event of a breach.

 Conditions

A condition is an important term going to the root of the contract.

Breach can result in damages or discharge or both. Discharge entitles the innocent party to repudiate the contract and claim damages.

Poussard v Spiers & Pond (1876)

Facts: A soprano, Madame Poussard, agreed to sing in a series of operas for Spiers. She failed to appear on the opening night and Spiers refused her services for subsequent nights.

Held: The obligation to appear on the opening night was a condition. Spiers was entitled to treat the contract as at an end and was therefore not himself in breach by refusing her services for the remaining nights.

Warranties

A warranty is a less important term, which is incidental to the main purpose of the contract.

Breach of warranty results in damages only.

Bettini v Gye (1876)

Facts: A tenor, Bettini, who agreed to sing in a series of concerts and to attend six days of rehearsals beforehand failed to appear for the first four rehearsal days. Gye in consequence refused Bettini's services for the balance for the rehearsals and performances.

Held: The obligation to appear for rehearsals was a warranty and therefore Bettini's breach did not entitle Gye to treat the contract as at an end. Gye was accordingly in breach of contract when he refused Bettini's services for the remainder of the contract.

Innominate terms

An innominate or indeterminate term is neither a condition nor a warranty.

The remedy depends on the effects of the breach:

- if trivial – damages only i.e. term is treated as if it were a warranty

- if serious – damages, discharge or both i.e. term is treated as if it were a condition.

The Hansa Nord (1976)

Facts: Citrus pulp pellets for use in animal food had been sold for £100,000 under a contract which provided for "shipment to be made in good condition." Part of the goods had not been so shipped and in addition the market value in such goods had fallen at the delivery date. The buyers rejected the goods which were later resold pursuant to a court order and eventually reacquired by the original buyers for just under £34,000. The buyers then used the goods for the originally intended purpose of making cattle food.

Held: The Court of Appeal held that rejection was not justified. The term as to shipment in good condition was neither a condition nor a warranty but an innominate term; and there was no finding that the effect of its breach was sufficiently serious to justify rejection. The buyers seem to have tried to reject, not because the goods were impaired, but because they saw an opportunity of acquiring them at well below the originally agreed price. In these circumstances their only remedy was in damages: they were entitled to the difference in value between damaged and sound goods.

Test your understanding 6

1 **Which one of the following is incorrect?**

   A   A condition is a term which the parties intended to be of fundamental importance.

   B   A warranty is a term which the parties did not intend to be of fundamental importance.

   C   If a condition is breached, then the contract must be terminated.

   D   If a warranty is breached, then the innocent party cannot terminate the contract.

2 **Dee Ltd has broken one of the terms of its contract with E Ltd. If that term is a warranty, which of the following is correct?**

   A   E Ltd may repudiate the contract with Dee Ltd

   B   E Ltd can avoid the contract and recover damages

   C   E Ltd is entitled to sue for damages only

   D   E Ltd is entitled to sue for damages or to repudiate the contract

3 **'An obligation, which though it must be performed, is not so vital that a failure to perform it goes to the substance of the contract' describes a:**

   A   Warranty

   B   Condition

   C   Innominate term

   D   Representation

4 **Which of the following statements is incorrect?**

   A   The remedies of the innocent party for breach of a warranty depend on the seriousness of the breach.

   B   The remedies for breach of a condition are repudiation and damages.

   C   The likely remedy for breach of an innominate term cannot be assessed at the outset of a contractual relationship.

   D   The remedy for breach of a warranty is a legal one and therefore available as of right.

8 Exclusion clauses

 Definition

An exclusion clause (or exemption clause) is a term that seeks to exclude or limit a party's liability for breach of contract.

Common law rules

In order to be valid an exclusion clause must satisfy two conditions:

- it must be incorporated into the contract
- its wording must cover the loss.

An exclusion clause can be incorporated into a contract by:

- signature
- notice
- previous dealings.

Signature

The case of **L'Estrange v Graucob (1934)** established that a clause is incorporated by signature even if the signatory did not read or understand the document.

However, the situation in **L'Estrange v Graucob (1934)** can be contrasted with **Curtis v Chemical Cleaning (1951)** in which it was held that a signature does not incorporate the clause if the effect of the term was misrepresented.

Curtis v Chemical Cleaning (1951)

Liability for damage to a wedding dress was not excluded due to misrepresentation of the clause.

Notice

For an exclusion clause to be incorporated by notice, reasonable steps must have been taken to bring it to the attention of the other party at the time the contract was made. What are 'reasonable steps' depend on the circumstances.

Thompson v LMS Railway (1930)

Facts: T bought a railway ticket, which stated that she would travel subject to the company's standard conditions of carriage. These conditions could be inspected at the station; one of them excluded liability for injury to passengers.

T was unable to read, and so was unaware of the clause. She was injured and claimed damages.

Held: The ticket was a document which should be expected to contain terms, being more than a mere receipt for payment. The railway company had taken reasonable steps to bring the exclusion clause to passengers' attention, by incorporating it into the contract document (the ticket). T was bound by the clause (even though she could not read: 'illiteracy is a misfortune, not a privilege') as were all other passengers.

Olley v Marlborough Court (1949)

A clause can be incorporated by notice, provided it was given before making the contract. A notice in a hotel room did not exclude liability as the contract was made at the reception desk.

Previous dealings

For an exclusion clause to be incorporated by previous dealings, there must have been a consistent course of dealings between the parties.

Spurling v Bradshaw (1956)

Facts: The defendant had dealt with the claimant for a number of years. On the contract in question he delivered four full barrels for storage. As usual, he later received a document which acknowledged receipt and contained a clause excluding liability for negligence. When he came to collect the barrels, he found they were empty.

Held: The exclusion clause had been incorporated into the contract, even though it was received after the contract was made. It had been incorporated through the previous course of dealings whereby he had been sent copies of documents containing the clause, even though he had never read them.

However, **Spurling v Bradshaw (1956)** can be contrasted with **Hollier v Rambler Motors (1972)** in which three or four deals between a garage and a private customer over a five-year period were held to be insufficient to constitute a course of dealings.

The wording must cover the loss

Under the contra proferentem rule, the courts interpret the words narrowly against the interests of the person seeking to rely on the clause.

Photo Productions Ltd v Securicor (1980)

Facts: Security guard burned down factory he was guarding. The contract between his employers and the factory owners limited employers' liability for injurious acts and defaults of guards.

Held: The clause was clear and unambiguous and effectively limited their liability even for this fundamental breach.

Statutory rules

Even if a clause passes the common law test, it must also satisfy the statutory rules. These are contained in:

- Unfair Contract Terms Act (UCTA) 1977

- Consumer Rights Act (CRA) 2015.

The law treats business to business contracts differently than it does business to consumer contracts.

Unfair Contract Terms Act (UCTA) 1977

UCTA 1977 applies to exclusion clauses in business to business contracts.

It states that a clause excluding liability for:

- death or personal injury due to negligence is void

- other loss due to negligence is void unless reasonable.

The burden of proving reasonableness is on the party seeking to rely on the clause. In assessing whether a term is unfair or unreasonable, the court has regard to:

- the strength of the bargaining positions of the parties

- whether the buyer received an inducement to agree to the term

- whether the buyer knew or ought to have known of the existence and extent of the term

- the ability of the party to insure against the liability.

St Albans City and District Council v International Computers Ltd (1994)

Facts: The defendants had been hired to produce a computer system which would calculate population figures on which the claimants would base their community charges. The contract contained a clause restricting liability to £100,000. The database that the computer system produced was seriously inaccurate and as a result the claimant sustained a loss of £1.3m.

Held: The clause was unreasonable. The defendants could not justify the limitation of £100,000 which was small both in relation to the potential risk and the actual loss. In addition, the defendants had insurance of £50m themselves. Therefore, it was reasonable to expect that those who stood to make the profit, and had been well able to insure and had insured, should carry the risk.

Consumer Rights Act 2015

The Act consolidates and combines previous legislation contained in the Unfair Contract Terms Act 1977 (UCTA 1977) and the Unfair Terms in Consumer Contracts Regulations 1999 (UTCRR 1999) in respect of consumer contracts.

A consumer contract is a contract between a business and a consumer. A **consumer** is defined as 'an individual acting for purposes that are wholly or mainly outside that individual's trade, business, craft or profession'. A **business** is referred to as a 'trader' under the Act and is defined as 'a person acting for purposes relating to their business, craft or profession, whether acting personally or through another person acting in the trader's name or on the trader's behalf'.

The legislation applies to standard form contracts as well as individually negotiated contracts.

Fairness

In essence a term in a consumer contract is unfair if, contrary to the requirement of good faith, it causes a significant imbalance in the parties' rights and obligations under the contract, to the detriment of the consumer.

To decide whether a term is unfair, the Act uses a fairness test which considers:

- the nature of the subject matter of the contract

- all the circumstances existing when the term was agreed

- all the other terms of the contract; and

- all the terms of another contract on which the contract depends. This is known as a 'secondary contract' which can be made subsequent to a main contract.

Transparency

A written term must be expressed in plain and intelligible language and consumers must be given a real chance, before entering into a contract, to see and understand all terms that could operate to their disadvantage.

Terms and notices

An important feature of the legislation is that it applies to all 'announcements, whether or not in writing, and any other communication or purported communication' which seek to limit liability to a consumer, or otherwise relates to the rights and duties between the trader and consumer.

This means that as well as the contract terms themselves, notices such as on a website or in business premises would also be subject to a fairness assessment.

Exemption for core terms

A term is not subject to a fairness assessment where the term:

- specifies the main subject matter of the contract; or

- relates to the appropriateness of the price payable under the contract.

These exemptions for the fairness assessment are only available where the term is transparent (plain and intelligible language) and prominent. A term is prominent if it is brought to the consumer's attention in such a way that the average consumer would be aware of it.

Automatically unenforceable

Some terms and notices are automatically unenforceable against consumers, referred to by the Competition and Markets Authority as blacklisted.

An example of this is a term that excludes or restricts responsibility for death or personal injury resulting from negligence.

Grey listed

Schedule 2 of the Act provides illustrations of the types of terms that may be considered unfair (referred to by the Competition and Markets Authority as the grey list) such as:

- consumers being tied into the contract beyond what they would normally expect

- the business not having to perform its obligations

- consumers unreasonably losing prepayments if the contract is ended

- the business determining the price or subject matter of the contract after the consumer has become bound by it.

How to challenge unfair terms

A consumer can report a trader to the local trading standards department or to the Competition and Markets Authority.

The consumer has the right to challenge a term as unfair in court. If the court decides that the term is unfair the consumer will not be bound by it.

The Competition and Markets Authority has produced the following flowchart which aims to provide a simplified approach to dealing with unfair terms.

Summary

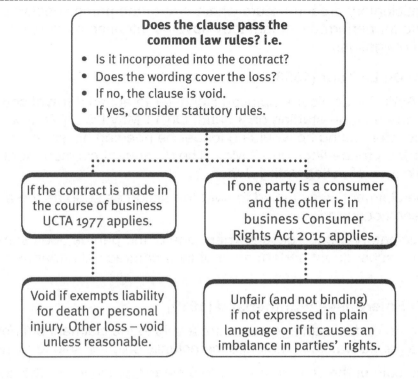

Does the clause pass the common law rules? i.e.
- Is it incorporated into the contract?
- Does the wording cover the loss?
- If no, the clause is void.
- If yes, consider statutory rules.

If the contract is made in the course of business UCTA 1977 applies.

If one party is a consumer and the other is in business Consumer Rights Act 2015 applies.

Void if exempts liability for death or personal injury. Other loss – void unless reasonable.

Unfair (and not binding) if not expressed in plain language or if it causes an imbalance in parties' rights.

9 Discharge of contract

A contract can be brought to an end in several ways:

By Performance

This is the way in which most contracts are discharged: both parties perform their obligations under the contract.

By Frustration

Where, after the contract is made, it becomes impossible to perform.

By Breach of Contract (see below)

10 Breach of contract

 What is meant by breach of contract?

Breach of contract occurs where one of the parties to the agreement fails to comply, either completely or satisfactorily, with their obligations under it.

 Types of breach

Actual breach is where the breach occurs on the due date for performance.

Anticipatory breach occurs where, before the due date for performance, a party shows an intention not to perform his contractual obligations. It is referred to as renunciation.

Anticipatory breach may be express or implied.

Express anticipatory breach occurs where one of the parties declares, before the due date for performance, that they have no intention of carrying out their contractual obligations.

Hochster v De La Tour (1853)

Facts: In April, De La Tour employed Hochster to act as a travel courier on his European tour, starting on 1 June. On 11 May De La Tour wrote to Hochster stating he would no longer be needing his services. Hochster started proceedings on 22 May. The defendant claimed there would be no cause of action until 1 June.

Held: The claimant was entitled to start the action as soon as the anticipatory breach occurred.

Implied anticipatory breach occurs where one of the parties does something which makes subsequent performance of their contractual undertaking impossible.

Omnium D'Enterprises v Sutherland (1919)

Facts: The defendant had agreed to hire a ship to the claimant but before the hire period was to commence, he actually sold the ship to someone else.

Held: The sale of the ship amounted to a clear repudiation of the contract. The claimant could sue for breach from that date.

What are the effects of anticipatory breach?

Anticipatory breach does not automatically bring the contract to an end. The innocent party has two options:

- treat the contract as discharged and bring an action for damages immediately, without waiting for the contractual date of performance as in **Hochster v De La Tour (1853)**

- elect to treat the contract as still valid, complete his side of the bargain and then sue for payment by the other side.

White & Carter (Councils) v McGregor (1961)

Facts: McGregor contracted with the claimants to have advertisements placed on litter bins which were supplied to local authorities. The defendant wrote to the claimants asking them to cancel the contract. The claimants refused to cancel, and produced and displayed the advertisements as required under the contract. They then claimed payment.

Held: The claimants were not obliged to accept the defendant's repudiation, but could perform the contract and claim the agreed price.

The effect of **White & Carter (Councils) v McGregor (1961)** apparently runs contrary to the duty to mitigate losses, as it involves the party in breach paying for more than the mere profit on the contract. There is, however, an element of danger in not accepting the repudiation of the contract when it first becomes apparent. For example, where the innocent party elects to wait for the time of performance, he takes the risk of the contract being discharged for some other reason and thus of losing his right to sue on the basis of the breach of contract.

11 Damages

Introduction

Damages are a common law remedy. They are available as of right for breach of contract.

Damages are intended to be compensatory not punitive.

Liquidated damages and penalty clauses

Where a contract provides for the payment of a fixed sum on breach, it may either be a liquidated damages clause or a penalty clause.

 Liquidated damages are a genuine pre-estimate of the expected loss. The amount stated is the amount of damages claimable. The clause is enforceable by the court.

Dunlop Pneumatic Tyre Co v New Garage and Motor Co (1915)

Facts: The claimant supplied the defendant with tyres, under a contract which imposed a minimum retail price. The contract provided that the defendant had to pay the claimant £5 for every tyre they sold in breach of the price agreement. When the defendant sold tyres at less than the agreed minimum price, they resisted the claim for £5 per tyre, on the grounds that it represented a penalty clause.

Held: The provision was genuine attempt to fix damages, and was not a penalty. It was, therefore, enforceable.

Old penalty clause test

If a clause was not considered to be a genuine pre-estimate of the expected loss then it was deemed a penalty clause and therefore not enforceable.

New penalty clause test

In 2015 the Supreme Court provided a new test on penalties which replaced the old test.

In **Cavendish v Makdessi; ParkingEye Limited v Beavis** the court ruled that the new test is whether the clause is a secondary obligation which imposes a detriment which is all out of proportion to the legitimate interest of the innocent party. If so it will be penal and therefore unenforceable.

Assessment of unliquidated damages

Where the contract does not make any provision for damages, the court will determine the damages payable. These are known as unliquidated damages.

There are two factors to consider in determining the amount of unliquidated damages:

- remoteness of loss (i.e. what losses can be claimed for?) and

- measure of damages (i.e. how much are those losses worth?).

Remoteness of loss

Damages cannot not be recovered for all losses suffered. Some losses are too remote.

A loss is not too remote:

- if it arises naturally from the breach (general damages or normal loss)

- it may reasonably be supposed to be within the contemplation of the parties, at the time they made the contract, as a probable result of the breach (special damages or abnormal loss).

Hadley v Baxendale (1854)

Facts: C owned a mill. One of the mill parts had broken and C made a contract with D for the transport of the old part to London as a pattern for making a replacement. D was responsible for a delay in delivering the part and as a result the mill was closed for a longer duration than would have been necessary if there had been no delay. C claimed for loss of profits during the period of delay.

Held: D did not know that the mill was inoperable without the part and whilst he was directly responsible for the delay itself, that stoppage was not a natural consequence of the delay in transportation. C could have had a spare part and did not alert D to the fact that the mill would be inoperable until the new part was made. Accordingly, D was not liable for the loss of profit.

Victoria Laundry v Newman Industries (1949)

Facts: A laundry required a new boiler to enlarge its plant. There was delay in the delivery of the boiler and as a result the laundry lost:

(a) a normal trading profit from the delay in bringing the new plant into use, and

(b) an extra large profit on certain government contracts.

Held: The boiler manufacturer was liable for the loss of normal profits; under the first branch of the rule, he or anyone else would know that an industrial boiler was essential to the operation of the plant and, therefore, to earning normal profits from it. He was not liable for the loss of profit on the government contracts, of which he had no information. (If, of course, he had known of them he would have been liable under the second branch of the rule.)

Jarvis v Swans Tours (1973)

Damages cannot usually be recovered for loss of enjoyment, unless the contract is one designed to give enjoyment. In this case, it was a holiday.

Measure of damages

The measure of damages is the amount which will put the claimant in the position he would have been in had the contract been properly performed.

This is sometimes described as damages for loss of bargain.

It is particularly difficult to measure damages in cases involving **building contracts** as there are two ways in which the damages could, in theory, be measured:

A the damages could be the difference in value between the building as it has been completed and its value if it had been properly completed, or

B the cost of rebuilding so that it meets the required specifications.

The usual measure of such damages is the cost of repairing the faulty work, known as the 'cost of cure'. However, this may not be the case where the costs of remedying the defects are disproportionate to the difference in value between what was supplied and what was ordered.

Ruxley Electronics and Construction Ltd v Forsyth (1995)

Facts: The parties had entered into a contract for the construction of a swimming pool. Although the contract stated that the pool was to be 7ft 6in deep at one end, the actual depth of the pool was only 6ft 9in. The total contract price was around £18,000. Fixing the error would have required a full reconstruction and would have cost about £21,000.

Held: The House of Lords considered that, as the costs of reinstatement would have been out of all proportion to the benefit gained, the difference in value only should be awarded. This was £0 as the pool as constructed was just as suitable for swimming and diving as one built to the original specification. However, the House of Lords did uphold the lower court's award of £2,500 for loss of amenity/enjoyment (although they commented that the amount was on the high side).

 Reliance damages enable the claimant to recover compensation for expenses incurred in performing his part of the contract before its breach. Where applicable, they are given in place of damages for loss of bargain; the claimant cannot receive both.

Anglia TV Ltd v Reed (1972)

Facts: R was engaged to play the leading role in a TV play. The claimants incurred expenses in preparing for filming. R repudiated the contract. Anglia could not find a suitable replacement and had to abandon the project.

Held: Anglia could recover the whole of their wasted expenditure from R.

Further points:

- If there is no actual loss, the claimant can recover only nominal damages.

- The claimant must take reasonable steps to mitigate (i.e. reduce) their loss.

Brace v Calder (1895)

Facts: Brace was employed by a partnership for a fixed period of two years, but after only five months the partnership was dissolved, thereby prematurely terminating his contract of employment. He was offered identical employment with a reconstituted partnership which was immediately formed to replace the previous one. He refused the offer and sued for wages he would have earned had his job continued for the agreed two year period.

Held: Brace had not mitigated the loss he suffered by his employer's breach of contract, thus he could only recover nominal damages.

- A notional deduction may be made to reflect taxation.

BTC v Gourley (1956)

Facts: A civil engineer was awarded damages by the British Transport Commission in respect of a railway accident. The award included an amount for loss of earnings. The question was whether the amount of damages should be paid to the recipient gross or net of deductions that would have been suffered by the individual had he remained in employment.

Held: It was held that the award should be made net of an amount that would reflect the deductions that would have been made for tax and national insurance in arriving at the settlement figure. The broad general principle which should govern the assessment of damages in cases such as this is that the tribunal should award the injured party such a sum of money as will put him in the same position as he would have been in if he had not sustained the injuries.

- Difficulty in evaluating losses does not prevent their recovery. In Chaplin v Hicks (1911), an amount was awarded representing the loss of opportunity to audition for a theatre role even though there was no guarantee of the claimant being awarded the role.

Test your understanding 7

In the event of a breach of contract, what is the purpose of damages?

(I)   To punish the contract breaker.

(II)   To compensate the innocent party.

(III)   To put the innocent party in the same position as if the contract had been carried out correctly.

A   (I) only

B   (II) and (III) only

C   (III) only

D   (I), (II) and (III)

12 Other common law remedies

Action for the price

If the breach of contract arises out of one party's failure to pay the contractually agreed price, then the creditor should bring an action to recover that sum.

If the contract is for the sale of goods, the action may only be brought if the property has passed to the buyer, unless the price has been agreed to be payable in a specific date.

Quantum meruit

Under this remedy, the value of the contractual work which has already been performed is measured.

This remedy is likely to be sought where one party has already performed part of his obligations and the other party then repudiates the contract.

13 Equitable remedies

Specific performance	Requires someone to perform their contractual obligations. Not available for personal service contracts. It enforces positive covenants within the contract.
Injunction	Orders someone to do something or not to do something. It enforces negative covenants within the contract.
Rescission	Restores the parties to their exact pre-contractual position.

Equitable remedies are only available at the discretion of the court. They are not granted if:

- damages are an adequate remedy

- the claimant has acted unfairly (i.e. he who comes to equity must come with clean hands)

- the order would cause undue hardship

- the order would require the constant supervision of the court

- there is undue delay in seeking the remedy (i.e. delay defeats the equities).

Warner Brothers Pictures Inc v Nelson (1936)

Facts: The film star, Bette Davis (Miss Nelson) entered into a contract with the claimants, whereby she agreed that she would not undertake other film work or any other occupation without the claimant's written consent. The claimant sought an injunction to restrain her from doing film work for another company in breach of this agreement.

Held: The injunction would be granted. However, no injunction would be granted to prevent her engaging in 'other occupations' as this would force her to work for the claimants.

Page One Records v Britton (Trading as The Troggs) (1967)

Facts: The claimants, as managers of a pop group (The Troggs), sought an injunction to restrain the group from breaching their contract by engaging another manager.

Held: As the group would have been unable to obtain an order of specific performance to compel the claimants to perform their personal services as managers, the claimants could not obtain an injunction against the defendants, as there was no mutuality between the parties.

Test your understanding 8

1   **Which of the following statements is correct?**

(I)   An order for specific performance will not be granted where damages provide an adequate remedy.

(II)   An order for specific performance will not be granted where the contract is for personal services.

A   (I) only

B   (II) only

C   Both (I) and (II)

D   Neither (I) nor (II)

2   Which one of the following contracts might be specifically enforceable?

A   Alan has contracted to sell his house to Bob but has changed his mind and no longer wishes to sell it.

B   Chris has contracted to buy a new Ford motor car but the garage is now refusing to honour the contract.

C   Diane has contracted to purchase a number of tins of fruit for her business but the seller has now stated that he no longer wishes to proceed with the contract.

D   Eduardo has contracted to sing at a concert organised by Fernando, but Eduardo has withdrawn as he has received a more lucrative offer from Giovanni.

3   Which one of the following is not an equitable remedy?

A   Damages

B   Specific performance

C   Rescission

D   Injunction

4   In breach of contract, C Ltd refused to sell a motor car to D Ltd at the agreed price of £10,000. If the type of motor car is readily available on the market at a price of £9,000, which one of the following is correct?

A   D Ltd is entitled to an order of specific performance, forcing C Ltd to carry out its contract.

B   D Ltd is entitled to damages of £1,000.

C   D Ltd is entitled to nominal damages only.

D   D Ltd is not entitled to damages.

14   Chapter summary

Test your understanding answers

Test your understanding 1

B

This is a definition of a 'simple' contract. It does not have to be in any particular form – e.g. it does not have to be in writing – to be binding on the parties.

Test your understanding 2

1   **D**

An advertisement, such as the statement in the newspaper, is an invitation to treat and is not an offer in itself. An invitation to treat is an invitation to others to make an offer.

2   **B**

The withdrawal of an offer can be made before acceptance, and if an offer is withdrawn, there cannot be offer and acceptance. In the case of **Dickinson v Dodds (1876)**, it was held that the withdrawal of an offer can be communicated by a reliable third party, and does not have to be made directly by the offeror to the offeree.

Test your understanding 3

1   **D**

For a contract to exist there must be an offer and an acceptance. The offer was made on 1 September, the acceptance was made on 6 September, within the 10-day period. The contract is valid from 6 September, the date of acceptance.

2   **B**

An advertisement is an invitation to treat, not an offer. When B Ltd placed an order for 100 television sets, it was making an offer. A Ltd can refuse to accept (but can make a counter-offer to sell the sets at £59).

3   **C**

For a contract to exist there must be offer and acceptance, so A and B are both incorrect, even though B might seem a logical position. D is clearly incorrect, since payment in advance is not a required condition for consideration in a contract. Since there has not yet been acceptance by either party, Alf is in a position to withdraw his offer, and can also refuse the offer by Bert.

Test your understanding 4

1 **B**

Based on **Williams v Roffey Bros and Nicholls (Contractors) Ltd (1990)**.

2 **B**

Consideration need not be adequate, but it must be sufficient.

Test your understanding 5

A

Statement (i) is correct. An agreement that is binding in honour only is not a contract as there is no intention to create legal relations. However, statement (ii) is incorrect. An enforceable contract does not have to be in writing.

Test your understanding 6

1 **C**

Conditions are the most important terms. Failure of a condition is so serious that the other party is not limited to seeking damages; he may also treat the contract as discharged by breach. However, it is incorrect to state that the contract must be terminated. The correct statements in the question provide a useful summary of the difference between conditions and warranties.

2 **C**

When a warranty is breached, the injured party can only claim damages.

3 **A**

A warranty is a term which is incidental to the main purpose of the contract. Failure to observe it does not cause the whole contract to collapse.

4 **A**

The remedy for breach of a warranty is damages. The remedies for breach of a condition are repudiation and damages.

KAPLAN PUBLISHING

Test your understanding 7

B

The aim of damages in contract is usually to put the injured party into the position he would have been in if the contract had been properly performed – often referred to as bargain loss. However, in some cases, the courts award 'reliance losses', i.e. losses incurred in trying to perform the contract prior to the breach. Both (ii) and (iii) are therefore purposes of awarding damages. Damages are not intended as a punishment of the person in breach of the contract.

Test your understanding 8

1   **C**

Although specific performance is given at the discretion of the court, there are certain circumstances where it will not be given. The two statements are examples of those circumstances.

2   **A**

In English Law, the sale of land and property must be by written contract (the transfer or title is by way of a Deed of Transfer or conveyance). If this contract has been signed, it may be specifically enforceable. (In common parlance, if the parties have 'exchanged contracts' for the purchase of a house, the contract is enforceable even though 'completion' is not until a later date.)

3   **A**

Damages are a remedy available under common law, not equity.

4   **C**

Damages are intended to be compensatory and not punitive. In this case, D Ltd has not suffered loss because he can obtain at a lower price the same item that C Ltd has refused to sell. D Ltd is therefore entitled to nominal damages only.

The law of torts

Chapter learning objectives

Upon completion of this chapter you will be able to:

- define a tort and show how it is different from a contract
- explain the elements of negligence
- discuss defences to an action in negligence
- relate the basic principles to accountants
- explain the basics of passing off.

1 Understand the nature of the law of tort

 What is a tort?

A tort is a type of civil wrong. It is a breach of a legal duty or an infringement of a legal right which gives rise to a claim for damages.

As a tort is a breach of a legal duty, there is no liability unless the law recognises that the duty exists.

Differences between contracts and torts

A contractual relationship does not have to be established for a claim in tort to be successful. Often the parties have never even met before. For example, in a claim for personal injury as a result of a road accident, the parties will often have had no previous relationship at all.

However, if a contract does exist and a tort has been committed, the claimant may choose the remedy most appropriate.

There are two options:

- Under a valid contract, the amount of damages awarded is intended to put the claimant back in the position he would have been in had the contract been properly performed.

- In tort, the amount of damages awarded is intended to put the claimant in the position he would have been in had the tortious act never taken place.

Limitation periods

- In contract the limitation period is six years from the breach of contract.

- In tort the limitation period is generally six years, but three years for personal injury.

The main elements of a tort

In order to be successful in an action for tort, the following conditions must be satisfied:

- There must be an act or omission by the defendant.

- The act or omission must have directly caused loss to the claimant.

- The courts must be able to establish a legal liability as a result of the damage.

A claim will only be successful if the loss suffered is not 'too remote' i.e. the loss must be as a direct consequence of something the defendant did/or did not do.

2 Negligence

Negligence is the breach of a legal duty to take care, which results in damage to another.

In order for an action in negligence to succeed, the claimant must prove the following:

- That a duty of care was owed to him by the defendant.

- The defendant breached that duty.

- As a consequence of that breach, damage or loss has been suffered.

Duty of care

There is a duty to take reasonable care not to cause foreseeable harm to others.

The 'neighbour principle'

The case of **Donoghue v Stevenson** (below) was the first to establish that a duty of care may be owed to a person, even where no contractual relationship exists.

Prior to this case, the belief was that to allow an action to be taken where there was no contractual relationship would undermine the principles of contract law. The doctrine of privity states that only parties to a contract can sue or be sued.

Donoghue v Stevenson changed this principle and, as a result, manufacturers of goods owe a duty of care to the ultimate consumer of the product.

Donoghue v Stevenson (1932)

Facts: Mrs Donoghue went to a cafe with a friend. The friend bought her a bottle of ginger beer which Mrs Donoghue drank. She then discovered that there was a decomposed snail in the bottom of the opaque bottle. Mrs Donoghue found this sight so upsetting that she suffered physical illness. She sued the manufacturer, claiming that they were under a duty to see that such outside bodies did not get into the ginger beer.

Held: There was a duty on behalf of the manufacturer to take reasonable care in the manufacture of their products. The manufacturer owes a duty to the consumer to take reasonable care to prevent injury.

Lord Atkin defined those to whom we owe a duty of care in the **'neighbour principle'**:

'You must take reasonable care to avoid acts or omissions which you ought reasonably foresee would be likely to injure your neighbour.'

He defined neighbours as:

...persons who are so directly affected by my act that I ought reasonably to have them in contemplation'.

The duty of care, which in **Donoghue v Stevenson** just related to physical harm has been extended in subsequent cases.

Bourhill v Young (1943)

In this case the court established that the duty of care could apply to nervous shock provided there was sufficient proximity i.e. that the shock was suffered by someone within the reasonable range of harm.

Facts: A motorcyclist was killed in a road accident for which he has responsible. A pregnant woman who got off a tram near the scene of the accident claimed that when she got to the scene of the accident she saw blood on the road and as a result suffered shock which put her into premature labour which resulted in the loss of her baby. She subsequently brought a claim in relation to nervous shock and the resulting loss.

Held: The House of Lords held that the motorcyclist did not owe a duty of care to the pregnant woman as she was not deemed to be a foreseeable victim. She was not present at the scene of the accident, she arrived after the accident occurred.

White v Chief Constable of South Yorkshire Police (1998)

Facts: The claimants were police constables on duty for maintaining law and order during a football match in April 1989 at Hillsborough Stadium. As a result of overcrowding and the consequent stampede, 95 people died and hundreds of others sustained injuries. The policemen on duty, including the claimants, had to tend to the victims for whom many of them suffered post traumatic stress disorder. Four of them were on duty at the stadium, and the fifth one was responsible for stripping bodies and completing casualty forms at a hospital. Resultantly, they claimed compensation for their psychiatric injury from the police department.

Held: The House of Lords overruled the decision of the Court of Appeal and rejected the claim. It was established that the claimants were a 'secondary victim'. A secondary victim is someone whose personal safety is not threatened, but who suffers psychiatric injury as a result of either fear for the safety of others or the trauma of witnessing a harrowing event. In order to succeed in their claim a secondary victim must satisfy three requirements. First, they must have close ties of love and affection with the person who suffers injury or death in an accident attributable to negligence. Second, they must have been present at the accident or on the scene in its immediate aftermath. And third, the psychiatric injury must have been caused by direct perception of the accident or its immediate aftermath and not upon receiving it second-hand. In this case the claimants did not meet the first criteria.

Economic or financial loss

The case of **Donoghue v Stevenson (1932)** established that an action could be taken if **physical damage was suffered**. However, the law still did not recognise liability in respect of 'pure' economic loss. Pure economic loss is monetary loss which is unconnected to physical injury to a person or damage to other property. Where there is economic loss that is connected to physical injury or damage to property then that is 'consequential' economic loss which is recoverable.

Spartan Steel & Alloys Ltd v Martin & Co (Contractors) Ltd (1973)

Facts: Spartan Steel and Alloys Ltd had a stainless steel factory which obtained its electricity by a direct cable from the power station. Martin & Co Ltd were doing work on the ground with an excavator and negligently damaged that cable. As a consequence, the factory was deprived of electricity for fifteen hours which has caused physical damage to the factory's furnaces and metal, lost profit on the damaged metal and lost profit on the metal that was not melted during the time the electricity was off. Spartan Steel claimed all the three heads of damage.

Held: The Court of Appeal held that Spartan Steel could only recover the damages to their furnaces, the metal they had to discard and the profit lost on the discarded metal. They could not recover the profits lost due to the factory not being operational for fifteen hours. Their main reasoning for this was that while the damage to the metal was "physical damage" and the lost profits on the metal was "directly consequential" upon it, the profits lost due to the blackout constituted "pure economic loss".

In respect of pure economic loss suffered as a result of professional misstatement the case of **Hedley Byrne v Heller** modernised the law in this area. The House of Lords refined the neighbour principle by acknowledging that a claim for financial loss suffered could be made if a 'special relationship' existed between the claimant and defendant (see later).

The limits of the duty of care

In the case of **The Nicholas H (Marc Rich & Co v Bishops Rock Marine) (1995),** four tests were laid down which should be followed in determining whether a duty of care exists.

The issues to be considered are:

- Was the damage reasonably foreseeable by the defendant at the time of the act or omission?

- Is there a neighbourhood principle or sufficient proximity (closeness) between the parties?

- Should the law impose a duty of care between the parties i.e. is it fair and reasonable to do so?

- Is there a matter of public policy which exists or requires that no duty of care should exist?

The **Nicholas H** case focused on financial loss, but these tests should also be applied when determining the duty of care for physical damage cases.

Illustration 1 – Negligence

A was given an ipod for his birthday by his uncle. Due to a design defect, it set fire to his bedroom and caused damage to carpets and furniture. A was made ill by smoke inhalation. A is entitled to claim damages from the iPod manufacturer for:

1   pain and suffering caused by smoke inhalation

2   any loss of earnings whilst he recovers

3   the cost of replacing furnishings and redecoration.

He is not entitled to claim the cost of replacing the defective ipod which would be pure economic loss.

The defect does not give rise to the liability: it is the resultant damage to person or property.

> ### Test your understanding 1
>
> **In assessing whether a duty of care exists, which of the following tests will be taken into consideration?**
>
> (I)   Was the damage reasonably foreseeable by the defendant at the time of the act or omission?
>
> (II) Was it fair and reasonable for the law to impose a duty of care?
>
> (III) Has the defendant intentionally caused physical damage or financial loss?
>
> (IV) Has the claimant taken reasonable steps to mitigate the loss suffered?
>
> A   (I) and (IV) only
>
> B   (I) and (II) only
>
> C   (III) and (IV) only
>
> D   All of the above

Breach of duty of care

In order for a claim to be successful, a claimant must not only prove that a duty of care existed, but also that the duty was breached by the defendant.

1   **As a question of fact the claimant shows that the defendant was in breach of his duty.**

The Breach

Establishing if there has indeed been a breach is a question of fact. Each case must be viewed separately on its own facts.

2   **As a question of law the claimant has to show the defendant has not shown the required standard of care.**

The standard of care

The test for establishing breach of duty is an objective one and was set out in **Blyth v Birmingham Waterworks Co (1856)** which stated that a breach of duty occurs if the defendant:

'...fails to do something which a reasonable man, guided upon those considerations which ordinarily regulate the conduct of human affairs, would do; or does something which a prudent and reasonable man would not do.'

The reasonable man is not expected to be skilled in any particular trade or profession.

The following principles have been established by case law:

- Probability of injury/vulnerability of claimant

The degree of care required has to be balanced against the degree of risk involved in the event of the duty being breached. This means that the greater the risk of injury the more that should be done in order to prevent the injury.

Glasgow Corporation v Taylor (1922)

Facts: A seven year old child died after eating poisonous berries he had picked from a bush in a park controlled by the defendant.

Held: The provision of a warning notice was not enough. The defendant had breached its duty of care to the child by leaving the berries on the bush.

Children are owed a higher standard of care and a lower standard can be expected from them.

The degree of care to be exercised may be increased if the claimant is more vulnerable i.e. is young, old or less able bodied. This is based on the rule that 'you must take your victim as you find him'.

Haley v London Electricity Board (1965)

Facts: In order to carry out some repairs the defendant made a hole in the pavement. They took sufficient precautions to make the area safe for a sighted person. However, the claimant who was blind fell into the hole, and sustained an injury which made him deaf.

Held: The defendant was in breach of its duty of care to pedestrians as it had failed to ensure that the area was safe for all pedestrians. Although it was reasonably safe for sighted persons clearly it was not for blind persons.

- Particular skill

    As a general rule, the level of skill and care required is that which a reasonable man would possess. However, if the defendant possesses a particular skill, i.e. he is a qualified solicitor or a qualified accountant, the standard of care expected will be that of a reasonable person with that skill.

    Hindsight is irrelevant, the degree of skill is the standard required at the time of the tort.

Roe v Ministry of Health (1954)

Facts: A doctor administered a spinal injection which had become contaminated as a result of minute cracks in the phials. As a result of that the patient was paralysed.

Held: There was no breach of duty since the doctor who had administered the injection had no way of detecting the contamination..

- Lack of skill

Lack of training or the peculiarities of the defendant are not relevant. Therefore, the standard of skill expected from a trainee accountant is the same as that of any reasonable accountant.

Nettleship v Weston (1971)

Facts: During a driving lesson, the defendant who was a learner driver lost control of the car and caused an accident in which the claimant was injured. The defendant argued that the claimant was well aware of her lack of skill and that the court should make allowance for her since she could not be expected to drive like an experienced motorist.

Held: The standard of care for a learner driver would be the usual standard applied to drivers: that of an experienced and skilled driver.

- Cost and practicability

Where there is a forseeable risk this must be balanced against the measures necessary to eliminate the potential risk. If the cost of these measures far outweighs the potential risk it will probably be concluded that there is no breach of duty in not eliminating the risk.

Latimer v AEC Ltd (1952)

Facts: A factory was flooded as a result of a heavy rainstorm and as a result made the floor of the factory very slippery. The defendant who owned the factory arranged for sawdust to be spread on the floor, however there was insufficient sawdust to cover the whole area. The claimant slipped and injured himself.

Held: The defendant was not in breach of its duty as it had taken all the reasonable precautions that would have been expected given the circumstances and had eliminated the risk as so far as was practicable.

- Common practice

Where a particular action is in line with common practice or custom that may be considered to be sufficient to meet the expected standard of care. However, this will not apply if the common practice itself is negligent.

Paris v Stepney BC (1951)

Facts: The defendant employed the claimant as a garage mechanic who had lost the sight of one eye during the war. In order to loosen a stiff bolt he struck it with a hammer; a piece of metal flew off and because he was not wearing goggles struck him in his good eye, causing him to become totally blind.

Held: The court made the point that not wearing glasses was common practice and in itself was not negligent and therefore could normally be used as a defence. However, because of the particular susceptibility of the defendant the employer should have taken more care and insisted that he wear goggles. For this reason, the employer was negligent.

Causality (loss caused by the breach)

A claimant must demonstrate that he has suffered loss or damage as a direct consequence of the breach. This is sometimes called the 'But For' test – but for the actions of the defendant the claimant would not have suffered the damage.

The claimant must establish a causal link between the defendant's conduct and the damage which occurred:

- If the damage was caused by something or someone else there will be no liability on the defendant's part.

- If the claimant would have suffered the loss regardless of the defendant's conduct then he has not caused the loss.

Barnett v Chelsea and Kensington Hospital Management Committee (1969)

Facts: The claimant's husband (Mr Barnett) went to hospital complaining of severe stomach pains and vomiting. He was seen by a nurse who telephoned the doctor on duty. The doctor told her to send him home and contact his GP in the morning. Mr Barnett died five hours later from arsenic poisoning.

Held: Even if the doctor had examined Mr Barnett at the time there was nothing the doctor could have done to save him. Therefore, the hospital was not liable as the doctor's failure to examine Mr Barnett did not cause his death.

- If something happened after the defendant's breach that caused or contributed to the damage then the defendant's liability will cease at that point.

- The following losses are normally recoverable:

    - loss as a result of personal injury

    - damage to property

    - financial loss directly connected to personal injury (i.e. loss of wages).

    As discussed earlier pure financial loss is very rarely recoverable.

- Even where the claimant is able to show the loss was suffered as a result of the defendant's breach the court will not allow recovery of that loss if it is considered to be too remote (see part 4 below) i.e. must be of a type of loss that is reasonably foreseeable.

Vicarious liability

Vicarious liability occurs when one person is held responsible for the negligence of another. Typically, this applies in an employment context, where the employer is responsible for the negligent acts of the employee which occur within the context of the employment relationship.

Lister and others v Hesley Hall Ltd (2001)

Facts: A school board employed a warden to manage a boarding house for vulnerable children. The warden committed sexual abuse of the children. The claimants (the abused children) sued the school board for vicarious liability.

Held: The court overruled earlier decisions to hold that the school was vicariously liable. These acts had been committed on the premises and during the time when the warden should have been complying with his duty to care for the children. The connection of time and place, and the inextricable link between the acts of abuse and the employment, were sufficiently close to establish liability.

Test your understanding 2

Which one of the following is not an essential element of the tort of negligence?

A   A duty of care owed to the claimant

B   A breach of the duty of care

C   An intention to cause loss or injury

D   Loss or injury caused by the defendant's breach

3   Professional advice and negligent misstatement

In practice there is no difference between liability arising from negligent misstatement and liability arising from negligent acts. A party can suffer damage by reliance on incorrect advice just as he can be injured by any other negligent conduct.

With respect to a negligent misstatement however, the consequences of this could be far-reaching and affect countless people. Because of this the law had been reluctant to impose a duty of care in the making of statements.

This situation changed in 1964 when the landmark case set out below marked a new approach to the law of negligent misstatement.

Hedley Byrne & Co Ltd v Heller & Partners Ltd (1964)

Facts: The claimants (Hedley Byrne) were advertising agents, who had contracted to place advertisements for their client's (Easipower) products. As this involved giving Easipower credit, they asked the respondents, who were Easipower's bankers, for a reference as to the creditworthiness of Easipower.

Heller gave favourable references (but stipulated that the information was given without responsibility on their part). Relying on this information, the claimants extended credit to Easipower and lost over £17,000 when the latter, soon after, went into liquidation. The claimants sued Easipower's bankers for negligence.

Held: The respondents' disclaimer was adequate to exclude the assumption by them of the legal duty of care. However, in the absence of the disclaimer, the circumstances would have given rise to a duty of care in spite of the absence of a contractual or fiduciary relationship. Thus, but for the disclaimer, the bank was liable on its misleading statement. Note: nowadays the disclaimer might be invalidated under Unfair Contract Terms Act 1977 (UCTA 1977).

The effect of Hedley Byrne

The above case created a new duty situation by recognising liability for negligent misstatement causing economic loss in circumstances where there exists a special relationship between the parties.

Cases involving negligent misstatement are usually concerned with establishing whether or not a duty arises and it is difficult to establish clear principles to apply as the law has evolved on a case-by-case basis.

The meaning of special relationship

A special relationship exists where a professional person advises a known person who relies on the statement for a known purpose.

For an action in negligent misstatement to succeed there must be a special relationship. The considerations outlined in the **Nicholas H** case will still be relevant.

It is clear that liability will only arise where the defendant is in the business of giving professional advice and the statement is given in that context i.e. not on a social or informal occasion.

One important consideration is the relationship of the parties in the context of the damage suffered, for example whether the preparation of accounts is for shareholders or a potential takeover.

Jeb Fasteners Ltd v Marks, Bloom & Co (1982)

Facts: The defendant accountants audited the accounts of X Co. The audit report was negligently prepared. The claimant then took over X Co.

Held: The defendants owed the claimants a duty of care because they knew the claimant company was considering taking over X Co. and thus were likely to rely on the audited accounts. However, the claimant's action for damages failed because they had taken over the company to obtain the services of X Co's two directors and not on the basis of the accounts, so that the breach did not cause the loss suffered and there was no resultant loss.

However the court did express the view that a duty of care was owed by the accountants to the claimant as it was reasonably foreseeable that a potential bidder would rely on the accounts.

If advice is given or financial statements prepared for a specific purpose, then a duty of care is owed to those who are relying on them for that specific purpose.

Morgan Crucible v Hill Samuel Bank (1991)

Facts: MC made a bid for FCE plc which then issued circulars containing profit records and forecasts recommending its shareholders not to accept the bid. Eventually MC increased its bid and, on the FCE board recommending acceptance, MC's bid succeeded.

Subsequently MC discovered that the accounts and the profit forecasts grossly overstated FCE's profits and that FCE was worthless. Had MC known the true facts it would never have made the bid, let alone increased it. MC sued FCE's merchant bank, directors and accountants in the tort of negligence in respect of circulars issued after the bid was first made.

Held: Here the defendants knew MC would rely on the circulars for the particular purpose of deciding whether or not to make an increased bid and intended that they should. Thus there might be proximity.

Where there is no special relationship

As a general rule, however, unless the defendant had prior knowledge that a certain bidder would rely on the statement made, no duty of care would exist.

The concept of special relationship has now been redefined in the following leading case:

Caparo Industries plc v Dickman and Others (1990)

Facts: C, a shareholder in F plc, bought more shares in the company after receiving the audited accounts. He later made a takeover bid.

After the takeover C sued the auditors alleging that the audited accounts had been misleading as they showed a profit when in fact there had been a loss. C said the auditors owed a duty of care to investors and potential investors as they should have been aware that a press release saying that profits would fall significantly had made F vulnerable to a takeover bid and that bidders might rely on the accounts.

Held: The court set out three criteria which had to be fulfilled in order to give rise to a duty of care:

1   The standard test of foreseeability applied.

2   The concept of proximity limits the duty to circumstances where the statement would be communicated to the claimant either as an individual or a member of an identifiable group in respect of transactions of a particular kind and that the claimant would rely on the statement. It is therefore necessary to look at the purpose for which the statement is made, the statement maker's knowledge of the person relying on the statement and the type of transaction in which it is used.

3   Whether it is just and equitable that a duty of care should be imposed so that imposing it would not be contrary to public policy. When the court applied these criteria to the Caparo case they found that auditors of a public company owe no duty of care to the public at large who rely on accounts when purchasing shares in a company nor was any duty owed to individual shareholders who purchase additional shares.

This approach is also illustrated in the following case:

James McNaughton Paper Group v Hicks Anderson (1991)

Facts: JMP entered into negotiations with MK Paper for an agreed takeover of MK. The chairman of MK asked its accountants, HA, to prepare draft accounts as quickly as possible for use in the negotiations. The accounts when prepared were shown by MK to JMP. After the takeover was completed, JMP discovered certain discrepancies in the accounts. JMP brought an action against MK's accountants in the tort of negligence.

Held: No duty of care was owed because of lack of proximity between JMP and HA. The prime reasons for lack of proximity included:

- the accounts were produced for MK's use in negotiations not for JMP's use

- draft accounts are not intended to be relied on as if they were final accounts.

Where there is a special relationship

If advice is given or financial statements prepared for a specific purpose, then a duty of care is owed to those who are relying on them for that specific purpose.

Test your understanding 3

Which one of the following is correct?

A   Professional advisors cannot be liable in respect of negligent advice in the tort of negligence but may be liable for breach of contract.

B   Professional advisors cannot be liable for breach of contract in respect of negligent advice, but may be liable in the tort of negligence.

C   Professional advisors may be liable in respect of negligent advice in either contract or tort.

D   Professional advisors cannot be liable in respect of negligent advice in either contract or tort.

Test your understanding 4

What forms the basis of the existence of a legal duty of care in negligence for misstatements resulting in economic loss to the claimant?

A   Proximity

B   Proximity and damage

C   Foreseeability

D   Foreseeability and proximity

Test your understanding 5

In **Hedley Byrne v Heller & Partners**, the House of Lords held that a banker would owe a duty of care on a reference for a client given voluntarily without consideration to a third party.

What was the basis of this decision?

A   That in such a case a duty is owed to persons generally.

B   That a duty is owed to those persons who could reasonably be foreseen as relying on the statement.

C   That a duty is owed to a person the defendant knew or ought to have known would rely on the statement.

D   That a duty is only owed to those with whom the defendant was in a fiduciary or contractual relationship.

4 Remedies and defences in negligence

Remedies in an action in negligence

The principal remedy in any case involving negligence will be an award of damages.

The damage caused to the claimant must be of a type that is 'reasonably foreseeable'.

A loss is reasonably foreseeable if a reasonable man would have foreseen the type of injury, loss or damage.

As a general rule it is for the claimant to prove that the defendant was in breach of the duty of care.

Exceptionally the defendant will have to prove that he was not negligent. This will only occur if:

- the harm would not have normally happened if proper care were taken

- there is no other explanation for what has occurred, known as res ipsa loquitor, the thing that speaks for itself

- the defendant was in control of the situation and the victim was not.

Ward v Tesco Stores Ltd (1976)

Facts: The claimant was injured when she slipped on some yoghurt which had been spilt on the floor. At the trial the defendant gave evidence that spillages occurred about ten times a week and that staff had been instructed that if they saw any spillage on the floor they were to stay where the spill had taken place and call somebody to clear it up. Apart from general cleaning, the floor was brushed five or six times every day on which the supermarket was open. There was, however, no evidence before the court as to when the floor had last been cleaned before the claimant's accident.

Held: Even though it could not be said exactly what happened, the yoghurt being spilled spoke for itself as to who was to blame. The claimant did not need to prove how long the spill had been there, because the burden of proof was on Tesco.

Remoteness of Damage

Overseas Tankship (UK) v Morts Dock and Engineering Co (The Wagon Mound) (1961)

Facts: Due to the defendants' negligence, oil was spilled and accumulated around the claimant's wharf. The oil ignited and the wharf suffered fire damage.

Held: The defendants were held not liable since, while damage to the wharf by oil pollution was foreseeable, damage by fire was not.

If the type of damage is reasonably foreseeable the defendant is liable. It is irrelevant that the defendant might not have been able to foresee its cause or its severity.

Hughes v Lord Advocate (1963)

Facts: The defendant telephone engineers left an inspection hole covered only by a tent and surrounded by paraffin lamps. A child claimant was badly injured when he fell down the hole carrying a lamp which exploded on impact causing a fireball.

Held: The defendants were liable as they should reasonably have foreseen that a child would be attracted by the lamps and might be burned when playing with them. It was irrelevant that they could not have foreseen the explosion or the severity of the burn damage.

Defences to a claim in negligence

There are four main defences to a charge of negligence:

- contributory negligence
- volenti non fit injuria
- novus actus interveniens
- exclusion clauses.

Contributory negligence

If the claimant is partly responsible for his own injuries, the defendant can plead the defence of contributory negligence. The court may then reduce any damages it awards to the claimant depending on the degree to which he is judged responsible for his loss.

The onus is on the defendant to show the claimant was at fault and therefore contributed to their own injury.

It is only a partial defence, the defendant is still liable but the damages are reduced to reflect the extent for which the claimant was responsible for their own injury.

Jones v Livox Quarries (1952)

Facts: The claimant was riding down a slope leading to the bottom of a quarry on the back of the defendants' vehicle, contrary to their orders, when another vehicle of the defendants was negligently driven into the back of the first vehicle. As a result, the claimant was injured.

Held: The claimant exposed himself not only to the risk of falling off the vehicle but also to the risk of being injured in the particular way in which he was injured. The court therefore found that he was contributorily negligent.

Sayers v Harlow Urban District Council (1958)

Facts: The claimant having paid to use a public toilet found herself trapped inside a cubicle which had no door handle. She attempted to climb out by stepping first on to the toilet and then on to the toilet-roll holder which gave way and as a result she was injured.

Held: The injuries she suffered were a natural and probable consequence of the defendant's negligence, but that the damages would be reduced by 25% since the claimant had been careless in depending for support on the toilet-roll holder.

Volenti non fit injuria

This applies where the claimant has freely consented to the tort. It amounts to an agreement by the claimant to exempt the defendant from a duty of care that he would otherwise owe. Consent can be given expressly where the claimant agrees to the risk of injury e.g. by signing a consent form, or may be implied from the claimant's conduct.

ICI v Shatwell (1964)

Facts: The claimant and his brother were certificated and experienced shot firers employed by ICI Ltd in a quarry owned by the defendant company. Part of the brothers' work included wiring up detonators and checking the electrical circuits. They ignored the defendant's rules relating to safety and tested the detonators without using the shelter provided. One of the brothers was injured and claimed his brother was 50 per cent to blame for the explosion and that the employer was vicariously liable.

Held: Both brothers had impliedly consented to the risks of their actions and therefore the defendant was not liable.

Consent acts as a complete defence and no damages would be awarded if it is shown to apply.

Novus actus interveniens

Where there is a new intervening act this may break the chain of causation removing liability from the defendant. There are three types of intervening act that will break the chain of causation.

1 Act of the claimant

Where the new intervening act is that of the claimant, the test is whether the claimant acted reasonably in the circumstances. If the claimant's actions are deemed reasonable the chain of causation remains intact and the defendant is liable for the actions of the claimant. If, however, the claimant's actions are unreasonable in the circumstances the chain of causation is broken and the defendant is not liable for the actions of the claimant.

McKew v Holland (1969)

Facts: The claimant sustained an injury at work due to his employer's breach of duty of care. He strained his back and hips and his leg was prone to giving way. Whilst in this state he attempted to climb unaided down a steep concrete staircase without a handrail unaided. He got part way down and felt his leg give way so he jumped 10 steps to the bottom. He suffered a fractured right ankle and was also left with a permanent disability. The defendant accepted liability for the injury sustained during his employment but disputed liability for the second injuries resulting from the claimant's action in jumping down the stairs.

Held: The claimant's action amounted to a novus actus interveniens because his action in attempting to climb the steps unaided, knowing that his leg might give way, was unreasonable. The defendant was therefore not liable for the injuries resulting from the incident on the stairs.

2   Act of a third party

Where the new act is of a third party, the test is whether the act was foreseeable. If the act of the third party is foreseeable, the defendant remains liable and the chain of causation remains intact. If the act of the third party is not foreseeable this will break the chain of causation and the defendant is not liable for the actions of the third party.

Lamb v Camden LBC (1981)

Facts: The defendant council negligently struck a water pipe outside the claimant's house. This caused extensive damage and the property had to be vacated. One year later the council had not undertaken the repairs. Squatters had also moved in and caused further damage. The claimant arranged for repairs to be done herself and submitted a bill to the council for the repairs and damage caused by the squatters.

Held: The local authority was not liable for the acts of the squatters. It was not foreseeable that squatters would move into an empty house.

3   Natural events

An intervening natural event will normally break the chain of causation unless it can be shown that the defendant's breach has either increased the likelihood of further damage from a natural event or has made the claimant more susceptible to damage.

Carslogie Steamship Co Limited v Royal Norwegian Government (1952)

Facts: The claimant's ship was damaged in a collision as a result of the defendant's negligence. The ship was en route to have the resulting repairs carried out. On the way the ship was damaged further by heavy weather and as a consequence took a longer period of time to repair. The claimant claimed compensation for the loss of profit for the period the ship was unusable due to the original incident.

Held: The claimant could not recover compensation for the time it would have taken to repair the ship in respect of the collision damage, as the ship would have been out of use in any case, due to the damage caused by the weather.

Exclusion clauses

An exclusion clause is one which seeks to exclude or limit liability for negligence. An exclusion clause may fall within the provisions of the Consumer Rights Act 2015 (see **Chapter 2**).

If an exclusion clause is found to be valid, this constitutes a viable defence against any action for negligence.

Act of God

In addition, liability is excluded if it is possible to say that the act occurred in the course of nature i.e. that it was an 'act of god'; something beyond human foresight which the defendant could not have been expected to provide against.

Test your understanding 6

In the tort of negligence, if a claimant is partly responsible for his own injuries then:

A   No compensation can be recovered from the defendant.

B   The defendant is fully liable if he was mainly responsible for the injuries.

C   If the defendant was negligent he remains fully liable for all the injuries caused.

D   The compensation will be reduced to take account of the claimant's share of the responsibility.

5   The tort of passing off

This tort protects the goodwill, reputation and profits of a business.

The tort of passing off arises:

*   where one business uses a name which is similar to that of an existing business, and

*   it misleads persons into believing that they are the same business, and

*   it causes actual damage to that business or will probably do so.

Ewing v Buttercup Margarine Co Ltd (1917)

Facts: Ewing who traded under the name Buttercup Dairy Company sued to restrain a newly registered company called Buttercup Margarine Company Ltd from using the name on the grounds that the general public might reasonably believe that there was a link between the two businesses.

Held: The court held that the word 'Buttercup' was so closely associated with Ewing dairy products as to be likely to cause confusion if used by the similar margarine business. An injunction was granted to prevent the defendant company from trading under its name.

If passing off is proved, the court may restrain the business from trading under that name and order that damages be paid to the person whose business has suffered loss.

If a company feels than another company has a name which is too similar to its own, it may object to the Company Names Adjudicator under CA 06. The Adjudicator will consider the case and then make their decision. In most cases the Adjudicator will require a name change, and in some cases the Adjudicator may state the new company name.

6   Chapter summary

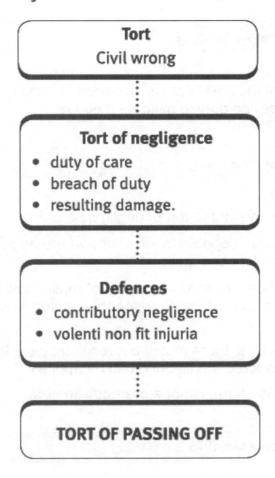

Test your understanding answers

Test your understanding 1

B

The intention of the defendant is irrelevant to a claim for negligence. The claimant is under no duty to mitigate their loss.

Test your understanding 2

C

The three elements of the tort of negligence are:

- Duty of care: It applies in situations where an individual owes a duty of care to someone else.

- Breach of duty of care: the claimant must show the defendant failed to take the care which a reasonable person would have done in the circumstances.

- Resultant loss: there must be a resultant loss, financial or otherwise, before the tort of negligence can be applied.

Intention to cause harm is not a prerequisite here.

Test your understanding 3

C

Professional advisers may be liable in respect of negligent advice in either contract or tort.

Test your understanding 4

D

The main element is proximity, but some likelihood of damage must have been foreseeable.

Test your understanding 5

C

A duty is owed to a person the defendant knew or ought to have known would rely on the statement. He must also know the purpose to which the information will be put.

Test your understanding 6

D

In the tort of negligence, if the claimant is partly responsible for his own injuries, the compensation awarded by the court will be reduced to take account of the claimant's share of the injuries.

Employment law

Chapter learning objectives

Upon completion of this chapter you will be able to:

- distinguish between employees and the self-employed

- explain the nature of the contract of employment and give examples of the main duties placed on the parties to such a contract

- distinguish between wrongful and unfair dismissal, including constructive dismissal

- explain what is meant by redundancy

- discuss the remedies available to those who have been subject to unfair dismissal or redundancy.

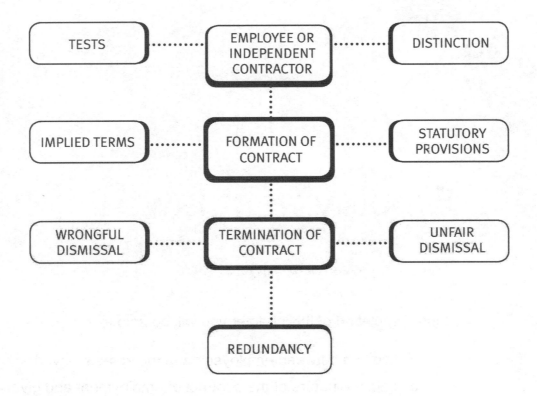

1   Employed versus self-employed

Introduction

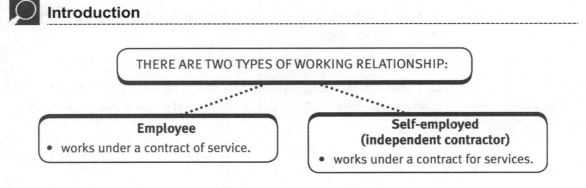

The tests used to determine employment

A number of tests can be used to determine if someone is employed or self-employed:

- **the control test** – employees are subject to control by their employer as to how, where and when they do their work: **Yewens v Noakes (1880)**. (Note, however, that this test is inappropriate for skilled workers.)

- **the integration test** – someone is regarded as an employee if their work is an integral part (i.e. part and parcel) of the business and not merely an accessory to it. (Note, however, that this test has become difficult to apply as a sole criterion.)

- **the economic reality test (or multiple test)** – under this test the court takes all the surrounding factors into account.

The test involves asking whether the person who is doing the work, is doing so as a person in business on his own account.

Relevant factors are:

- control

- provision of his own equipment

- whether he hires his own helpers

- degree of financial risk he undertakes

- degree of responsibility he bears for investment and management

- the extent to which he has an opportunity of profiting from sound

- management in the performance of his task

- whether there is a regular method of payment

- whether the person works regular hours

- whether there is mutuality of obligations.

Ready Mixed Concrete (South East) Ltd v Minister of Pensions & National Insurance & Others (1968)

Fact: The driver of a lorry had a contract with a company under which he drove his lorry only on company business, obeyed instructions of the foreman and wore company colours. He provided his own lorry which he had obtained from the company on hire purchase and which was painted in company colours. He could employ a substitute driver. He was paid on the basis of mileage and quantity of goods delivered. He paid the expenses of repair and maintenance of the lorry and his own national insurance and income tax. The Minister of Pensions claimed that he was an employee and the company had therefore to make the employer's national insurance contributions.

Held: Although the employer exercised some control over his work, the other factors were not consistent with there being a contract of service. In particular, the fact that he owned his own equipment and was operating at his own financial risk to a degree (i.e. was 'a small businessman') meant that he was an independent contractor.

Control test

An example of this test in operation may be seen in **Walker v Crystal Palace Football Club (1910)** in which it was decided that a professional footballer was an employee of his club on the basis that he was subject to control in relation to his training, discipline and method of pay.

However, with developing technology and specialisation, the control test became inappropriate as employers would hire people for particular skills (e.g. a chemical engineer), of which the employer did not have sufficient knowledge or skill to instruct as to the manner in which they carried out their work.

Integration test

An example of the application of the integration test may be seen in **Whittaker v Minister of Pensions & National Insurance (1966)** in which the court found that the degree to which a circus trapeze artist was required to do other general tasks in relation to the operation of the circus in which she appeared, indicated that she was an employee rather than self-employed. As a consequence, she was entitled to claim compensation for injuries sustained in the course of her employment.

The economic reality test

Market Investigations Ltd v Minister of Social Security (1968)

Facts: A market research interviewer worked on and off under a series of contracts whereby she interviewed for a company in accordance with interview instructions issued by the company. She had to complete the work within a specified period, but otherwise had no specified hours of work. There was no provision for holiday or sick pay and she was free to work for others while working for the company.

Held: The company did have some control over the manner in which she did her work and the terms of the contract were consistent with a contract of service. The court emphasised that she did not provide her own tools and took no risk. She was therefore not 'in business on her own account' and was an employee and not an independent contractor. The court also emphasised that there was 'no exhaustive test compiled, nor strict rules laid down' as to the factors which identified a contract of service.

Temporary or casual workers

There are real problems in determining the status of temporary or casual workers.

O'Kelly v Trusthouse Forte plc (1983)

Facts: A wine waiter was called a 'regular casual' because he was given work when it was required in the banqueting hall. He had no other employment and it was generally accepted that he would be offered work in preference to others when work was available, and that he would accept such work when offered.

Held: He was an independent contractor because there was 'no mutuality of obligation' in that the company was under no duty to offer him work and he was under no duty to accept it. However when at work he wore a company uniform, did not use his own equipment, did not share in the profit and had no investment in the business (aside from his time as a waiter).

Home workers or outworkers

There are also problems with home workers or outworkers. Generally such people will be paid by the number of pieces they produce and will supply their own equipment. Their position is ambiguous and many consider themselves to be self-employed, but the law does not always take this view.

Nethermere (St Neots) Ltd v Taverna and Gardiner (1984)

Facts: Two women, who sewed trousers at home, let the company know when to deliver the material and collect the finished garments. They rarely refused work, but did give warning if they did not want it, e.g. going on holiday. They submitted time sheets and were paid at the same rate as the workers in the factory. The company relied on the work they produced. The company provided the machines.

Held: They were employees because, by the giving and taking of work regularly over a continuous period of time, they had built up a mutuality of obligation (i.e. the company to provide work and the women to accept it).

The importance of the distinction

The type of working relationship has a number of consequences:

- employees receive statutory protection (e.g. unfair dismissal/redundancy)

- there are implied terms in a contract of employment (e.g. duty of obedience)

- an employer is vicariously liable for the acts of employees when they act in the course of the employer's business. The employer is not liable for the acts of independent contractors

- on the insolvency of the employer, an employee is a preferential creditor, whereas someone who is self-employed ranks as an ordinary unsecured creditor

- employees receive their pay net of income tax and national insurance under the PAYE system. Independent contractors are taxed under the trading income provisions

- certain state benefits (e.g. statutory sick pay) are only available to employees.

Test your understanding 1

1   **Which of the following statements suggest that John is an independent contractor in relation to the work he carries out for Zed Ltd?**

   (I)   He is required to provide his own tools.

   (II)   He is required to carry out his work personally and is not free to send a substitute.

   (III)   He is paid in full without any deduction of income tax.

   A   (I) and (II) only

   B   (II) and (III) only

   C   (I) and (III) only

   D   (I), (II) and (III)

2   H plc carries on its business using both employees and independent contractors. It is important for H plc to be able to distinguish between its employees and independent contractors for a number of reasons.

   Which one of the following is incorrect?

   A   Employees have a right not to be unfairly dismissed, but this does not apply to independent contractors.

   B   H plc must deduct income tax and national insurance contributions from the wages paid to its employees, but not from the amount paid to independent contractors.

   C   Both employees and independent contractors can enforce contractual rights against H plc.

   D   Both employees and independent contractors would rank as preferential creditors in respect of unpaid wages, if H plc went into insolvent liquidation.

3   **Which of the following is a test to determine a worker's status?**

A   The neighbour test

B   The multiple test

C   The reasonableness test

D   The test of remoteness

4   **Which of the following statements is correct?**

(I)   An employer is vicariously liable for the torts of employees committed in the course of their employment.

(II)   An employer is vicariously liable for the torts of independent contractors, if they were committed whilst carrying out work for the employer.

A   (I) only

B   (II) only

C   Both (I) and (II)

D   Neither (I) nor (II)

2   The contract of employment

Contents

A contract of employment will consist of:

- express terms
- terms implied by the courts
- terms implied by statute.

Express terms

Express terms are those agreed by the parties themselves. The agreement may be written or oral.

The Employment Rights Act 1996 (ERA 1996) requires an employer to provide an employee with a written statement of prescribed particulars of their employment within two months of the commencement of employment.

This must include a principal statement which must include details of:

- the business's name
- the employee's name, job title or a description of work and start date
- if a previous job counts towards a period of continuous employment, the date the period started
- how much and how often an employee will get paid

- hours of work (and if employees will have to work Sundays, nights or overtime)

- holiday entitlement (and if that includes public holidays)

- where an employee will be working and whether they might have to relocate.

As well as the principal statement, a written statement must also contain information about:

- how long a temporary job is expected to last

- the end date of a fixed-term contract

- notice periods

- collective agreements

- pensions

- who to go to with a grievance

- how to complain about how a grievance is handled

- how to complain about a disciplinary or dismissal decision.

Any change must be notified by written statement within one month.

The statement is not a contract unless both parties agree and it is called a contract. It is strong prima facie evidence of the terms of the contract, but is not conclusive.

Terms implied by the courts

The courts have implied various duties into the employment contract.

Duties of the employee

Duty to obey lawful and reasonable orders

Pepper v Webb (1968)

Facts: A gardener refused to plant the plants where instructed by the employer.

Held: He was in breach of the duty of obedience and this, coupled with the fact that he was rude and surly, justified his summary dismissal.

Duty of mutual co-operation (or the duty to perform the work in a reasonable manner)

The duty of the employer to give, and the employee to obey, lawful instructions is often expressed as the duty of mutual co-operation. The courts have begun to imply a term that the employer must not act in a manner calculated to damage the mutual trust and confidence and this is taken into account in considering the reasonableness of the order. The courts have interpreted the duty to obey lawful and reasonable orders as a duty not to frustrate the commercial objectives of the employer.

Secretary of State for Employment v ASLEF (1972)

Facts: Railway workers 'worked to rule', i.e. obeyed the British Rail rule book to the letter. This resulted in considerable delays in the train service.

Held: There was an implied term that each employee in obeying instructions would not do so in a wholly unreasonable way which had the effect of disrupting the service he was there to provide.

Duty to exercise reasonable care and skill

The employee must act with reasonable care in performing his duties. The standard of care will depend on the circumstances. It is generally accepted that a single act of negligence, unless it is gross negligence, will not justify summary dismissal. There are certain occupations, such as airline pilots, where a single act of negligence in performing essential duties may warrant dismissal.

An extension of this duty of care is a duty to indemnify the employer for any damages which he has had to pay as a result of his vicarious liability for the employee's negligence.

Lister v Romford Ice & Cold Storage Ltd (1972)

Facts: An employee negligently ran over another employee with a fork-lift truck.

Held: He was liable in damages to his employer for breach of contract.

Duty of good faith – a duty to give honest and faithful service

The employee cannot use the employer's property as his own, and must account to his employer for any money or property which he receives in the course of his employment.

Sinclair v Neighbour (1967)

Facts: An employee secretly borrowed from the shop till. He repaid the money the next day.

Held: He was in breach of the duty of good faith and, since this was a serious breach of contract, the employer was justified in summarily dismissing him.

The employee may do other work in his own time. However, the law imposes a duty not to do spare time work which competes with that of his employer and may cause his employer damage.

An employee must not disclose trade secrets to a third party nor misuse confidential information he has acquired in the course of his employment. This implied duty may continue after the employment has ceased. Clearly an employee who uses or sells secret processes, such as chemical formulae, or photocopies list of customers and sells them or uses them for his own purposes will be in breach.

The real problem arises in drawing a line between trade secrets/confidential information and general knowledge and skill acquired by the employee in the course of his employment. An employee may always use skills he has learnt in his employment.

Hivac Ltd v Park Royal Scientific Instruments Ltd (1946)

Facts: Two employees of a company which manufactured sophisticated components for hearing aids worked at the weekends for a rival company.

Held: An injunction was granted as there was potential for misuse of the secret information.

Duty to render personal service

Employees may not delegate the performance of their work to someone else unless they have their employer's express or implied permission to do so.

Duties of the employer

Duty to pay reasonable remuneration

This will be implied in the absence of an express provision regarding pay.

Duty to indemnify the employee

The employer must indemnify his employee where the employee has incurred a legal liability or necessary expenses whilst acting on the employer's behalf.

Duty to provide a safe system of work

At common law the employer is under a duty to take reasonable care for the health and safety of his employees. Breach of this duty exposes the employer to liability in negligence to his employees.

In addition, the employer is under various statutory duties, e.g. the Factories Act 1961, the Offices, Shops and Railway Premises Act 1963, and the Health and Safety at Work etc. Act 1974 all regulate work conditions.

The requirement at common law is to take reasonable care to provide a safe system of work and this encompasses such matters as the selection of staff and provision for their supervision; and ensuring that premises, plant and materials are safe.

In assessing the reasonableness of the employer in these matters a number of factors must be considered. For example: what was the risk of injury? What was the cost of prevention? What were the characteristics of the employee?

If the employer has not acted unreasonably, he has not been negligent, and has no common law liability.

Latimer v AEC Ltd (1953)

Facts: Following flood damage, the employer carefully strewed sawdust over a factory floor to prevent employees slipping until the floor could be properly cleared. A small patch remained uncovered and L slipped and was injured.

Held: The employers had not acted unreasonably. They were not liable to L for his injuries.

Duty to give reasonable notice of termination of employment

In practice this implied duty rarely arises since most contracts of employment contain express provision stating the exact length of notice or stating that the contract is to be for a fixed term. Also there are statutory minimum periods of notice.

Duty of mutual co-operation

This duty has already been discussed in respect of employees' duties. The employer has a duty not to behave in a manner calculated to damage the relationship of trust and confidence, e.g. by abusively reprimanding an employee.

Provision of work

There is no general common law duty to provide work. However, such a term may be implied, under the business efficacy test, where failure to provide work would deprive the employee of a benefit contemplated by the contract. For example, if the contract expressly provides for remuneration on a piecework or commission basis it may be possible to imply a duty on the employer to provide sufficient work to enable the employee to earn a reasonable sum.

Similarly, where the employee is skilled and needs practice to maintain those skills, there may be an obligation to provide a reasonable amount of work.

William Hill Organisation Ltd v Tucker (1998)

Facts: T worked as a senior dealer (one of only five authorised to do so) operating in the field of spread betting. He served notice to terminate his contract in order to work for a competitor. WH insisted that he remain on the payroll for the notice period, but stayed at home 'on garden leave'. T sought to start his new job immediately, arguing that WH was in breach of contract in refusing to allow him to work.

Held: WH was in breach by not providing work because T had particular skills which must be exercised to maintain them.

Provision of a reference

There is no duty to provide a reference but, if one is provided, it must be truthful, as shown in:

Spring v Guardian Assurance (1994)

Facts: The claimant had worked as a representative for a company but was dismissed after their sale to Guardian Assurance. He applied to work for the insurance company Scottish Amicable. Guardian Assurance provided Scottish Amicable with a bad reference in respect of the claimant who claimed damages for negligent misstatement. The reference was, the judge said, 'so strikingly bad as to amount to . . . the 'kiss of death' to his career in insurance'.

Held: The defendants did owe the claimant a duty of care in providing a reference, knowing that a bad one might damage his prospects of employment, and that they were in breach of that duty.

Terms implied by statute

ERA 1996	Gives employees certain rights, such as a right not to be unfairly dismissed, a right to a redundancy payment if made redundant and a right to a minimum period of notice to terminate the contract.
Working Time Regulations 1998	Limit the **hours** of work to an average of **48 a week**. It also gives the right to **four weeks' paid leave** a year and **one day off each week**.
Employment Act 2002	Gives **parents of children under seventeen or disabled children under eighteen** the right to request **flexible working** arrangements. The employer must give serious consideration to such a request and can only reject it for clear business reasons. The Act also introduced paternity and adoption leave.
Equality Act 2010	Deals with protecting people from discrimination in the workplace (and in wider society). Recognises 'protected characteristics'. In terms of remuneration deals not only with pay, but other terms, e.g. holiday and sick leave. **Implies an equality clause** into all contracts of employment if workers of the opposite sex do the same job or a different job of equal value.
National Minimum Wage Act 1998	Imposes minimum levels of pay.

Test your understanding 2

1 **Which one of the following is normally implied into a contract of employment?**

   A   A duty to provide a reference

   B   A duty to provide work

   C   A duty to pay reasonable remuneration

   D   An employee's duty to disclose his own misconduct

2 **Which one of the following statements is correct?**

   A   An employer is obliged to provide a careful and honest reference.

   B   An employer is obliged to provide a safe system of work.

   C   An employer is obliged to provide employees with smoking facilities during authorised breaks at work.

   D   An employer is obliged to give two days off a week.

3 **Which of the following are sources of terms of a contract of employment?**

   (I)   Custom and practice.

   (II)   A collective agreement between the union and the employer.

   A   (I) only

   B   (II) only

   C   Both (I) and (II)

   D   Neither (I) nor (II)

4 **Which of the following statements are correct with regard to the terms of the Employment Act 2002?**

   (I)   Parents of children under seventeen years old have the right to request a flexible working arrangement.

   (II)   An employer receiving a request from an employee for a flexible working arrangement, in accordance with the Act, is obliged to offer such an arrangement.

   A   (I) only

   B   Both (I) and (II)

   C   (II) only

   D   Neither (I) nor (II)

Test your understanding 3

Eric and Freda have worked together as partners for many years. They have decided to take on staff in order to expand the business. They are unsure as to what rights and obligations this will entail.

A **Fill in the gaps.**

The choice of status of worker is between that of an .... and an....................These are distinguished mostly by the use of the .... test. Three of the factors in determining that a worker is an...............................are:

B **Fill in the gaps.**

Under the...............................a .... must be given to employees within two months of starting work. That statement must be in writing/can be oral and these are three examples of what it must contain:

C **State the main common law duties owed by an employee to employer**

3 Wrongful and unfair dismissal

Minimum notice periods

If a period of notice is not expressly agreed, the ERA 1996 imposes the following minimum notice periods:

Notice by employer

Continuous employment	Period of notice
1 month – 2 years	1 week
2 – 12 years	1 week per complete year
12 years +	12 weeks

Notice by employee

An employee with at least four weeks' continuous employment must give his employer at least one week's notice of his terminating of the contract.

Wrongful dismissal

A claim for wrongful dismissal is a common law action for breach of contract. The claim is available to both employees and independent contractors. The usual rules of breach of contract will apply.

Wrongful dismissal occurs where the employer terminates the contract:

- without giving proper notice or
- during its fixed term.

 Dismissal without notice is known as summary dismissal.

Summary dismissal is usually wrongful dismissal unless the employee:

- waives their rights or accepts payment in lieu of notice
- repudiates the contract themselves or is in fundamental breach (e.g. wilful refusal to obey orders; failure to show professed skill; serious negligence; breach of duty of good faith).

Remedies

An individual who believes he has been wrongfully dismissed may sue in the County court or High Court for damages. The limitation period for such a claim is six years.

Alternatively, if he is an employee, he can bring a claim to the employment tribunal provided he does so within three months of his dismissal and the claim is for £25,000 or less.

Test your understanding 4

Mario is entitled to one month's notice. Consider both of the following situations and state whether he has been wrongfully dismissed:

A   The employer dismisses Mario on one month's notice, but gives him no reason for the dismissal.

B   The employer dismisses Mario without notice for fighting in the workplace with another employee.

Unfair dismissal

This is a statutory right under the Employment Rights Act 1996. Only employees can bring an action for unfair dismissal.

 The employer terminates the contract without justifiable reason.

Must be continuously employed for 2 years.

Must serve grievance notice on employer.

Claim to employment tribunal within 3 months of dismissal.

Employee must prove he was dismissed
(presumption raised that dismissal is unfair).

Employer must prove reason for dismissal: **Devis W & Sons Ltd v Atkins (1977)**.
Employer must prove that it is within one or more of five statutory fair reasons.

The tribunal must be satisfied that the employer has acted reasonably.

If found unfair, entitlement to reinstatement, re-engagement or compensation.

The requirement to be continuously employed for two years is for an employment contract which started on or after 6th April 2012. For employment contracts which started before this date the qualifying period is one year.

Types of dismissal

- Contract terminated by employer with or without notice.
- Fixed-term contract expired and not renewed.
- Constructive dismissal.

Constructive dismissal

Normally employees who resign deprive themselves of the right to make a claim for redundancy or unfair dismissal. However, s95 ERA 1996 covers situations where 'the employee terminates the contract with, or without, notice in circumstances which are such that he or she is entitled to terminate it without notice by reason of the employer's conduct'. This is known as constructive dismissal.

In **Western Excavating (ECC) Ltd v Sharp (1978)** it was held that an employee is entitled to treat himself as constructively dismissed if the employer is guilty of conduct which is a significant breach going to the root of the contract of employment, or which shows that the employer no longer intends to be bound by one or more of the essential terms of the contract. Whether the employee leaves with or without notice, the conduct must be sufficiently serious to entitle him to leave at once. However, he must act quickly, for if he continues for any length of time without leaving, he will be regarded as having elected to affirm the contract and will lose his right to treat himself as discharged.

Where such a repudiatory breach occurs the employee resigns and will have an action against the employer for wrongful dismissal.

Donovan v Invicta Airways (1970)

Facts: The employer put pressure on the employee, an airline pilot, to take abnormal risks on a flight. The employer did this three times in rapid succession. Each time the employee refused. Relations with management deteriorated and he left.

Held: The employer had committed a serious breach of contract amounting to constructive dismissal. The employee succeeded in an action for wrongful dismissal.

Simmonds v Dowty Seals Ltd (1978)

Facts: S had been employed to work on the night shift. When his employer attempted to force him to work on the day shift he resigned.

Held: He could treat himself as constructively dismissed because the employer's conduct had amounted to an attempt to unilaterally change an express term of the employment contract.

Kevin Keegan v Newcastle United Football Club Limited (2010)

Facts: A football club manager resigned from his position and claimed he was constructively dismissed. He contended that when he was appointed manager of the club it was agreed that he would have the final say regarding the transfer of players into the club. The club breached this term by signing a particular player against his express wishes and that he 'had no option but to resign'.

Held: The manager had been constructively dismissed and was awarded in the region of £2m in damages.

In **British Aircraft Corporation v Austin (1978)** a failure to investigate a health and safety complaint was held to be conduct sufficient to entitle the employee to treat the contract as terminated.

If the employee does not resign in the event of the breach, he is deemed to have accepted the breach and waived any rights. However, he need not resign immediately and may legitimately wait until he has found another job: **Cox Toner (International) Ltd v Crook (1981)**.

Statutory fair reasons for dismissal

Dismissal for one of the following reasons is fair **unless the employer acted unreasonably** in dismissing for the reason given:

- capabilities/qualifications of employee
- conduct of employee
- redundancy (see below)
- continued employment would contravene statute
- some other substantial reason.

Reasons for dismissal

An employer can only rely on a given reason for dismissal where he knew of it at the date of the dismissal.

Devis W & Sons Ltd v Atkins (1977)

Facts: The employer dismissed the employee and afterwards discovered that the employee had been guilty of dishonesty.

Held: Dishonesty was not the reason for the dismissal and therefore the employer could not rely on it in order to justify the dismissal as fair.

Stevenson v Golden Wonder Ltd (1977)

Facts: A technical manager took part in an unprovoked assault on another employee at a company social function held outside working hours in the company canteen.

Held: This was a fair reason for the dismissal, it was serious misconduct.

An example of 'some other substantial reason' justifying dismissal is the case of **Singh v London Country Bus Services (1976)**, where an employee in a position of trust was convicted of a criminal offence of dishonesty (which he committed off duty).

Reasonableness of employer

Once the employee has shown they were dismissed and the employer has shown that it was for one or more of the six fair reasons it is then for the tribunal to decide whether the dismissal was fair or unfair.

S98(4) ERA 1996 states that the determination of this question 'depends on whether in the circumstances (including the size and administrative resources of the employer's undertaking) the employer acted reasonably or unreasonably in treating it (the reason) as a sufficient reason for dismissing the employee'. The question 'shall be determined in accordance with equity and the substantial merits of the case'.

Case law shows that this 'reasonableness test' involves two questions:

- Whether the reason given was sufficiently serious to justify dismissal.
- Whether the employer adopted reasonable procedures both in coming to the decision to dismiss and in the manner of the dismissal.

The Arbitration, Conciliation and Advisory Service (ACAS) has issued codes of practice for procedures to be followed in coming to the decision to dismiss an employee (e.g. warnings, proper inquiry into alleged misconduct, etc.) which the employment tribunal has regard to. These were illustrated by the House of Lords in **Polkey v Dayton (AE) Services (1987)** where it was stated that:

- in a case of incapability, the employer will normally not act reasonably unless he gives the employee fair warning and an opportunity to mend his ways and show he can do the job

- in a case of misconduct, the employer will normally not act reasonably unless he investigates the complaint fully and fairly and hears whatever the employee wishes to say in his defence or in explanation or mitigation

- in a case of redundancy (this was the situation in **Polkey**) the employer will normally not act reasonably unless he warns and consults any employees affected or their representative, adopts a fair basis upon which to select for redundancy and takes such steps as may be reasonable to avoid or minimise redundancy by redeployment within his own organisation.

Inadmissible reasons for dismissal

Dismissal for one of the following reasons is automatically unfair. This means that there is no need to meet the length of employment condition. The tribunal will also make an additional award of compensation.

The inadmissible reasons are:

- victimisation of health and safety complainants or whistleblowers. A whistleblower is a person who raises a concern about wrongdoing occurring in an organisation. The revealed misconduct may be classified in many ways; for example, a violation of a law, rule, regulation and/or a direct threat to public interest, such as fraud, health/safety violations, and corruption

- pregnancy or the exercise of maternity leave rights

- trade union membership/non-membership/activities

- assertion of a statutory right e.g. the exercise of paternity leave rights

- unfair selection for redundancy (see **section 4**).

Remedies for unfair dismissal

Reinstatement – Employee treated as if not dismissed. Returned to same job with no loss of seniority. **OR** **Re-engagement** – Employee given comparable employment.	Only awarded if the applicant wishes and if it is practicable. The employer's failure to comply with an order for reinstatement or re-engagement results in compensation.

Basic award	Compensatory award	Additional award
18 – 21 years of age – 1/2 weeks pay for each year of service. 22 – 40 years of age – 1 week pay for each year of service. 41 plus – 1.5 weeks pay for each year of service. Maximum – 20 years service at £508 a week.	Discretionary award of up to £83,682. Based on employee's losses and expenses. Reduced if the complainant contributed to his dismissal.	Given where: • the employer ignores an order for reinstatement or re-engagement • the dismissal is unfair because of race, sex or disability discrimination • the reason cited for dismissal is an inadmissible one.

Under the Small Business, Enterprise and Employment Act 2015 non-payment of an award by the Employment Tribunal can lead to a fine between £100 – £5000, payable to the Treasury.

Test your understanding 5

You have recently been appointed personnel director of a major plc. The board has asked for a review and report on various employment law issues relevant to the employees and working practices within the firm. You investigate the relevant areas of law discussed below.

A **Fill in the gaps.**

The.....................sets out a number of reasons why a dismissal will be ....unfair.

The five major reasons are:

I

II

III

IV

V

B **Explain the remedies for unfair dismissal available to a tribunal.**

4 Redundancy

An employee is redundant if his dismissal is wholly or mainly attributable to the fact that:

- the employer has **ceased**, or intends to cease, **business** for the **purposes** for which the employee has been employed

- the employer has ceased, or intends to cease to carry on the business in the **place** where the employee was employed, or

- the requirements of that business for employees to carry out work of a **particular kind**, or for them to carry out the work in the place where they were so employed, have ceased or diminished.

Note that the work may have ceased altogether or only in the place where the employee was employed.

Redundancy consultation process

If you fail to consult employees – and their representatives if applicable – in a redundancy situation, the redundancy dismissals will almost certainly be unfair.

If you plan to make 20 or more employees redundant in one place of work within a 90-day period, known as a collective redundancy situation, you must:

- Notify the Department for Business, Energy and Industrial Strategy; and

- Consult with workplace representatives. These may be either trade union representatives or, where no union is recognised, elected employee representatives instead. If your employees choose not to elect employee representatives, you must give the relevant information directly to each individual.

Consultation must start in good time – when redundancy proposals are in their formative stage – and at least:

- 30 days before the first redundancy where there are 20 to 99 proposed redundancies

- 45 days in advance where there are 100 or more proposed redundancies.

Procedure:

> Must be continuously employed for **2 years**.

> **Claim** to employment tribunal within **six months** of dismissal.

> Employee must prove he was dismissed.

> Employer must prove employee not redundant (i.e. there is a **presumption** that he is **redundant**).

> If found redundant, **pay as per basic** award for unfair dismissal.

Is the employee redundant?

European Chefs Catering v Currell (1971)

Facts: A pastry cook was dismissed because the requirement for his specialty (éclairs and meringues) had ceased. He was replaced by a new pastry cook whose specialty was the new requirement (continental pastries).

Held: It was held that the dismissed pastry cook had been dismissed for redundancy as the need for the particular work he contracted to do had ceased.

Vaux and Associated Breweries v Ward (1969)

Facts: A quiet public house was modernised by installing a discotheque. The 57-year-old barmaid, Mrs Ward, was dismissed in order to make way for a younger more glamorous barmaid.

Held: Mrs Ward had not been dismissed for redundancy as there was no change in the nature of the particular work being done.

The place where a person is employed means in this context the place where he is habitually employed and any place where, under his contract, he can be required to work. There will not, therefore, be a redundancy situation where the transfer of location is reasonable or where the contract gives the employer an express or implied right to move (a mobility clause may have been agreed in the contract) the employee in question from one place to another. This is not the case, though, if the employer has no such right: **O'Brien v Associated Fire Alarms (1969)**.

Redundancy pay

Redundancy pay is calculated in the same way as the basic award for unfair dismissal.

However, an employee is not entitled to redundancy pay if they unreasonably refuse an offer of fresh employment (made before the old contract expires) to start within four weeks on the same or suitable terms. The employee must be allowed at least a four-week trial period in the new job.

Whether the alternative employment offered is suitable, or the offer was unreasonably refused, are both questions of fact to be determined by reference to such matters as the employee's skill and working conditions, the requirements of his family, change in earnings, age, health, sex, etc. Any dispute arising in this respect is for the tribunal to determine and the onus of proof is on the employer.

Taylor v Kent County Council (1969)

Facts: T was headmaster of a school. The school was amalgamated with another school and a new head appointed to the combined school. T was offered employment in a pool of teachers, standing in for short periods in understaffed schools. He would retain his current salary.

Held: T was entitled to reject this offer and claim a redundancy payment: the new offer was substantially different, particularly in regard to status.

5 Chapter summary

Test your understanding answers

Test your understanding 1

1 **C**

Independent contractors would have their own tools, and would be paid in full for their work without deduction of income tax. They may do the work personally; alternatively, they may send a substitute. Items (i) and (iii) therefore apply, but not (ii).

2 **D**

On a company being wound up, arrears of wages due to employees for four months up to the commencement of the winding up rank as preferential debts. Arrears of money owing to independent contractors do not rank as preferential debts.

3 **B**

The multiple test is one of the tests used to determine a worker's status. It is sometimes called the economic reality test.

4 **A**

An employer is vicariously liable for the torts of employees whilst they are at work, but is not liable for the torts of any independent contractor providing services to the employer.

Test your understanding 2

1 **C**

A duty to pay reasonable remuneration is normally implied in a contract of employment.

2 **B**

An employer does not have to provide a reference for an employee leaving to work somewhere else. Nor does an employer have to provide smoking facilities at work – you might have seen employees standing outside their place of work, smoking in the street, because there is nowhere on the premises to smoke. An employer is obliged to give only one day off a week. However, an employer is under an obligation to provide a safe system of work.

3 **C**

The terms of a contract of employment might be subject to a collective agreement between an employer and a trade union, so (ii) is quite clearly correct. In addition, some terms of employment might be derived from custom and practice.

4 **A**

The right of a parent to ask for a flexible working arrangement applies to parents of children under seventeen and disabled children under eighteen. Statement (i) is correct. An employer is obliged to consider such requests seriously, but may refuse where there is a clear business reason. Statement (ii) is therefore incorrect.

Test your understanding 3

A   Employee

independent contractor

multiple/economic reality

employee

Any three of the following:

- control
- provision of his own equipment
- whether he hires his own helpers
- the degree of financial risk he undertakes
- the degree of responsibility he bears for investment and management
- the extent to which he has an opportunity of profiting from sound management in the performance of his task
- whether there is a regular method of payment
- whether the person works regular hours
- whether there is mutuality of obligations.

B   Employment Rights Act 1996

Statement of Particulars

Must be in writing

Any three of the following:

- how pay will be calculated and paid
- job title and nature of the work
- date on which employment began
- intervals of pay
- hours of work
- holidays and holiday pay
- sick pay/leave
- pension scheme details
- place of work
- any collective agreement
- length of notice required
- names of employer and employee.

C   Duties to obey lawful reasonable orders, of mutual co-operation (care and skill), of good faith and of personal service.

Test your understanding 4

A   Mario has not been wrongfully dismissed as he has been given the appropriate amount of notice.

B   Mario has not been wrongfully dismissed as his conduct puts him in serious breach of his contract.

Test your understanding 5

A   Employment Rights Act 1996 automatically

   I   Complaints/actions by an employee under the Health and Safety at Work etc. Act 1974

   II   Pregnancy or childbirth

   III Trade union related activities

   IV Assertion of statutory right

   V   Unfair selection for redundancy

B   A complainant can be compensated, re-instated under the same contract or re-engaged under a different contract in the same organisation.

Agency law

Chapter learning objectives

Upon completion of this chapter you will be able to:

- define the role of the agent and give examples of such relationships, paying particular regard to partners and company directors

- explain how the agency relationship is established

- define the authority of the agent

- explain the potential liability of both principal and agent.

1 Definition of an agent

 An agent (A) is a person who is authorised to act for another (the principal (P)) in the making of legal relations with third parties.

The resulting contracts are made between the principal and the third party, and not directly with the agent.

An agency relationship exists in lots of situations:

- A director acts as an agent for his company.

- A partner acts as an agent for his partnership.

- An estate agent is appointed by a seller of a house to find a buyer.

- A travel agent is appointed by a holiday company to make bookings with customers.

2 How the agency relationship arises

Introduction

An agency relationship can be established in one of five ways:

- express agreement
- implied agreement
- by necessity
- by ratification
- by estoppel.

Express agreement

This is where P actually appoints A as his agent. The agreement can be made orally or in writing.

Implied agreement

This is where P has not expressly agreed that A should be his agent. However, the agreement can be implied from the parties' conduct or relationship.

By necessity

This requires four conditions to be satisfied:

- P's property is entrusted to A
- an emergency arises making it necessary for A to act
- it is not possible to communicate with P
- A acts in the interest of P.

Prager v Blatspeil (1924)

Facts: A bought skins as the agent for P but was unable to send them to P because of prevailing war conditions. Since A was also unable to communicate with P, he sold the skins before the end of the war.

Held: A was not an agent of necessity, because he could have stored the skins until the end of the war. There was no real emergency.

Great Northern Railway v Swaffield (1874)

Facts: There was a contract between the two parties whereby GNR agreed to transport the defendant's horse to a particular railway station from where it would be collected.

When no one arrived to pick it up, the station master, having tried unsuccessfully to contact the defendant, placed the horse in a stable overnight.

Held: GNR was entitled to recover the costs of stabling because it had become the agent of the defendant by necessity.

By ratification

If a properly appointed agent exceeds his authority, or a person having no authority purports to act as an agent, the principal has no liability on that contract unless the principal 'ratifies' the contract.

The effect of ratification is to backdate A's authority to act as agent. This requires P to:

- have the contractual capacity to make the contract

- have been in existence both when the contract was made and at the date of ratification

- be identified when the contract is made

- be aware of all the material facts

- clearly signify his intention to ratify the whole contract within a reasonable time.

Note that a void or illegal contract cannot be ratified.

Kelner v Baxter (1866)

Facts: The promoters of a company entered into a contract on behalf of a company before it was incorporated, to purchase some property. The other party was not paid.

Held: As the company did not exist at the time the contract was made, the company could not ratify the contract. The promoters were personally liable to the seller.

By estoppel

This arises where P holds out that A is his agent even though he is not. He is then prevented or 'stopped' from denying A's authority (see **Freeman & Lockyer v Buckhurst Park Properties Ltd** in **section 3**).

Test your understanding 1

Peter advertised his car for sale in a local newspaper and then went on holiday leaving his car in the drive. While Peter was away, Tom, having seen the advertisement, went to look at the car and decided to make an offer for it. Peter's neighbour, Alf, pretending to act with Peter's authority, entered into negotiations with Tom and eventually accepted Tom's offer on Peter's behalf.

Alf had no authority to act in this way. When Peter returned from his holiday, he wrote to Tom saying that he was ratifying Alf's act.

Advise Tom as to whether he is bound by the contract.

3 Authority

The authority of an agent is a central issue in the concept of agency. It determines:

- the powers that the agent has on behalf of the principal, and

- for which acts the principal is liable.

If the agent exceeds his powers the principal may still be liable to the third party, but he may have rights against the agent for breach of contract.

There are three ways in which authority may be given:

Express actual authority	This is authority that P has explicitly given to A.
Implied actual authority	An agent has implied authority to do things which: • are reasonably incidental to the performance of an expressly authorised act • an agent occupying that position would usually have authority to do • have not been expressly prohibited by P. See **Watteau v Fenwick (1893)** below.
Apparent/ostensible authority	Such authority arises where A is held out by P as having authority. The representation by P may arise from previous dealings (allowing A to make contracts in the past is a representation that A has authority to continue to do so in the future). See **Freeman & Lockyer v Buckhurst Park Properties Ltd (1964)** below. However, a third party cannot rely on apparent authority when he knows of the lack of actual authority.

Watteau v Fenwick (1893)

Facts: The new owners of a hotel continued to employ the original owner as the manager. In the agency agreement the new owners ordered the agent not to buy certain items, including cigars. The manager still bought cigars from a third party. The owners then refused to pay for the cigars.

Held: The purchase of the cigars was within the usual authority of a manager of a hotel. The contract was binding on the owners. (If a limitation on the usual authority is going to be effective, it must be communicated to the third party before any contract is made.)

Freeman & Lockyer v Buckhurst Park Properties Ltd (1964)

Facts: The defendant company had four directors, none of whom had been appointed as the managing director. One director effectively ran the business by himself and entered into a number of contracts with the claimants. On previous occasions, the board on behalf of the company had honoured the contracts and paid the claimants. However, on this occasion, the board refused to pay arguing that the director had no express authority to make the contract because he was not the managing director.

Held: Although the director had no express authority to make the contract, the director had apparent authority. This was because by honouring similar contracts in the past, the company (as the principal) had given the impression that the director had the authority to make this sort of contract. The claimants had relied on this representation by continuing to deal with the director when purporting to act on behalf of the company.

Test your understanding 2

Harry wanted to insure the contents of his house against all loss and damage and appointed Colin to effect a policy, instructing him to 'insure any furniture'. Having obtained quotes from various companies, Colin eventually took out insurance with Hawk Star Limited. Sometime later vandals broke into Harry's house and did substantial damage to his furniture. They did not steal anything. When Harry claimed, Hawk Star refused to pay as the policy covered loss by theft or fire but not damage by vandals.

Advise Harry as to whether he can recover the value of damaged furniture from Colin.

Breach of warranty of authority

As discussed earlier if an agent has no authority or exceeds it the principal may ratify the contract and become liable. However, if the principal does not ratify, then the agent will be liable to the third party for breach of warranty of authority because he warranted or promised that he had authority which he did not possess.

4   Liability

Where the agent acts for a disclosed principal

A principal is disclosed where the existence of the principal has been made known to the third party. It is not necessary for the principal to be identified to the third party.

As a general rule, the contract is between the principal and the third party. The agent is neither liable nor entitled under the contract. However, the agent will be personally liable in the following exceptional circumstances:

- where the agent showed an intention to undertake personal liability, e.g. by signing a written contract in his own name

- trade usage or custom

- where the agent refuses to identify the principal

- where the agent is acting on behalf of a fictitious principal.

Where the agent acts for an undisclosed principal

An undisclosed principal is where the principal's existence has not been made known to the third party. When the third party discovers the existence of P, he can elect to treat P or A as bound by the transaction.

Agent's fiduciary duty

An agent has a fiduciary relationship with his principal. This is a position similar to that of a trustee. It has the following consequences:

- A must not allow his personal interests to conflict with those of P.

- A must always act in the best interests of P.

- A must not make a secret profit.

- A has a duty to account to P for all money and property received.

Where an agent is in breach of his fiduciary duty, the following remedies are available:

- P can repudiate the contract with the third party.

- A can be dismissed without notice.

- P can refuse to pay any money owed to A or recover any money already paid.

- P can recover any secret profit made or any bribe.

Principal's liability to the agent

The agent has the right:

- To claim remuneration or commission for services performed.

  Usually the amount of remuneration or commission to be paid is stated in the agency agreement. Where it is not specified and it is a commercial agreement, the court will imply a term into the agreement requiring a reasonable amount to be paid.

- To claim an indemnity against P for all expenses reasonably incurred in carrying out his obligations.

- To exercise a lien over P's property. The lien allows the agent to retain possession of P's property that is lawfully in A's possession until any debts due to A, e.g. arrears of remuneration, have been paid by P.

5 Chapter summary

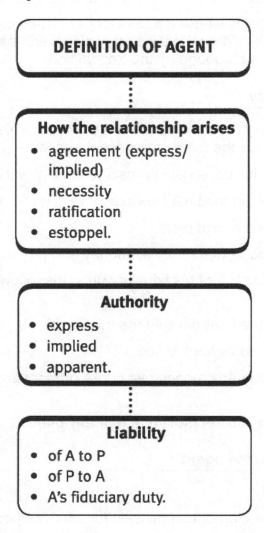

DEFINITION OF AGENT

How the relationship arises
- agreement (express/ implied)
- necessity
- ratification
- estoppel.

Authority
- express
- implied
- apparent.

Liability
- of A to P
- of P to A
- A's fiduciary duty.

Test your understanding answers

Test your understanding 1

Where a person purports to act as another's agent, even though he has no authority to do so, the principal is only bound by the contract if he decides to ratify it.

The principal can only ratify the contract if certain requirements are satisfied. The principal must have the contractual capacity to make the contract both at the time the contract is made and at the time of ratification. The principal must have been identified to the third party at the time the contract was made.

The principal must be aware of all material facts and ratify the contract within a reasonable time. The principal must ratify the whole contract.

It would appear that all these requirements can be satisfied in this situation. Therefore Peter is able to ratify the contract.

When the principal ratifies the contract, it is binding on the parties from the date on which it was originally made. Therefore Tom is bound by the contract.

Test your understanding 2

When an agent is appointed, he is given express authority to act on behalf of the principal. However, where the terms of authority are ambiguous or where the agent is given discretion to act the law implies authority to enable an agent to carry out his express duties. The agent must always act in the best interests of the principal.

Colin's authority is very ambiguous. He can decide which policy to take out 'to insure the principal's furniture'.

If Colin can show that when he made the decision to take this policy as opposed to any other, that he was acting in Harry's best interests, Colin will be acting within his authority. Harry will not be able to recover the value of the damaged furniture from Colin.

Types of business organisation

Chapter learning objectives

Upon completion of this chapter you will be able to:

- distinguish between different types of business organisation
- explain the meaning of the different types of partnership
- in relation to general or ordinary partnerships:
  - discuss how they are established
  - explain the authority of the partners in relation to partnership activity
  - outline the liability of the partners for partnership debts – explain the ways in which they can be brought to an end.

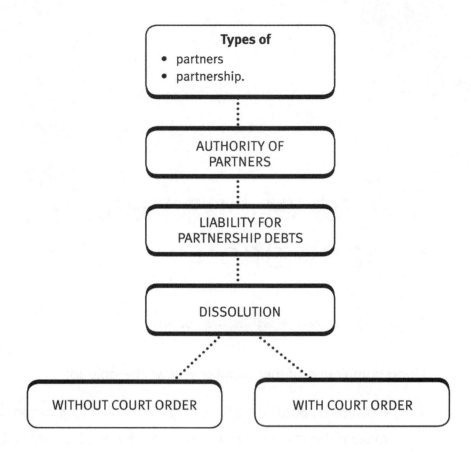

1 Types of business organisation

Different forms of business organisation

Sole trader/sole practitionership	• The owner 'is' the business – owns the assets and is liable for all the debts. • No legal formalities are required to set up a sole trader business/practitionership. • This form of business is inappropriate for large businesses or those involving a degree of risk.
General partnership	Defined by Partnership Act 1890 (PA 1890) as the relationship which subsists between persons carrying on a business in common with a view to profit. (See below.)
Limited partnership	Formed under the Limited Partnerships Act 1907. (See below.)
Limited liability partnership	An artificial legal entity where the liability of the members is limited to the amount of capital they have agreed to contribute. (See below.)
Company	A corporation is an artificial legal person. (See Chapter 7.)

The rest of this chapter will focus on partnerships.

2   Types of partnership

 Definition

A partnership is a relationship which subsists between two or more persons carrying on a business in common with a view to profit: s1 Partnership Act 1890 (PA 1890).

A partnership can be a small operation or as with some large firms of solicitors and accountants partnerships with several hundred partners.

Types of partners

General partner	Actively involved in the day-to-day business.
Sleeping partner	Takes no active part in the running of the business. However, is jointly and severally liable for the debts and contracts of the business.
Limited partner in a limited partnership	Contributes a specific amount of capital. Liability limited to that amount. Cannot take part in the management of the firm.
Salaried partner	Will received a fixed amount in income. Not a real partner unless he also receives a share of the profits.

Types of partnership

General or ordinary partnership	Governed by Partnership Act 1890 – this is the default position if a partnership is not formed under either of the two Acts below.
Limited partnership	Governed by Limited Partnership Act 1907.
Limited liability partnership (LLP)	Governed by Limited Liability Partnerships Act 2000. Legally separate from its members.

Characteristics of a partnership

In order for a partnership to exist, a business must be carried on with a view to profit. This means that the persons involved in the partnership intend the business to yield a profit and they are all entitled to share in that profit.

The following do not necessarily create a partnership:

- joint ownership of property
- the sharing of gross returns
- the sharing of expenses.

Cox v Coulson (1916)

Facts: C agreed with M that M would put on a play at C's theatre. C was to have 60% and M 40% of the gross box office receipts. C paid the expenses of running the theatre and M paid the expenses of putting on the play. During a performance the claimant, who was in the audience, was accidentally shot by one of the actors. The claimant sued C alleging that C was M's partner and was jointly liable with M.

Held: C was not M's partner because they merely shared gross box office receipts.

A partnership begins as soon as the partners start their business activity. The actual agreement may be made earlier or later than that date.

No formalities are required to form general partnerships, no documentation and no registration. The reason for this is that The Partnership Act 1890 applies to every partnership whether written or oral. Many of the Act's provisions apply, unless they are excluded by a **partnership agreement**. The PA 1890 provides that partners shall share profits equally, but in cases where partners contribute different amounts of capital this may not be appropriate and partners will need to agree specific profit sharing arrangements within their partnership agreement.

The partnership agreement is a contract. Like any contract it may be:

- express (e.g. oral, in writing or by deed), or

- implied.

The partners are contractually bound by the terms they have agreed, even if they conflict with PA 1890.

 Limited partnerships under Limited Partnership Act 1907

A limited partnership is a partnership in which the liability of one or more partners is limited to their capital contribution.

A limited partnership must fulfil the following conditions:

- There must be at least one partner with unlimited liability (s4(2) LPA 1907).

- The partnership must be registered with the Registrar of Companies as a limited partnership (s5 LPA 1907).

- Limited partners may not participate in the management of the business. If they do, they forfeit their limited liability (s6(1) LPA 1907).

- A limited partner has no power to bind the firm to contracts, i.e. unlike the unlimited partners, he is not an agent of the firm (s6(1) LPA 1907).

3 Authority of partners

Agency relationship

When entering into a contract to carry out the business, each partner is acting as the agent of all the partners:

- The express authority of a partner is set out in the partnership agreement.

- The implied authority is set out in s5 PA 1890.

S5 PA 1890 states that every partner is the agent of the firm and of the other partners. This means that each partner has the power to bind all partners to business transactions entered into within their express or implied authority.

Implied authority

Under s5 every partner is presumed to have the implied authority to:

- sell the firm's goods

- buy goods necessary for, or usually employed in, the business

- receive payments of debts due to the firm

- engage employees

- employ a solicitor to act for the firm in defence of a claim or in the pursuance of a debt.

Trading partnerships

The above implied powers apply to both trading and non-trading partnerships. Partners in trading partnerships have additional powers, such as to borrow money.

In order to be acting within his implied authority, the individual partner must be acting within the usual scope of a partner's powers in the particular business concerned.

Mercantile Credit Co v Garrod (1962)

Facts: P and G entered into a partnership to let lock-up garages and repair cars. P ran the business and G was a sleeping partner. The partnership agreement expressly stated that the firm would not buy and sell cars. P sold a car to a finance company, M. M sued G to recover the £700 which it had paid to P for the car. G denied liability claiming that P when selling the car had been acting outside the agreed limits of the firm's business and therefore P had no actual or apparent authority to make the contract. Evidence was given that other garage businesses of the type carried on by P and G did deal in cars.

Held: The test of what is the firm's business is not what the partners agreed it should be but 'what it appears to the outside world' to be. Under that test P appeared to M to be carrying on business of a kind carried on by such a firm. This contract was within the apparent authority of P and therefore the contract was binding on G.

Test your understanding 1

Jekyll and Hyde are in partnership providing support services to police services. The partnership agreement states that all scientific equipment is to be supplied by James and that neither partner may incur liability of more than £2,000 without consulting the other. Jekyll, although he contributed all the firm's initial capital, does not have any active involvement and visits its premises rarely. Hyde receives a salary, as well as a share of the profits, and works full-time for the firm.

Jekyll now seeks your advice as he has found out that Hyde has ordered £5,000 worth of equipment from Edgar. Advise him.

4 Liability for partnership debts

Is there liability in contract?

The firm is liable for contracts made by a partner if he was acting within his express or implied authority.

The firm is not bound by the implied authority of a partner if:

- the third party knows the partner has no express authority, or
- the partner has no express authority and the third party does not know or believe him to be a partner.

Holding out

Every person who by his words or conduct represents himself (or knowingly allows himself to be represented) as a partner is liable as if he is a partner to anyone who thereby gives credit to the firm: s14 PA 1890.

Martyn v Gray (1863)

Facts: G went to Cornwall to discuss the possibility of investing in a tin mine belonging to X. Nothing came of the discussions, but while G was in Cornwall he was introduced by X to M as 'a gentleman down from London, a man of capital'. M later gave X credit believing he was in partnership with G.

Held: The introduction amounted to a representation that G was in partnership with X, and so G was liable for the debt incurred subsequent to the introduction. He should have made the true position clear by correcting the impression made.

Liability in tort

The concept of vicarious liability was discussed in Chapter 4 in the context of the employer-employee relationship. The same principles apply in the context of a partnership. Where a tort is committed during the ordinary course of the partnership's business, or by a partner acting with the authority of the other partners, the partners are jointly and severally liable to the person who has suffered loss.

Misapplication of money or property

The partnership is liable to make good the loss where a third party's money or property is misapplied:

- after being received by a partner within his actual or apparent authority, or

- while it is in the custody of the firm, such as in the partnership bank account.

Which partners are liable?

General rule	Every partner is jointly and severally liable for the debts and contracts of the business.
	Outsiders can sue one partner alone or the firm. The Civil Liability Act 1978 provides that a judgment against one partner does not bar a subsequent action against the other partners.
New partners	A new partner is not personally liable for debts incurred before they became a partner.
Retiring partners	A retiring partner remains liable for any debts incurred while he was a partner. If no notice of the retirement is given, the firm continues to be bound by his actions as he is still being held out as a partner.
Change in partners	Where a third party deals with a partnership after a change in partners, all of the partners of the old firm are still treated as partners, until the third party receives notice of the change:
	• Previous customers require actual notice.
	• Third parties who were not existing customers can be notified by a notice in the London Gazette: s36 PA 1890. This is known as constructive notice.
	Notification must take place prior to retirement if the retiring partner is to avoid liability for contracts entered into after his retirement.

Novation	A creditor agrees with the outgoing, continuing and/or incoming partners that liability for an existing debt will be that of the continuing and incoming partners.
	(Thus the liability of the outgoing partner is removed and the incoming partner becomes liable for the debt even though it was incurred before he became a partner.)
Indemnity	The continuing and incoming partners may agree to indemnify the outgoing partner against debts incurred pre- and/or post-retirement.

Test your understanding 2

Following their earlier dispute, Jekyll and Hyde do not believe that they can continue in partnership. It is proposed that Jekyll will retire and Edgar will be admitted as a partner.

What will be the liability for the firm's debts of (i) Jekyll and (ii) Edgar once these changes have been made?

5 Dissolution

Without court order

The partnership will automatically end in the following situations:

- The expiry of a fixed term or the completion of a specific enterprise.

- One of the partners gives notice (unless the partnership agreement excludes this right).

- Death or bankruptcy of a partner (the partnership agreement will usually make provision for the partnership to continue if a partner should die).

- Where continuation of the partnership would be illegal.

Hudgell, Yeates and Co v Watson (1978)

Facts: Practising solicitors are required by law to have a practising certificate. One of the partners in a firm of solicitors forgot to renew his certificate which meant that it was illegal for him to practice.

Held: The failure to renew the practising certificate brought the partnership to an end, although a new partnership continued between the other two members.

By court order

Under s35 PA 1890, the court can bring a partnership to an end in any of the following situations:

- Partner has mental disorder or permanent incapacity.

- Partner engages in activity prejudicial to the business.

- Partner wilfully or persistently breaches the partnership agreement.

- Partner conducts himself in a way that it is no longer reasonably practicable for the others to carry on in business with him.

- Business can only be carried on at a loss.

- It is just and equitable to do so.

Distribution of assets

In the event of dissolution the assets of the partnership will be used to pay off the debts of the partnership. As a partnership does not have the advantage of limited liability status, if the proceeds on the sale of the assets does not cover the debts then the partners' personal wealth will be called upon to make up the shortfall.

The proceeds from the sale of the assets will be applied in the following order:

(i)   paying debts to outsiders

(ii) paying the partners any advance they made to the firm beyond their capital contribution i.e. a loan

(iii) paying the capital contribution of the partners.

If there is a residue remaining this will be divided between the partners in the same proportion in which they share the profits of the partnership.

In the event that the assets are insufficient to meet the debts to outsiders then profits held back from previous years or partners' capital will be used to make good the shortfall. If these are also insufficient then the partners will individually contribute in the proportion to which they shared in the profits.

6   LLPs

A limited liability partnership (LLP) is a corporate body which combines the features of a traditional partnership with a company.

LLP's are covered in the next chapter once we have covered the characteristics of a company.

7 Chapter summary

Partners
- general
- sleeping
- limited
- salaried.

TYPES

Partnerships
- partnership
- limited partnership
- LLP.

Authority of partners
- express /actual
- implied /apparent
- trading partnerships.

Liability for partnership debts
- which partners are liable?
- LLPs.

DISSOLUTION

Without court order
- expiry of term
- notice
- death
- bankruptcy
- continuation is illegal.

With court order
- just and equitable
- activity prejudicial to business
- breach of partnership agreement.

Test your understanding answers

Test your understanding 1

PA 1890 states that a partnership is a relationship which subsists between two or more persons carrying on a business with a view to profit. Each partner is liable for the debts of the firm.

Jekyll is a sleeping partner who takes no part in the running of the business, but he is treated as any other partner with respect to his liabilities.

Hyde is a salaried partner which means that he can run the business. Any act done within the ordinary course of the firm's business is binding on all partners and they are jointly and severally liable for the debts of the business.

When Hyde enters into the contract with Edgar, he is exceeding the actual authority given to him in the partnership agreement. However, the partnership agreement is not a public document and Edgar could not be expected to know of any limitation imposed upon Hyde's authority. In addition to actual authority, every partner has the apparent authority under s5, to enter into contracts on behalf of the business. As long as the equipment could be used in the ordinary course of the business, the contract will be binding on both parties.

When Hyde enters into the contract with Edgar, he is acting in breach of the partnership agreement. Jekyll can sue for breach of agreement and recover damages for any loss he suffers.

Test your understanding 2

A partner who has retired from the firm is not liable for any debts that arise after his or her retirement. He or she must notify the partnership's usual suppliers of his retirement and make sure that his name is taken off the list of partners including from the firm's stationery. This is actual notice.

A notice should also be placed in the London Gazette to give notice to the persons who have not previously dealt with the firm that he is no longer a partner. This will be constructive notice.

Jekyll will continue to be liable for the debts that arose while he was still a partner. However, it is possible to avoid this by agreement with Hyde, Edgar and the creditors.

An incoming partner is only liable for the debts arising after he became a partner. However, if there is an arrangement with the creditors by which the new partners assume the obligations of the old, Edgar will be liable for the old debts as well. This agreement can be express or it can be implied from the conduct of the partnership.

Corporations and legal personality

Chapter learning objectives

Upon completion of this chapter you will be able to:

- explain the meaning and effect of limited liability

- explain meaning of LLPs and compare companies and partnerships

- analyse the different types of companies, especially public and private companies

- illustrate the effect of separate personality

- recognise instances where separate personality will be ignored

- explain the role and duties of company promoters

- describe the procedure for registering companies, both public and private

- describe the contents of model articles of association

- analyse the effect of a company's articles

- explain how articles of association can be changed

- describe the statutory books, records and returns that companies must keep or make.

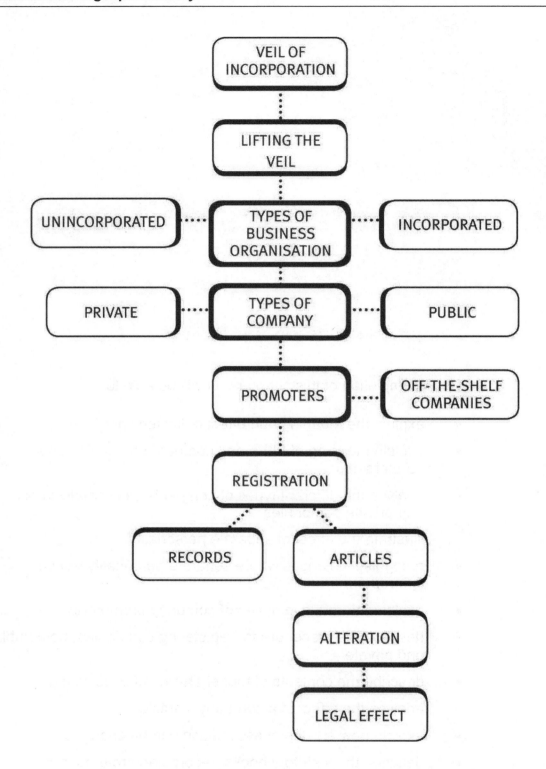

1 The doctrine and veil of incorporation

 Meaning

The company is separate legal entity (i.e. separate from its shareholders, the part owners and its directors, the managers).

Salomon v Salomon & Co Ltd (1897)

Facts: S transferred his business to a limited company. He was the director and majority shareholder and a secured creditor. The company went into liquidation and the other creditors tried to obtain repayment from S personally.

Held: S as shareholder and director had no personal liability to creditors, and he could be repaid in priority as a secured creditor. This enshrined the concepts of separate legal personality and limited liability in the law.

Lee v Lee's Air Farming Ltd (1960)

Facts: This case concerned an aerial crop-spraying business. Mr Lee owned the majority of the shares (all but one) and was the sole working director of the company. He was killed while piloting the aircraft.

Held: Although Lee was the majority shareholder and sole working director of the company, he and the company were separate legal persons. Therefore he could also be an employee of the company for the purposes of the relevant statute with rights against it when killed in an accident in the course of his employment.

Macaura v Northern Life Assurance (1925)

Facts: M owned a forest. He formed a company in which he beneficially owned all the shares and sold his forest to it. He, however, continued to maintain an insurance policy on the forest in his own name. The forest was destroyed by fire.

Held: He could not claim on the policy since the property damaged belonged to the company, not him, and as shareholder he had no insurable interest in the forest.

Consequences of incorporation

There are a number of consequences of being a separate legal entity:

- Limited liability. A company is fully liable for its own debts. If a company fails, the liability of the shareholders is limited to any amount still unpaid on their share capital (or any amount they have agreed to contribute if the company is limited by guarantee). The consequence that a company's members have limited liability for its debts gives protection to the members from the company's creditors and from the risk of the business collapsing.

- A company enters into contracts in its own name and can sue and be sued in its own name.

- A company owns its own property.

- A company has perpetual succession, irrespective of the fate of shareholders.

- The management of a company is separated from its ownership.

- A company is subject to the requirements of the Companies Act 2006 (CA06) and the Small Business, Enterprise and Employment Act 2015 (SBEEA 2015).

- Where a company suffers an injury, it is the company itself that must take the appropriate remedial action. This is known as the rule in **Foss v Harbottle**.

Foss v Harbottle (1843)

Facts: Two minority shareholders initiated legal proceedings against, among others, the directors of the company. They claimed that the directors had missapplied the company's assets.

Held: The court dismissed the claim and held that when a company is wronged by its directors it is only the company that has standing to sue.

2 Lifting the veil of incorporation

Meaning

The phrase 'lifting the veil of incorporation' means that in certain circumstances the courts can look through the company to the identity of the shareholders.

The usual result of lifting the veil is that the members or directors become personally liable for the company's debts.

 Statutory examples

There are a number of occasions on which statute will intervene to lift the veil:

- S399 of CA06 requires accounts to be prepared by a group of related companies, therefore recognising the common link between them.

- Under the Insolvency Act 1986 (IA 1986), members and/or directors liable for wrongful or fraudulent trading may be personally liable for losses arising as a result. (See chapter 12).

- If a public company starts to trade without first obtaining a trading certificate, the directors can be made personally liable for any loss or damage suffered by a third party: S767 CA06.

- Under the Company Directors Disqualification Act 1986, if a director who is disqualified participates in the management of a company, that director will be jointly or severally liable for the company's debts.

Case law examples

Sham companies

The veil will be lifted only where **'special circumstances** exist indicating that it is a mere facade concealing the true facts': **Woolfson v Strathclyde Regional Council (1978).**

Gilford Motor Co Ltd v Horne (1933)

Facts: An employee had a covenant in his contract of employment which stated that he would not solicit his former employer's customers. After he left their employment he formed a company to solicit those customers and claimed it was the company approaching the customers and not him.

Held: The court held that the company could be restrained from competition, as the previous employee had set it up to evade his own legal obligations. An injunction was granted against him and the company.

Jones v Lipman (1962)

Facts: Mr. Lipman contracted to sell his land and thereafter changed his mind. In order to avoid an order of specific performance he transferred his property to a company.

Held: The veil was lifted in order to prevent the seller of a house evading specific performance. An order of specific performance was granted against him and the company to transfer the property to the buyer.

Nationality

In times of war it is illegal to trade with the enemy. It may be possible to lift the veil of incorporation so as to impute to a company the same nationality as its members.

Daimler v Continental Tyre & Rubber Co (1916)

Facts: C sued D for debts owing. C was a UK company, however all shareholders but one were German. D argued that they should not pay the debt to German individuals to prevent money going towards Germany's war effort.

Held: As C was German, D need not discharge their debt to C since effective control of the latter was in enemy hands and hence to do so would be to trade with the enemy.

Groups

Although each company within a group is a separate legal entity, there have been a number of cases where the courts have lifted the veil between a holding company and its various subsidiaries. This has generally been done in order to:

- benefit the group by obtaining a higher compensation payment on the compulsory purchase of premises.

- benefit creditors of an insolvent company by making other companies within the group liable for its debts.

DHN Food Distributors v London Borough of Tower Hamlets (1976)

Facts: DHN carried on business from premises owned by a subsidiary. The subsidiary itself had no business activities. Both companies had the same directors. The local authority acquired the premises compulsorily but refused to pay compensation for disturbance of the business since the subsidiary, which owned the premises, did not also carry on the business.

Held: The companies were, in economic terms, mutually interdependent on each other and therefore they should be regarded as a single economic entity. Thus there was a valid claim for disturbance since ownership of the premises and business activity were in the hands of a single group.

The above case can, however, be contrasted with the more recent case of **Adams v Cape Industries (1990)** which represents the current position:

Adams v Cape Industries (1990)

Facts: Cape was an English registered company. One of its subsidiaries, CPC, a company incorporated and carrying on business in the United States, had a court judgement against it.

Held: It was unsuccessfully argued that the veil should be lifted between the companies so as to enable the judgement to be enforced against Cape. The Court of Appeal said there were no special circumstances indicating that CPC was a mere facade for Cape such as was the situation in **Jones v Lipman**.

There was no agency as CPC was an independent corporation under the control of its chief executive.

The DHN doctrine of economic reality would not be extended beyond its own facts to facts such as these where the effect would be to make a holding company liable for its subsidiary's debts.

3 LLPs

Ordinary (or general) partnerships lack the characteristics of a company in the sense that they do not have limited liability or separate legal personality. Over time the government was pressurised to recognise the needs of some partnerships (especially professional partnerships such as solicitors, accountants and auditors) to limit their liability and have separate legal personality without having to form a company. This resulted in the Limited Liability Partnerships Act 2000 (LLPs).

LLPs have similar features to private limited companies, for example, their members (i.e. not called partners) are not directly responsible for the debts of the partnership.

Incorporation	• Incorporation document must be delivered to registrar stating name of LLP, location and address of registered office, names and addresses of members (minimum two).
	• Must send a declaration of compliance that LLP satisfies requirements of the Limited Liability Partnerships Act 2000.
	• Registrar issues a certificate of incorporation.
Membership	• First members sign incorporation document. Later members join by agreement with the existing members.
	• Membership ceases on death, dissolution or in accordance with agreement with other members.
	• Rights and duties are set out in membership agreement. If no agreement, governed by Limited Liability Partnership Regulations 2001.
	• Each member acts as an agent of the LLP.
Designated members	• Perform the administrative and filing duties of the LLP.
	• Incorporation document specifies who they are.
	• Must be at least two designated members. If there are none, all members will be designated members.
Name	• Must end with Limited Liability Partnership, llp or LLP.
	• Rules on choice are the same as for companies.
Taxation	• Members are treated as if they are partners carrying on business in a partnership, i.e. they pay income tax, not corporation tax.
Registers	The LLP must maintain the following registers:
	• Register of members
	• Register of members usual residential addresses
	• Register of people with significant control.
	The LLP can keep these registers at its registered office or choose to send the information to the Registrar of Companies to be kept on the public register at Companies House.

Liability for debts	• The liability of a member of an LLP to contribute to its debts is limited to his capital contribution. However, there is no requirement for a capital contribution, and any contribution made can be withdrawn at any time.
	• If an LLP goes into liquidation, the court can order the members to repay any drawings made in the previous two years if it can be shown that the member knew or had reasonable grounds to believe that the LLP:
	– was unable to pay its debts at the date of withdrawal, or
	– would become unable to pay its debts because of the withdrawal: s214A Insolvency Act 1986 (IA 1986).
	The fraudulent and wrongful trading provisions of IA 1986 apply to members of LLPs in the same way as they apply to - directors of companies **(see chapter 12)**.
Differences between LLP and partnership	• The liability of the members of an LLP is limited to the amount of capital they have agreed to contribute.
	• The LLP must file annual accounts and an annual report with Companies House.
	• LLP is an artificial legal entity with perpetual succession. It can hold property in its own right, enter into contracts in its own name, create floating charges, sue and be sued.

Company versus partnership

Company	General Partnership
Created by registration – with a written constitution.	No special formality required for creation.
Separate legal person, i.e. can own property, sue or be sued, and contract in own name.	Not a separate legal person – the partners own any property, are jointly liable on contracts and are liable if sued.
Shares are transferable. However, the articles of private companies usually restrict transfer.	Limits on transfer of shares (may require dissolution of partnership or consent of other partners to enable partners to realise their share).
Can create both fixed and floating charges as security for borrowing.	Can only create fixed charges as security for borrowing. More usual to have personal guarantees.

Managed by directors, who may or may not also be shareholders.	Managed by partners, who are also the owners of the business.
The company cannot usually return capital to its members (except on dissolution).	Partners may withdraw their capital.
The company is liable for its debts. (No personal liability for shareholders beyond any unpaid portion of the price of their shares or the amount they have agreed to contribute.)	The partners are personally liable for the debts of the firm. Their liability is joint and several.
Must make information about financial affairs and ownership publicly available.	Private business. No disclosure of results.
The business is run by the directors. Members have no right to participate.	Every partner has the right to take part in the management of the business.
Must comply with Companies Act requirements concerning meetings, special resolutions, filing accounts and annual return.	No administrative requirements regarding meetings.
Formal dissolution procedure (known as liquidation). Death/bankruptcy of any member/director does not dissolve the company.	May dissolve by agreement. Automatically dissolved on the death/bankruptcy of any partner.
Companies pay corporation tax.	Partners pay income tax.

Test your understanding 1

1   **X Ltd, Y Ltd and Z Ltd have formed the XYZ partnership. If the partnership should become insolvent, which of the following statements is correct?**

A   The shareholders of each company are fully liable for the firm's debts.

B   X Ltd, Y Ltd and Z Ltd are fully liable for the firm's debts.

C   The directors of each company are fully liable for the firm's debts.

D   The liability of X Ltd, Y Ltd and Z Ltd for the firm's debts is limited to the amount of their capital contributions.

2   **In relation to E Ltd, a company limited by shares, which one of the following statements is correct?**

A   The liability of the company and its shareholders is limited, but the directors are fully liable for the company's debts.

B   The liability of the company and its directors is limited, but the shareholders are fully liable for the company's debts.

C   The liability of the company, its directors and shareholders is limited.

D   The liability of the directors and shareholders is limited, but the company is fully liable for its own debts.

3   Mr X owns shares in Y Ltd. This means that Mr X:

(I)   is a part-owner of Y Ltd

(II)   is a part-owner of Y Ltd's property.

Which of the above is/are correct?

A   (I) only

B   (II) only

C   Both (I) and (II)

D   Neither (I) nor (II)

4   Types of company

Introduction

Private company versus public company

The following table summarises the basic differences between public companies and private companies.

	Public companies	**Private (limited) companies**
Definition	Registered as a public company.	Any company that is not a public company.
Name	Ends with plc or public limited company.	Ends with Ltd or limited.
Capital	In order to trade, must have allotted shares of at least £50,000 of which at least ¼ of the nominal value should be paid up.	No minimum (or maximum) requirements.
Raising capital	May raise capital by advertising its securities (shares and debentures) as available for public subscription.	Prohibited from offering its securities to the public.
Start of trading	Must obtain trading certificate from registrar before commencing trading.	Can begin from date of incorporation.
Directors	Minimum two.	Minimum one.
Secretary	Must have one. Must be qualified.	Need not have one.
Accounts	Must file accounts within 6 months.	Need not lay accounts before general meeting. Must file within 9 months.
Audit	Accounts must be audited.	Audit not required if turnover below £6.5m.
AGM	Must be held each year.	Need not hold an AGM.
Resolutions	Can't pass written resolutions.	Can pass written resolutions.

Unlimited companies

An unlimited company is a separate legal entity and, if it has assets, it will have the benefits arising from separate legal personality. However, if the company's assets are insufficient to meet its liabilities, all members are liable to contribute without limit towards paying its debts and the cost of liquidation.

Such companies do have the advantage that they need not have their accounts audited, and need not deliver annual copies to the Registrar of Companies.

Community interest companies

Since 2004 it has been possible to form a 'Community Interest Company' for those wishing to establish social enterprises. The company's object must be considered by a reasonable person to be of benefit to the community and any surpluses made by the company should be reinvested for the purposes of the company.

Such a company must first be registered as a company limited by guarantee or as a company limited by shares and then apply to the Regulator of Community Interest Companies for Community Interest Company status.

These companies may be used as vehicles for community interests such as a local crime prevention group. The company name must end in C.I.C.

Test your understanding 2

1 **Which one of the following statements is incorrect in relation to a public company limited by shares?**

   A   The company must have at least one director.

   B   The company must have a qualified company secretary.

   C   The company must have an allotted share capital of at least £50,000.

   D   The company must be registered as a public limited company.

2 **What is the main requirement of the Companies Act 2006 relating to a private company?**

   A   The allotted capital must not exceed £50,000.

   B   It must not have more than 50 members.

   C   The liability of its members must be limited.

   D   It must not invite the public to subscribe for its shares.

Test your understanding 3

Spencer and his brother Trevor have decided to leave their employment as software engineers and set up a consultancy. Spencer has come to you for advice; he is unsure about the type of business organisation he should commence trading as.

A   **Fill in the gap, delete as appropriate and complete the sentence.**

The term 'partnership' is defined in . People..............................can form such organisations informally or formally and they need/do not need written agreements.

The definition of a partnership is ...

(Your answer must not exceed 20 words.)

B   **Fill in the gaps, delete as appropriate and complete the sentence.**

The major advantage of incorporating a business is that the..of the...is .... On company insolvency, the amount the shareholders/directors can be obliged to contribute to the company's assets is ....

(Your answer must not exceed 10 words.)

C   **Delete as appropriate.**

The formalities required to form a company are less/more onerous than for other types of business organisation. In addition there is less/more regulation in relation to the officers of a company compared to partners. Partnerships are also less/more private in that they do/do not have to publish annual accounts.

D   **Spencer and Trevor may one day wish to become a public company. What are the main characteristics of this business entity?**

(Your answer must not exceed 20 words.)

5   Promoters

Definition

There is no statutory definition of a promoter.

According to case law, a promoter is a person who 'undertakes to form a company and who takes the necessary steps to accomplish that purpose': **Twycross v Grant (1878)**.

The definition excludes people just acting in a professional capacity, such as accountant or solicitor.

Duties

A promoter is under a fiduciary duty to:

- disclose any interest in transactions to the company and not to make a 'secret profit'

- disclose any benefit acquired to an independent board and/or to the shareholders.

If a promoter does make a secret profit, the company may:

- Rescind the contract – but this is not always possible, e.g. if a third party has acquired rights under the contract.

- Obtain damages – but this requires the company to prove loss.

- Recover the profit – the company must prove that the promoter has failed to disclose his profit from a transaction.

Erlanger v New Sombrero Phosphate Co (1878)

Facts: Erlanger bought the lease of an island for phosphate mining for £55,000. He then set up the New Sombrero Phosphate Co. Eight days after incorporation, he sold the island to the company for £110,000 through a nominee. After eight months, public investors found out the fact that Erlanger had bought the island at half the price the company had paid for it. The company sued to rescind the contract and recover its money.

Held: The contract could be rescinded. The promoters of a company stand in a fiduciary relationship to investors, meaning they have a duty of disclosure.

 ### Pre-incorporation contracts

A pre-incorporation contract is where a person enters into a contract before a company has been registered.

The position at common law is that a company, prior to its incorporation, does not have contractual capacity and after its formation it cannot ratify or formally adopt a pre-incorporation contract. The promoter is therefore personally liable under any such contract. (This is because a company does not legally exist until it is incorporated.)

Kelner v Baxter (1866)

Facts: A, B and C entered into a contract with the claimant to purchase goods on behalf of the proposed Gravesend Royal Alexandra Hotel Co. The goods were supplied and used in the business. Shortly after incorporation the company collapsed.

Held: As the Gravesend Royal Alexandra Hotel Co was not in existence when the contract was made it was not bound by the contract and could not be sued for the price of the goods. Neither could it ratify the contract after incorporation.

S51 CA06 reinforces the common law position by providing that, subject to any agreement to the contrary, the person making the contract is personally liable. Clear and express words are needed in order to negate liability: **Phonogram Ltd v Lane (1981).**

The promoter can protect his position by:

- including a term in the contract giving the company the right to sue under the Contracts (Rights of Third Parties) Act 1999 (see Privity of Contract: **Chapter 2**)

- postponing finalising contracts until the company is formed

- entering into an agreement of novation (this involves discharging the original contract and replacing it with a new one) or assigning (transferring) the contract. All parties must agree

- agreeing with the company that there is no personal liability for the promoter

- buying an 'off-the-shelf' company, so it is ready to contract without waiting for incorporation.

Off-the-shelf companies

An 'off-the-shelf' company is one that has already been formed. Buying off the shelf has a number of advantages as follows:

- cheap and simple

- can trade immediately

- no problem of pre-incorporation contracts.

Test your understanding 4

1   **Which of the following statements is true in respect of a promoter in breach of their duty not to make a secret profit?**

A   The company can always sue the promoter for damages.

B   The company can only rescind the contract with the promoter when the promoter owned the property before the promotion began.

C   The company can always rescind the contract with the promoter.

D   The company can only rescind the contract with the promoter when the promoter acquired the property after the promotion began.

2   **Which of the following are correct?**

(i)   Purchasing an 'off-the-shelf' company enables a business to commence more quickly.

(ii)   It is generally cheaper to purchase an 'off-the-shelf' company than to arrange for a solicitor or accountant to register a new company.

(iii) Incorporating a company by registration enables the company's documents to be drafted to the particular needs of the incorporators.

A   (i) and (ii) only

B   (ii) and (iii) only

C   (i) and (iii) only

D   (i), (ii) and (iii)

3   **A company's contractual capacity before incorporation is limited in that it may:**

A   only make contracts necessary to form the company.

B   only ratify, once formed, contracts necessary to form the company.

C   only make or ratify, once formed, contracts necessary to form the company.

D   not make or ratify, once formed, any contract even if necessary to form the company.

Test your understanding 5

Alfred and Betty have carried on a business as a partnership for some years. They have now decided to incorporate their business.

A   **Explain the difference in liability for business debts between partners and shareholders.**

(Your answer must not exceed 25 words.)

B   **Fill in the gaps, delete as appropriate and complete the sentence.**

Alfred bought some stationery on credit before the date of incorporation. Alfred is/is not personally liable for the debt because...

(Your answer must not exceed 10 words.)

The company can/cannot unilaterally adopt the contract.

A range of better solutions might have included...............................

(Your answer must not exceed 25 words.)

---

6 Registration

Documents to Registrar

The following must be submitted to the Registrar in order to form a company.

Memorandum of association	• Used to be a more important document under previous company legislation. • Signed by all subscribers (first shareholders) and stating that they wish to form a company and agree to become members of the company. • In relation to a company limited by shares, the memorandum provides evidence of the members' agreement to take at least one share each in the company. • Is not possible to amend or update the memorandum of a company formed under CA06.
Application for registration	S9 CA06 sets out the information that must be delivered to the Registrar when an application for registration is made. In all cases, the application form must include: • the proposed name of the company • whether the members will have limited liability (by shares or guarantee) • whether the company is to be private or public • details of the registered office.

Documents to be sent with application:	
Statement of capital and initial shareholdings **OR**	Essentially is a 'snapshot' of a company's share capital at the point of registration. This must state: • the total number of shares to be taken by the subscribers to the memorandum • their aggregate nominal value • the class of shares and the rights which attach to them • the aggregate amount unpaid on the total number of shares • a contact address for each subscriber.
Statement of guarantee	This states the maximum amount each member guarantees to contribute in a winding up.
Statement of consent to act	The company confirms that the director or secretary has given their consent to act.
Statement of compliance	This provides confirmation that CA06 has been complied with. It may be made in paper or electronic form.
Registration fee	Currently £20 approximately.

Note: As the model articles will apply if no articles are supplied, it is not a requirement that articles must be sent, although all companies will have articles.

Registrar's duties

On receipt of the above documents the registrar must:

- **Inspect the documents** and ensure that Companies Act requirements are fulfilled.

- **Issue** certificate of incorporation which is conclusive evidence that Companies Act requirements have been fulfilled: s1 5 CA06. The company exists from the date on the certificate of incorporation.

Trading certificate – public companies only

A plc cannot commence trading until the registrar has issued a trading certificate.

In order to obtain a trading certificate, an application must be made to the registrar which states:

- The nominal value of allotted share capital ≥ £50,000.

- That at least a quarter of the nominal value and all of any premium have been paid up (i.e. at least £12,500 of nominal capital).

- The amount of preliminary expenses and who has paid or is to pay them.

- Any benefits given or to be given to promoters.

If it trades before the certificate is issued:

- The company and any officers in default are liable to a fine.

- It is a criminal offence to carry on business, but any contracts are still binding on the company.

- Any transactions are valid. However, if the company fails to comply with its obligations 21 days after being called upon to do so, the directors become jointly and severally liable for those obligations.

- It is a ground for winding up if not obtained within one year: s122 IA 1986.

Test your understanding 6

1   Bob and Mike decided to form a company. On 1 March 20X6, they sent the necessary documents to the registrar. On 10 May 20X6, they received the certificate of incorporation dated 1 May 20X6. Subsequently they discovered that the company was registered on 1 June 20X6.

What was the date of incorporation?

A   1 March 20X6

B   1 May 20X6

C   10 May 20X6

D   1 June 20X6

2   **Which of the following documents need not be submitted to register a company limited by shares?**

A   A memorandum of association.

B   Articles of association.

C   A statement of consent to act.

D   A statutory declaration of compliance with the requirements of the Companies Acts.

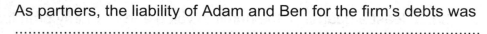

Test your understanding 7

Adam and Ben have carried on business together in partnership for a number of years. They have now decided to operate their business through the medium of a private company limited by shares called AB Ltd.

A **Complete this sentence.**

As partners, the liability of Adam and Ben for the firm's debts was

....

(Your answer must not exceed 3 words.)

B **In order to register a private company limited by shares the partners will need to submit the following documents to the Registrar of Companies.**

C **Complete this sentence:**

If the Registrar of Companies is satisfied with the documents submitted to him for registration, he will issue a .... which enables the company to commence trading immediately.

D **Explain the liability of Adam and Ben in the event of AB Ltd becoming insolvent.**

(Your answer must not exceed 20 words.)

Name of company

The name of the company must comply with the following rules:

- It must have limited (Ltd) or public limited company (plc) at the end as applicable.

- It cannot be the same as another in the index of names.

- It cannot use certain words which are illegal or offensive.

- It must have the Secretary of State's consent to use certain words (e.g. England, Chartered, Royal, National, University, Insurance, etc.) or any name suggesting a connection with the government or any local authority.

- It must avoid the tort of passing off (see **chapter 3**).

The Secretary of State can force a company to change its name in the following circumstances:

Reason	Period
The name is the same as, or too like, an existing registered name.	12 months
The name gives so misleading an indication of the nature of the company's activities as to be likely to cause harm to the public.	No time limit
Misleading information or undertakings were given when applying for a name that required approval.	5 years

S77 CA06 allows a company to change its name by special resolution.

As discussed at the end of chapter 3 if a company feels that another company has a name which is too similar to its own, it may object to the Company Names Adjudicator.

Test your understanding 8

1   **Which of the following names could not without further consent be a permissible name under the Companies Act for a company, the main object of which is to contract refuse collection services for Westminster City Council?**

   A   Westminster City Refuse Services Ltd

   B   Council (Refuse Collection) Services Ltd

   C   Refuse Collection (Westminster) Ltd

   D   City Waste Disposal Ltd

2   **Which of the following statements is correct?**

   (I)   It is not possible to register a company limited by shares with the same name as a company already on the register.

   (II)   Once on the register, a company limited by shares cannot change its registered office.

   A   (I) only

   B   (II) only

   C   Both (I) and (II)

   D   Neither (I) nor (II)

3   **A business has been registered under the name 'The Mark Jones Partnership Co Ltd'. What type of business organisation must this be?**

   A   A partnership

   B   A private limited company

   C   A public limited company

   D   Any of the above as this is a business name

7   Articles of association

Introduction

The articles of association form the company's internal constitution. They:

- set out the manner in which the company is to be governed and

- regulate the relationship between the company, its shareholders and its directors.

There are no mandatory contents.

Model articles

For companies incorporated under Companies Act 2006, model articles have been prescribed by the Secretary of State.

There are three model articles which cover the following companies:

- private companies limited by shares; or

- private companies limited by guarantee; or

- public companies.

These model articles will apply where a company is formed without registering articles or where the articles registered do not exclude or modify the model articles.

A company:

- may adopt the model articles in full or in part

- is deemed to have adopted the model articles if there is no express or implied provision to exclude them; or

- may draft its own unique articles.

Contents of Articles

Companies Act 2006 states that the articles should be contained in a single document which is divided into consecutively numbered paragraphs.

Articles should contain rules on a number of areas, the most important of which are as follows:

- Appointment and dismissal of directors

- Powers, responsibilities and liabilities of directors

- Director's meetings

- Member's rights

- Dividends

- Communication with members

- Issue of shares

- Documents and records.

8 Legal effect of company's constitutional documents

S33 CA06 states that the provisions of a company's constitution bind the company and its members to the same extent as if there were covenants on the part of the company and of each member to observe those provisions. This means that the articles form a statutory contract between the company and its members, and between the members themselves, even if they do not sign them.

1 The articles are enforceable by the company against the members.

Hickman v Kent or Romney Marsh Sheepbreeders' Association (1915)

Facts: The company's articles included a clause to the effect that all disputes between the company and its members were to be referred to arbitration. A member brought court proceedings against the company.

Held: The proceedings were stopped. The company could enforce the arbitration clause against a member.

2 The articles are enforceable by the members against the company.

Pender v Lushington (1877)

Facts: The articles provided for one vote per ten shares, with no member to have more than 100 votes. A member with more than 1,000 shares transferred the surplus to a nominee and directed him how to vote. The chairman refused to accept the nominee's votes.

Held: The right to vote was enforceable against the company and should have been recognised by the company as a breach of the articles.

3 The articles also operate as a contract between individual members in their capacity as members.

Rayfield v Hands (1958)

Facts: The articles required the directors to be members, i.e. to hold qualification shares and to purchase shares from any member who wished to sell.

Held: This was enforceable against the directors in their capacity as members.

However, the articles do not bind the company to non-members nor do they bind the members in any other capacity.

Eley v Positive Government Security Life Assurance Co (1876)

Facts: The articles provided that Eley should be solicitor to the company for life.

Held: This was not a right given to him as a member and he could not rely on the articles as a contract for professional services. The right to be a director of a company has also been held to be an outsider right (i.e. a non-membership) right.

Beattie v EF Beattie (1938)

Facts: The company's articles contained an arbitration clause. B, a member and director of the company, was in dispute with the company concerning his rights as director. He brought court proceedings against the company.

Held: He was not bound by the arbitration clause since he was acting in his capacity as director, not a member.

However, even where the articles are not a relevant contract for this purpose, the terms may be evidence of another contract made independently.

New British Iron Co, ex parte Beckwith (1898)

Facts: The articles stated that directors were entitled to be paid £1,000 on taking office.

Held: The contract was implied from the directors' action in taking office. The provision in the articles was merely evidence of that separate contract.

It is important in an examination question to check the capacity in which the person is claiming. Is it as a member, or in some other capacity, such as a director or an accountant? Obviously the articles have no effect as a contract between the company and a person who is not a member even if they are named in them and given apparent rights against the company. In **Eley's** case above, Eley's membership was irrelevant to his claim; as solicitor he had no claim – he was attempting to enforce an employment right not a member's right.

9   Alteration of articles

General rule

- The articles can usually be altered by a special resolution (75% majority).

- Copies of the amended articles must be sent to the Registrar within 15 days.

Exceptions

1   Entrenchment

It is possible to entrench some of the articles. This means that a specified procedure (e.g. unanimous consent) may be required to change them.

2   Members increase liability

S25 CA06 prevents a member being bound by any alteration made after he becomes a member that requires him to increase his liability or contribute further to the company.

3 Common law restriction

Any change to the articles must be 'bona fide in interests of the company as a whole': **Allen v Gold Reefs of Africa (1900)**.

- It is for the members to decide whether the change is bona fide in the interests of the company as a whole.

- The court will not interfere unless no reasonable person would consider the change to be bona fide (**Greenhalgh v Arderne Cinemas Ltd (1950)**, **Brown v British Abrasive Wheel Co (1919)** and **Sidebottom v Kershaw, Leese & Co (1920)**.

- If the change is bona fide, it is immaterial that it happens to inflict hardship or has retrospective operation.

- The change will be void if actual fraud or oppression takes place.

- An alteration is not invalid merely because it causes a breach of contract – but that does not excuse breach (**Southern Foundries (1926) Ltd and Federated Foundries Ltd v Shirlaw (1940)**).

Greenhalgh v Arderne Cinemas Ltd (1950)

Facts: The issue was the removal from the articles of the members' right of first refusal of any shares which a member might wish to transfer; the majority wished to make the change in order to admit an outsider to membership in the interests of the company.

Held: The benefit to the company as a whole was held to be a benefit which any **individual hypothetical member** of the company could enjoy directly or through the company and not merely a benefit to the majority of members only. The test of good faith did not require proof of actual benefit but merely the honest belief on reasonable grounds that benefit could follow from the alteration.

In several cases the court has held that actual and foreseen detriment to a minority affected by the alteration was not in itself a sufficient ground of objection if the benefit to the company test was satisfied.

Brown v British Abrasive Wheel Co (1919)

Facts: The articles were altered to enable the majority to purchase at 'a fair value the shares of the minority'. The intention was to invoke the clause against some minority members who were refusing to inject further capital into the company. They objected to the alteration.

Held: This was not a bona fide alteration as it would benefit the majority shareholders, rather than the company as a whole.

Sidebottom v Kershaw, Leese & Co (1920)

Facts: The company altered its articles to empower the directors to require any member who carried on a business competing with that of the company, to sell his shares at a fair price to persons nominated by the directors. The minority against whom the new article was aimed did carry on a competing business and they challenged the validity of the alteration on the ground that it was an abuse of majority power to 'expel' a member.

Held: The Court of Appeal held that the evidence showed that the claimant might cause the defendant company loss by information which he received as a member, and as the power was restricted to expulsion for competing, the alteration was for the benefit of the company as a whole and was valid.

Allen v Gold Reefs of West Africa Ltd (1900)

Facts: Z held fully paid up and partly paid up shares in the company. The company's articles provided for a lien for all debts and liabilities of any member upon all partly paid shares held by the member. The company by special resolution altered its articles so that the lien was available on fully paid up shares as well.

Held: The company had power to alter its articles by extending the lien to fully paid shares.

Southern Foundries (1926) Ltd and Federated Foundries Ltd v Shirlaw (1940)

Facts: Following a merger the members of the new group of companies agreed to make alterations in the articles regarding directors. The amended articles gave the group the power to remove any director of the company and also stipulated that a managing director should cease to hold office if he ceased to be a director. Shirlaw was removed from office as a director which meant that he could no longer be a managing director, however, his contract still had some time to run.

Held: The House of Lords held that the company could not be prevented from altering its articles but that the only remedy for an alteration which has caused a breach of contract was damages.

Test your understanding 9

Which of the following statements is/are correct?

(I)   The articles of association of a company limited by shares contain the internal regulations of the company.

(II)   The articles of association form a contract between the shareholders and the company.

A   (I) only

B   (II) only

C   Both (I) and (II)

D   Neither (I) nor (II)

Test your understanding 10

Explain the meaning and effect of a company's articles of association, paying particular attention to the following issues:

A   the operation of the model articles of association

B   the effect of the articles on both members and non-members

C   the procedure for altering the articles of association.

(Adapted from ACCA June 2004 examination)

10   Statutory books, returns and records

Registers

Register	Contents
Members	Names, addresses, date became/ceased, number of shares, class of share, amount paid up.
	Any member of the company can inspect the register without charge. A member of the public has the right of inspection but must pay.
Directors and company secretary	Names (present and former), address, date of birth, occupation, residency, nationality, other directorships within the last five years.
	The register does not include shadow directors (see **chapter 9**).
	The register must be open to inspection by a member without charge or by any other person for a fee.

Charges	This register contains details of fixed or floating charges created over the company's property (see **chapter 8**).
	The register will have details of the name of chargee, type of charge, brief description of property charged, amount and date created.
	The company must also keep copies of every instrument creating a charge at its registered office or some other place of which the Registrar has been notified.
	Any member or creditor may inspect the register free of charge, any other member of the public can inspect for a fee.
Persons with significant control	A person with significant control (PSC) is anyone in the company who:
	• owns more than 25% of the company's shares
	• owns more than 25% of the company's voting rights
	• has the right to appoint or remove a majority of the board of directors
	• has significant influence or control over the company
	• has significant influence or control over a trust or firm.
	The register should have details of name, service address, residential address, country and state of residence, nationality, date of birth, date they became a PSC and the nature of company control.
Other documents	Minutes of general meetings.
Resolutions and meetings	Records must be kept for a minimum period of 10 years.

The registers must normally be kept at the company's registered office (although the register of members and register of directors' interests can be kept where they are made up) and must be available for public inspection by a member free of charge or by any other person for a fee.

Requests for inspection must provide details about the person seeking the information, the purpose of the request and whether the information will be disclosed to others. The company may apply to the court for an order that it need not comply with the request.

The register of directors' addresses should now contain service addresses rather than details of the directors' residential addresses. The service address can be simply 'the company's registered office'.

The company must also keep a separate register of the directors' residential addresses. Both the service and the residential addresses will need to be supplied to the Registrar of Companies.

The residential addresses will be withheld from the public register. However, they will generally remain available to the Registrar and certain specified public bodies and credit reference agencies.

Under the SBEEA 2015 private companies can opt out of maintaining separate private registers and instead keep certain information on the public register at Companies House.

Annual confirmation statement

The annual confirmation statement must be filed with Companies House which states that the company has provided all of the information it was required to provide within the previous 12 months. This statement must be provided within 14 days of expiry of the previous 12 month period. For new companies, the first statement should be provided 12 months from the date of incorporation of the company.

The confirmation statement must include changes to any of the following:

- the address of the company's registered office

- the type of company

- the company's principal business activities

- details of directors and company secretary where applicable (see **chapter 10**)

- a statement of capital

- details of the members of the company as at the return date

- details of members who have cease to be members since the last return was made

- details of the number of shares of each class held by members at the return date.

Accounting records

The company must keep accounting records containing sufficient information to show and explain the company's transactions and its financial position.

At any time it should be possible:

- to disclose with reasonable accuracy the company's financial position at intervals of not more than six months

- for the directors to ensure that any accounts that needs to be prepared comply with Companies Act 2006 and International Accounting Standards.

In particular the records **must** show:

- daily entries of all money received and spent
- a record of assets and liabilities
- statement of stocks at end of the financial year
- statements of stocktaking to back up the above
- statements of all goods sold and purchased, showing the goods and the buyers and sellers (except in the retail trade).

Accounting records must be kept for three years in the case of a private company and six years in that of a public one. They should be kept at the company's registered office or at some other place thought fit by the directors.

Failure to keep sufficient accounting records is an offence by the officers in default.

Annual financial statements

Companies are required to produce annual financial statements for each accounting reference period. This includes a:

- balance sheet/statement of financial position and profit and loss account/statement of comprehensive income showing true and fair view
- directors' report stating the amount of any dividend and likely future developments.

The annual financial statements must be approved and signed on behalf of the board of directors and a copy filed with Registrar.

11 Chapter summary

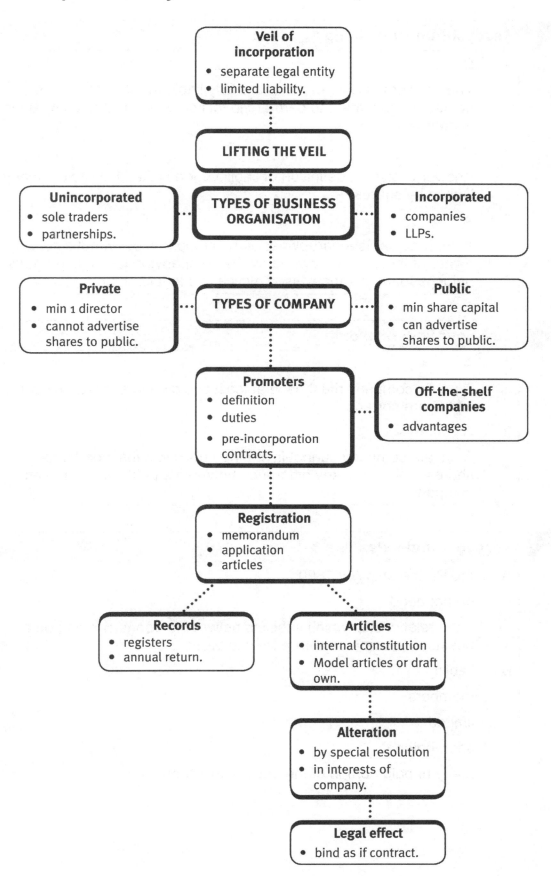

Test your understanding answers

Test your understanding 1

1   B

The partners of a partnership are fully liable for all of the firm's debts. The fact that the partners in this case are limited companies is irrelevant.

2   D

Answer D gives a definition of liability for a limited liability company limited by shares.

3   A

A shareholder is a part-owner of the company, but is not a part-owner of the property owned by the company. In law, this property belongs to the company itself, which is a legal person.

Test your understanding 2

1   A

A public company must have at least two directors. Statements B, C and D are correct.

2   D

A private company cannot invite the public to subscribe for its shares. This is the key difference between a public and a private company.

Test your understanding 3

A   the Partnership Act 1890

do not need

...the relationship which subsists between persons carrying on a business in common with a view to profit.

B   liability

members

limited

shareholders

...any unpaid portion of the price of their shares.

C   more

    more

    more

    do not

D   A public limited company must have a minimum allotted share capital of £50,000 and a trading certificate.

Test your understanding 4

1   **A**

    The company can always sue the promoter for damages. However, the right to rescission may be lost where, for example, there has been unreasonable delay.

2   **D**

    Buying a company off the shelf means that the company has already been incorporated. It saves the time of going through the procedures for incorporation. Other non-urgent changes can then be made, such as changing the company name. A company can be bought off-the- shelf for about £100, which is much cheaper than using a solicitor or accountant to register a new company. However, the registered details (such as the name and directors) may need to be changed. All three statements are therefore correct.

3   **D**

    The position at common law is that a company cannot be bound by a contract that was made before it was formed, and after its formation it cannot ratify or formally adopt a pre-incorporation contract. S51 CA06 provides that a person acting for the company should have personal liability on a pre-incorporation contract that he enters into.

Test your understanding 5

A   Partners are liable for business debts to the extent of their personal wealth, whereas shareholders' liability is limited to the unpaid portion of their shares.

B   is

    the company cannot make contracts before it comes into existence.

    cannot

    assigning the contract, making an agreement of novation or acquiring an 'off-the-shelf' company before making the contract.

Test your understanding 6

1   **B**

Regardless of the actual date of registration, the only date that matters is the date on the certificate of incorporation.

2   **B**

It is not necessary to submit articles of association and if a company limited by shares (or guarantee) does not do so, the model articles will apply.

Test your understanding 7

A   joint and several

B   (i)   An application

(ii)   Articles of Association (unless the model articles are to apply)

(iii)   Memorandum of Association

(iv)   A statement of capital and initial shareholdings

(v)   A statement of consent to act

(vi)   A statement of compliance

C   Certificate of incorporation

D   Adam and Ben are only liable for any unpaid portion of the price of their shares

Test your understanding 8

1   **B**

S54 CA06 prohibits a company, unless given approval by the Secretary of State for the Department for Business, Energy and Industrial Strategy from having a name that would be likely to give the impression that the business is carried on in connection with the government or a local council. Here, the use of the word 'Council' in the business name would not be permitted.

2   **A**

A company cannot take the same name as a company that has been registered already with the same name. Once registered, a company can change its registered office, and must notify the registrar of any such change.

3   **B**

The fact that the name ends with the letters 'Ltd' indicates that it is a private limited company.

Test your understanding 9

C

The articles of association form a contract between the shareholders and the company, in respect of the rights of the ordinary shareholders. The articles set out the internal regulations or constitution of the company, e.g. the articles set out the rights of shareholders and the powers of the directors.

Test your understanding 10

A   Model articles are prescribed by the Secretary of State. They apply where a company is formed without registering articles or where the articles registered do not exclude or modify the model articles.

A company:

    –   may adopt the model articles in full or in part

    –   is deemed to have adopted the model articles if there is no express or implied provision to exclude them; or

    –   may draft its own unique articles.

B   S33 CA06 states that the provisions of a company's constitution in the company and its members to the same extent as if there were covenants on the part of the company and of each member to observe those provisions. This section has three effects.

    (i)   The documents establish a contract which binds each member to the company. Thus in **Hickman v Kent or Romney Marsh Sheepbreeders' Association (1920)**, the company was able to enforce an article against a member that provided that disputes involving the member and the company should go to arbitration.

    (ii)   The company is contractually bound to each of its members. On this basis in **Pender v Lushington (1877)** a member was able to sue in respect of the wrongful denial of his right to vote at a company meeting.

    (iii)   The articles constitute a contract between the members. In **Rayfield v Hands (1958)**, the articles of the company provided that, where shareholders wished to transfer their shares, they should inform the directors of the company, who were obliged to take the shares equally between them at fair value. When the directors refused to purchase the plaintiff's shares, the court held that the directors were bound as members by the articles and therefore had to comply with the procedure set out there.

Articles only operate as a contract in respect of membership rights and obligations. Consequently it has been held that, although members can enforce them, non-members, or members suing in some other capacity than that of a member, will not be able to enforce promises established in the company's articles. In **Eley v Positive Government Security Life Assurance Co (1876)**, the articles of a company stated that the plaintiff was to be appointed as the company's solicitor. It was held that Eley could not use the articles to establish a contract between himself and the company as those articles only created a contract between the company and its members. Although Eley was in fact a member, he was not suing in that capacity but in the capacity of solicitor, which was not a membership right.

C   A company can normally alter its articles by passing a special resolution. However, if certain provisions are entrenched, they can only be altered by following the specified procedure; this may require unanimous consent.

Any alteration must be made 'bona fide in the interest of the company as a whole', although the exact meaning of this phrase is not altogether clear. It is evident that it involves a subjective element in that those deciding the alteration must actually believe they are acting in the interests of the company. There is additionally, however, an objective element. In **Greenhalgh v Arderne Cinemas Ltd (1950)** it was stated that any alteration had to be in the interests of the 'individual hypothetical member'.

In **Brown v British Abrasive Wheel Co (1919)** an alteration to the articles of the company was proposed to give the majority shareholders the right to buy the shares of the minority. It was held that the alteration was invalid as it would benefit the majority shareholders rather than the company as a whole. However, in **Sidebottom v Kershaw, Leese & Co (1920)**, an alteration to the articles gave the directors the power to require any shareholder, who entered into competition with the company, to transfer their shares to nominees of the directors at a fair price. It was held that under those circumstances the alteration was valid as it would benefit the company as a whole.

Capital and financing

Chapter learning objectives

Upon completion of this chapter you will be able to:

- understand the different meanings of capital

- illustrate the difference between various classes of shares

- explain the procedure for the variation of class rights

- define companies' borrowing powers

- explain the meaning of debenture

- distinguish loan capital from share capital

- explain the concept of a company charge and distinguish between fixed and floating charges

- describe the need and the procedure for registering company charges

- explain the doctrine of capital maintenance and capital reduction

- examine the effect of issuing shares at either a discount or a premium

- explain the rules governing the distribution of dividends in both private and public companies.

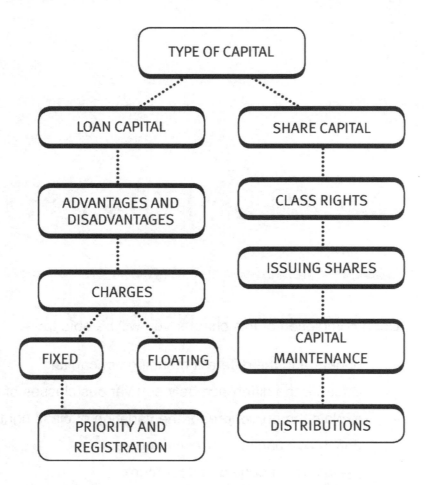

1   Share capital

Definition of a share

A share is 'the interest of a shareholder in the company measured by a sum of money, for the purpose of a liability in the first place, and of interest in the second, but also consisting of a series of mutual covenants entered into by all the shareholders': **Borland's Trustee v Steel Bros & Co Ltd (1901)**.

A shareholder is a member of the company and therefore has voting rights, depending on the class of shares held. They are also entitled to dividends depending on the availability of profits.

In the event of liquidation, depending on the type of share, a shareholder receives payment after all other creditors, but can participate in surplus assets.

2 Types of shares

	Preference shares	Ordinary shares
Voting rights	None, or restricted by the articles of association.	Full.
Dividend rights	Fixed dividend paid in priority to other dividends, usually cumulative.	Paid after preference dividend. Not fixed.
Surplus on winding up	Prior return of capital, but cannot participate in surplus.	Entitled to share surplus assets after repayment of preference shares.

Test your understanding 1

Freeco is a public limited company. Geoffrey owns 11,000 6% £1 preference shares in the company and his sister, Gertrude, owns 10,000 £1 ordinary shares.

A **Delete as appropriate and complete the sentence.**

Both Geoffrey and Gertrude are/are not members of the company. Geoffrey can/cannot attend general meetings. He can/cannot usually vote in the same way as Gertrude. Gertrude and Geoffrey can/cannot receive a dividend.

On liquidation, the position of both in relation to creditors is ....

(Your answer must not exceed 20 words.)

B **Explain why Geoffrey's investment may be seen as less risky than Gertrude's.**

(Your answer must not exceed 30 words.)

3 Class rights

What are they?

Class rights are the special rights attached to each class of shares, such as dividend rights, distribution of capital on a winding up and voting. (See above concerning the different rights that normally attach to ordinary shares and preference shares.)

How can they be varied?

The procedure for varying class rights depends on whether any procedure is specified in the articles:

Is procedure to vary specified?	Method of variation
Yes	Procedure set out in articles must be followed.
No	Variation needs special resolution or written consent of 75% in nominal value of the class: S630 CA06.

Minority protection

Under S633 CA06, the holders of 15% of the nominal value of that class, who did not consent to the variation, may ask the court to cancel the variation within 21 days of the passing of the resolution.

The court may confirm or cancel the variation. However, it will only cancel the variation if the petitioner proves it is unfairly prejudicial.

The court draws a distinction between:

- a variation that affects the value, enjoyment or power derived from the rights and

- a variation that changes the rights themselves.

The court will only intervene in the latter case.

Cumbrian Newspapers Group Ltd v Cumberland & Westmorland Herald (1986)

Facts: The claimant and the defendant were both publishers of newspapers. They negotiated a transaction whereby D would acquire one of C's papers and C would acquire 10 per cent of D's share capital. D issued the 10 per cent share holding and as part of the agreement under which the shares were issued amended its articles to give C certain rights including pre-emption rights over other ordinary shares. The purpose of such rights was to enable C as a shareholder to prevent a takeover. Subsequently, a few years later D called a meeting to pass a special resolution to cancel the articles which gave special rights to C. C sought a declaration that the rights were class rights which could not be cancelled without his consent.

Held: The declaration was granted. The special rights granted were rights which could not be varied or cancelled without C's consent.

White v Bristol Aeroplane Co (1953)

Facts: The company made a bonus issue of new ordinary and preference shares to the existing ordinary shareholders who alone were entitled to participate in bonus issues under the articles. The existing preference shareholders objected on the basis that this reduced their proportion of the class of preference shares and was a variation of class rights to which they had not consented.

Held: Bonus issue is not a variation of class rights since the existing preference shareholders had the same number of shares as before.

Greenhalgh v Arderne Cinemas Ltd (1950)

Facts: The company had two classes of ordinary shares, 50p and 10p shares, with every share carrying one vote. A resolution was passed to subdivide each 50p share into five 10p shares, thereby multiplying the votes of that class by five.

Held: The subdivision of shares is not a variation of class rights. The rights of the original 10p shares had not been varied since they still had one vote per share as before.

4 Terminology

Issued share capital	Issued share capital comprises share capital that has actually been issued, released or sold by the company.
Paid up share capital	The amount which shareholders have actually paid on the shares issued.
Called up share capital	The amount of unpaid share capital which has been called for from shareholders but not yet paid.
Uncalled share capital	The amount of unpaid share capital that has not yet been called for from shareholders and therefore also remains unpaid.
Statutory pre-emption rights	New shares offered to existing shareholders in proportion to their shareholdings. Raises new funds. Purpose is not to dilute individual member shareholding. Only applies to ordinary shares which must be paid for in cash. The offer is open for 21 days. Pre-emption rights can be disapplied by provision in the articles of association or by a special resolution being passed by the members.

Bonus issues	Also referred to as scrip issue or capitalisation issue.
	Are normally issued at no cost to the shareholders in which case do not raise any new funds. Sometimes the company issues partly paid-up bonus shares in which case the shareholders may have to make some contributions in the future.
	Carried out by using some of the company's non-distributable reserves to issue shares to existing shareholders in proportion to their shareholdings. For example, a company may issue two free preference shares for every ordinary share held.
	Must never be funded from a company's ordinary capital.
Rights issues	New shares offered to existing shareholders in proportion to their shareholdings to raise new funds. Must be made in writing (hard copy or electronic).
	Can be used where the statutory pre-emption rights have been disapplied.
	Offer is open for 21 days during which it cannot be withdrawn.
	Shares usually offered at discount to current market value (but not at discount to nominal value).
	Shareholders who do not want to buy the new shares themselves may sell the rights to a third party.
	Any shares which are not accepted may then be allotted on the same (or less favourable) terms to non-members.

Test your understanding 2

A public company with a stock market listing has just sold a new issue of ten million £1 ordinary shares. All the shares were bought by existing shareholders in the company.

Which one of the following conclusions can be inferred from this statement?

A   The company has undertaken a rights issue.

B   The company has raised exactly £10 million to finance the expansion of the business.

C   As a new issue, the shares could be sold only to personal shareholders and not to institutional shareholders.

D   Since there were no new shareholders, the company's share capital was not extended.

5   Issuing shares

Allotment of shares

This is where the shares are allocated to a person under a contract of allotment. Once the shares are allotted and the holder is entered in the register of members, they become a member of the company.

Authority

The directors need authority in order to allot shares. This may be given:

- by the articles, or

- by passing an ordinary resolution.

The authority must state:

- the maximum number of shares to be allotted

- the expiry date for the authority (maximum five years).

The directors of a private company with only one class of shares may allot shares of that class unless it is prohibited by the articles: S550 CA06.

Issue at discount

Every share has a **nominal value** which is fixed at the time of incorporation of the company in the statement of capital and initial shareholding. The nominal value of the share represents the extent of a shareholders potential liability.

The common law rule is that a company cannot issue its shares for a consideration which is at a discount on their nominal value.

Ooregum Gold Mining Co of India v Roper (1892)

Facts: Shares in a company which had a nominal value of £1 were trading at a market price of 12.5p. In an honest attempt to refinance the company, new £1 preference shares were issued and credited with 75p as paid up. The company subsequently went into liquidation.

Held: The holders of the shares were required to pay a further 75p per share.

The common law rule is given statutory effect in S580 CA06. In addition S582 CA06 states that shares are only treated as paid up to the extent that the company has received money or money's worth.

If this rule is breached the issue is still valid, but the allottee must pay up the discount plus interest. This applies to any subsequent holder of such a share who was aware of the original underpayment: S588 CA06.

Under S590 CA06 it is an offence to contravene these rules and the company and any officers in default are liable to a fine.

Issue at premium

Where a share is allotted at a value greater than its nominal value, the excess over the nominal value is share premium. This is where the market value of the share is greater than the fixed nominal value.

S610 CA06 requires any premium to be credited to a share premium account, which may only be used for:

- writing off the expenses of the issue of new shares
- writing off any commission paid on the issue of new shares
- issuing bonus shares.

Paying for shares – private companies

Private companies may issue shares for non-cash consideration. The court will interfere with the valuation only if there is fraud or the consideration is 'illusory, past or patently inadequate'.

Paying for shares – public companies

There are a number of additional rules relating to the issue of shares in public companies contained in CA06:

S584	Subscribers to the memorandum must pay cash for their subscription shares.
S585	Payment for shares must not be in the form of work or services.
S586	Shares cannot be allotted until at least one-quarter of their nominal value and the whole of any premium have been paid.
S587	Non-cash consideration must be received within five years.
S593	Non-cash consideration must be independently valued and reported on by a person qualified to be the company's auditor. The valuation must be carried out in the six months prior to the allotment.

Test your understanding 3

What can the share premium account be used for?

6 Capital maintenance

Purpose

The share capital of a limited company is regarded as a buffer fund for creditors. (Note that the creditors' buffer is an accounting fund, not real money. The actual cash or assets subscribed can be used by the company.)

The rules on maintenance of capital exist in order to prevent a company reducing its capital by returning it to its members, whether directly or indirectly. This means that, as a general rule, a limited company cannot reduce its share capital. There is, however, an exception to this general rule which is discussed below.

Exception

Reduction of capital

Under S641 CA06, a company can reduce its capital at any time, for any reason.

Reduce or cancel liabilities on partly-paid shares, i.e. the company gives up any claim for money owing.

Return capital in excess of the company's needs, i.e. the company reduces its assets by repaying cash to its shareholders.

Cancel the paid-up capital that is no longer represented by the assets, i.e. if the company has a debit balance on reserves it can write this off by reducing capital and thereby does not need to make good past losses.

Procedure for public companies:

Pass a special resolution

Apply to the court to confirm the special resolution.

If reduction involves one of the first two methods above, court must require company to settle a list of creditors entitled to object.

The court must not confirm the reduction until it is satisfied that all creditors have either consented to the reduction or had their debts discharged or secured.

The company must file documents with the Registrar. If the share capital of a public company falls below £50,000, it must re-register as a private company.

Simplified procedure for private companies:

> Pass a special resolution supported by a solvency statement.

> The solvency statement is a statement by each of the directors that the company will be able to meet its debts within the following year.

> A solvency statement made without reasonable grounds is an offence punishable by fine and/or imprisonment.

> Copies of the resolution, solvency statement and a statement of capital must be filed with the Registrar within 15 days.

Test your understanding 4

A public company limited by shares may reduce capital by:

A   passing an ordinary resolution and obtaining the court's permission

B   passing a special resolution and obtaining the court's permission

C   passing an ordinary resolution with special notice

D   passing a special resolution with special notice

7   Treasury shares

Definition

These are created when a company purchases its own shares from distributable profits. The shares do not have to be cancelled. Up to 10% of the shares can be held 'in treasury' which means they can be re-issued without the usual formalities.

Previously treasury shares could only be created by public companies but since 30 April 2013 they can be created by private companies as well.

General Rule

Shares which are purchased by a company must be cancelled and the amount of the company's share capital account reduced by the nominal value of the cancelled shares.

Exception

Under S724 CA 2006, companies can buy, hold and resell their shares.

The shares must be purchased from distributable profits and the company can cancel or sell them at any time.

Under S726 CA 2006, the shares will not give the company any voting rights in respect of those shares. In addition, no dividend or other form of distribution can be made in respect of them.

S728 CA 2006 prescribes that when treasury shares are sold or transferred for the purposes of an employees' share scheme, the company must deliver a return to the Registrar not later than 28 days after the shares are disposed of.

Any consideration received on a sale of treasury shares is to be treated as profits for distribution purposes.

Under S729 CA 2006, in the event the shares are cancelled, there will be a reduction in capital but there is no need for a special resolution of the members or authorisation by the court.

S730 CA 2006 states that where treasury shares are cancelled, the company must deliver a return to the Registrar not later than 28 days after the shares are cancelled. The return must state with respect to shares of each class cancelled.

(a)   the number and nominal value of the shares, and

(b)   the date on which they were cancelled.

The notice must be accompanied by a statement of capital which must state with respect to the company's share capital immediately following the cancellation

(a)   the total number of shares of the company

(b)   the aggregate nominal value of those shares

(c)   for each class of shares

    (i)   prescribed particulars of the rights attached to the shares,

    (ii)   the total number of shares of that class, and

    (iii)   the aggregate nominal value of shares of that class, and

(d)   the amount paid up and the amount (if any) unpaid on each share (whether on account of the nominal value of the share or by way of premium).

Treasury shares can also be created when a company initially issues shares to the public but keeps a portion in its treasury to be sold at a later date.

8   Distributions

Introduction

A company can only make a distribution (e.g. pay a dividend) out of profits available for that purpose, i.e. distributable profits.

Distributable profits

Distributable profits are the accumulated realised profits (so far as not previously utilised by distribution or capitalisation) less the accumulated realised losses (so far as not previously written off in a reduction of capital): S830 CA06.

Profit and loss

This can be from trading activities and capital transactions.

Accumulated

This looks at the cumulative profit/loss, not just the current year in isolation. For example, if a company made a trading loss of £1,000 in year 1 and £2,000 in year 2, but a trading profit of £1,000 in year 3, it must make a profit in excess of £2,000 in year 4 before any dividend can be paid.

Realised

A profit or loss is deemed to be realised if it is treated as realised in accordance with generally accepted accounting principles.

Provisions such as depreciation are deemed realised.

If a general revaluation of all the fixed assets has taken place and results in a deficit, that deficit does not need to be treated as realised.

Additional rules for a public company

A public limited company can only declare a dividend if both before and after distribution its net assets are not less than the aggregate of its called up share capital and undistributable reserves.

Undistributable reserves are:

- share premium account
- capital redemption reserve
- unrealised profits (i.e. revaluation reserve)
- reserves that the company is forbidden to distribute.

The latest audited accounts are used to make the calculations.

Model articles

Under the model articles, the directors recommend the payment of a dividend and the company declares it by passing an ordinary resolution. The amount paid cannot exceed the amount recommended by the directors.

However, a shareholder is not entitled to a dividend as of right.

Test your understanding 5

A company had a balance on its profit and loss account reserve at the beginning of its accounting year of losses of £3,000. During the year the company made trading profits of £7,000 and revalued its fixed assets by £5,000.

What are the profits available for distribution?

Consequences of an unlawful dividend

If a dividend is not paid in accordance with the rules on distributions then the company can recover the distribution from:

- shareholders who knew or had reasonable grounds to know the dividend was unlawful

- any director unless he can show he exercised reasonable care in relying on properly prepared accounts

- the auditors if the dividend was paid in reliance on erroneous accounts.

However, if a director has to make good to the company an unlawful dividend he may claim indemnity from the shareholders who when they received the dividend knew it was an unlawful dividend.

9 Loan capital

All companies have the implied power to borrow for the purpose of business.

Loan capital comprises all the longer term borrowing of a company such as:

- permanent overdrafts at the bank

- unsecured loans either from a bank or other party

- loans secured on assets either from a bank or other party.

Companies often issue long-term loans in the form of **debentures**.

Debentures

A debenture is a document issued by a company containing an acknowledgment of its indebtedness whether charged on the company's assets or not.

There are three main types of debentures:

- a single debenture e.g. a company obtains a secured loan or overdraft facility

- debentures issued as a series and usually registered

- debenture stock subscribed to by a large number of lenders.

Advantages of debentures

- The board does not (usually) need the authority of a general meeting to issue debentures.

- As debentures carry no votes they do not dilute or affect the control of the company.

- Interest is chargeable against the profit before tax.

- Debentures may be cheaper to service than shares.

- There are no restrictions on issuing debentures at a discount or on redemption.

- They are freely transferable.

Disadvantages of debentures

- Interest must be paid out of pre-tax profits, irrespective of the profits of the company. If necessary must be paid out of capital.

- Default may precipitate liquidation and/or administration if the debentures are secured.

- High gearing will affect the share price.

Test your understanding 6

Edward and Frederick wish to invest in Fizz, a listed plc. They have the choice of investing by buying shares or by subscribing to an issue of debentures.

A   **Fill in the gaps and complete the sentence.**

Most people understand a debenture to mean a

....

Strictly speaking it is a ....

(Your answer must not exceed 10 words.)

B   **Fill in the gaps and delete as appropriate.**

Edward and Frederick will have the choice of being .... shareholders or   ...shareholders. The   .. have the real voting rights while the   .. will have a less risky investment.

C   **List three differences between debentures and shares.**

---

10 Fixed versus floating charges

Fixed charge

 A fixed charge is a legal or equitable mortgage on a specific asset (e.g. land), which prevents the company dealing with the asset without the consent of the mortgagee.

A fixed charge has three main characteristics:

- It is on an identified asset.

- The asset is intended to be retained permanently in the business.

- The company has no general freedom to deal with (e.g. sell) the asset.

In certain circumstances a fixed charge can be set aside by a liquidator or an administrator if it can be shown that the company sought to put a creditor in a preferential position. This is covered in more detail in Chapter 12.

Floating charge

The judge in **Re Yorkshire Woolcombers' Association (1903)** stated that a floating charge has three main characteristics:

- It is on a class of assets, present and future.

- The assets within the class will change from time to time.

- The company has freedom to deal with the charged assets in the ordinary course of its business.

A floating charge cannot be created by a partnership.

Crystallisation

A floating charge does not attach to any particular asset until crystallisation.

Crystallisation means the company can no longer deal freely with the assets. It occurs in the following cases:

- liquidation

- the company ceases to carry on business

- any event specified (e.g. the company is unable to pay its debts; the company fails to look after its property; the company fails to keep stock levels sufficiently high).

Advantages of a floating charge

A floating charge has the following advantages for the company:

- The company can deal freely with the assets.

- A wider class of assets can be charged.

Disadvantages of a floating charge

A floating charge has a number of disadvantages for the chargee:

- The value of the security is uncertain until it crystallises.

- It has a lower priority in order of repayment than a fixed charge.

- It may be challenged by a liquidator if it was created within 12 months preceding a winding up. This is to prevent a company from giving preference to one of its unsecured creditors by giving a floating charge over its assets.

Test your understanding 7

JIH Ltd has borrowed money from K Bank plc and has provided security by executing a fixed charge debenture in favour of the bank.

A fixed charge is:

A   a charge over specific company property that prevents the company from dealing freely with the property in the ordinary course of business

B   a charge over a class of company assets that enables the company to deal freely with the assets in the ordinary course of business

C   a charge over specific company property that enables the company to deal freely with the assets in the ordinary course of business

D   a charge over company land enabling the company to deal freely with the land in the ordinary course of business

11 Priority and registration of charges

Priority

The priority of a charge depends on the type of charge and whether or not it has been registered:

- Equal charges – first created has priority.

- Fixed charge – has priority over a floating charge.

- An unregistered registerable charge has no priority over a registered charge.

- A chargeholder can prohibit the creation of a later charge with priority, but the prohibition is only effective if a subsequent chargee has notice of the prohibition as well as the charge.

Registration

The company must also notify the registrar within 21 days of the creation of the charge.

Registration can be undertaken by:

- the company
- the chargeholder.

Failure to register:

- renders the charge void against the liquidator
- results in a fine on the company and every officer in default
- renders the money secured immediately repayable.

If the charge relates to land it must also be registered with the Land Registry.

The company must also include all charges in its own register of charges. However, failure to include the charge in the company's own register does not invalidate the charge.

12 Loan capital versus share capital

Loan capital versus share capital

	Loan capital	**Share capital**
Definition	A debenture is a document issued by a company containing an acknowledgment of its indebtedness.	A share is the interest of a shareholder in a company measured by a sum of money. It is a bundle of rights and obligations.
Voting rights	A debenture is a creditor of the company and therefore has no voting rights.	A shareholder is a member (owner) of the company and therefore has voting rights, depending on the class of shares held.
Income	A debenture has a contractual right to interest, irrespective of the availability of profits.	Dividends depend on the availability of profits.
Liquidation	A debenture has priority with respect to repayment.	Depending on the type of share, shareholders receive repayment after creditors, but can participate in surplus assets.
Maintenance of capital	Does not need to be maintained.	Must be maintained.

13 Chapter summary

Test your understanding answers

Test your understanding 1

A   are

       can

       cannot

       can

       ...that they cannot receive any payment until all amounts due to creditors have been paid.

B   The dividend is fixed. Preference shares have priority when dividends are declared and on winding up. Dividends are cumulative and arrears of dividend will be paid when profits are available.

Test your understanding 2

A   A sale of a new issue of shares to the existing shareholders is a rights issue.

Test your understanding 3

The share premium account may only be used for:

- writing off the expenses of the issue of those shares
- writing off any commission paid on the issue of those shares
- issuing bonus shares.

Test your understanding 4

B

Once the special resolution to reduce the share capital has been passed, it must be approved by the court. The procedure involving a special resolution supported by a solvency statement is only available to private companies.

Test your understanding 5

The company can distribute up to £4,000. This represents the £7,000 profit for the year, less the accumulated losses of £3,000. The unrealised profit on the revaluation of fixed assets is excluded.

Test your understanding 6

A   loan

...written acknowledgment by a company of an amount owed.

B   ordinary

preference

ordinary shareholders

preference shareholders

C

(i)   Shareholders are members, debenture holders are creditors.

(ii)   Shareholders receive a dividend, debenture holders receive interest.

(iii) Shares cannot be issued at a discount, debentures can.

Test your understanding 7

A

A fixed charge is a charge over a specific asset which attaches to the asset immediately upon its creation. This means that the company cannot deal freely with the asset in the ordinary course of business.

Chapter

9

Directors

Chapter learning objectives

Upon completion of this chapter you will be able to:

- explain the role of directors in the operation of the company

- discuss the ways in which the directors are appointed, can lose their office or be subject to a disqualification order

- distinguish between the powers of the board of directors, the managing director and individual directors to bind the company

- explain the duties that directors owe to their companies

- demonstrate an understanding of the way in which statute law has attempted to control directors.

PER

One of the PER performance objectives (PO4) is to contribute effective governance in your area. You evaluate, monitor and implement risk management procedures, complying with the spirit and the letter of policies, laws and regulations. Working though this chapter should help you understand how to demonstrate that objective.

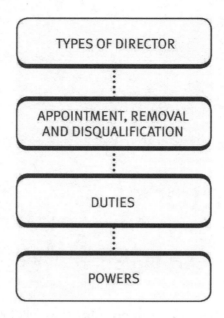

1 Directors

Definition of director

The term 'director' includes 'any person occupying the position of director, by whatever name called': s250 CA06.

The decision as to whether someone is a director is therefore based on their function, not their title.

A director must normally be aged at least 16. Under the SBEEA 2015 all directors must be natural persons.

De Jure Director

A person who is formally and legally appointed or elected as director in accordance with the articles of association of the company and gives written consent to hold the office of a director.

De Facto Director

A person who is not a de jure director but performs the acts or duties of a director.

Any person, who is not technically a director, but according to whose directions and instructions other directors and employees are accustomed to act, is legally deemed a de facto director.

A de facto director owes the same duties to the company as a de jure director, i.e. he is subject to both statutory duties and prohibitions, and he also owes fiduciary duties to the company.

Types of director

Managing director (Chief executive officer (MD/CEO)	<ul><li>A director appointed to carry out overall day-today management functions.</li><li>The model articles allow the board to delegate to the MD/CEO any powers they see fit.</li><li>The MD/CEO has a dual role – member of board and also executive officer.</li><li>**Freeman & Lockyer (A Firm) v Buckhurst Park Properties (Mangal) Ltd (1964)** – the MD/CEO has the apparent authority to enter into all contracts of a commercial nature.</li></ul>
Shadow director	<ul><li>A person in accordance with whose directions or instructions the directors of a company are accustomed to act': s251 CA06. As discussed earlier this means that it is the person's function rather than their title that defines them as a director.</li><li>Used to regulate activity by those who exercise control over a company but try to evade their responsibilities and potential liabilities as a director.</li><li>All the rules of company law are equally applicable to shadow directors.</li><li>Not a shadow director if advice is given only in a professional capacity e.g. accountants and lawyers.</li></ul>
Executive director	<ul><li>Likely to be a full-time employee involved in management.</li><li>Performs a specific role under a service contract.</li><li>May be distinguished by a special title such as 'Sales Director' or 'Finance Director'.</li></ul>
Non-executive director (NED)	<ul><li>Part-time.</li><li>Not an employee.</li><li>Brings outside expertise to board.</li><li>Contributes an independent view.</li><li>Exerts control over executive directors.</li><li>Subject to the same duties, controls and potential liabilities as executive directors.</li></ul>

Chairman of board	• Chairs meetings of board. • Acts as spokesman for the company. • Has a casting vote.
Alternate director	• Appointed by a director to attend and vote for them at board meetings which they are unable to attend. • Can be another director within the same company or more usually an outsider.

2 Appointment, disqualification and removal

Appointment

First Directors	• Public companies need a minimum of two; private companies need one. • There is no statutory maximum, but the articles may specify a maximum number.
Appointment procedure	• Usually appointed by the existing directors or by ordinary resolution. • Directors of public companies should generally be voted on individually: s160 CA06. • A director's actions are valid notwithstanding that his appointment was defective: s161 CA06.
Model articles for public companies	• At the first annual general meeting (AGM) all the directors retire and offer themselves for re-election by ordinary resolution. • At each AGM one-third retire (those most senior). They can be re-elected. • Casual vacancies are filled by the board until the next AGM when the new directors must stand for election.
Publicity	• The company must notify Companies House within 14 days of new appointments and any changes in particulars. It must also enter details in the register of directors.

Service contracts	• Cannot exceed two years unless they have been approved by the shareholders by ordinary resolution: s188 CA06.
	• If s188 CA06 is breached the service contract is deemed to state that the company can terminate the contract at any time by giving reasonable notice.
	• The service contract must be kept open for inspection at the company's registered office.
	• The directors of a quoted company must prepare a directors' remuneration report for each financial year of the company. The report will contain for each person who was a director during the year:
	(a) date of the contract, the unexpired term and the details of any notice periods
	(b) any provision for compensation payable upon early termination of the contract; and
	(c) such details of other provisions in the contract as are necessary to enable members of the company to estimate the liability of the company in the event of early termination of the contract.
Compensation for loss of office	• Gratuitous payments must be disclosed to all members and approved by ordinary resolution. If not approved, director holds payment on trust for the company.

Disqualification

Model articles – Directors must vacate their office if they become bankrupt.

Company Directors (Disqualification) Act 1986 (CDDA 1986)

The CDDA 1986 was introduced to prevent the misuse of the limited liability status of companies by directors who would set up a new company to carry on essentially the same business as an old company which had ceased trading with unpaid debts.

A disqualified director cannot be concerned in the management of a company directly or indirectly or act as a liquidator, receiver or promoter.

The CDDA 1986 identifies three distinct categories of conduct:

- General misconduct in connection with companies. This includes:
  - Conviction of a serious offence in connection with the management of a company either in the UK or abroad (maximum fifteen years disqualification).
  - Persistent breaches of CA06, e.g. failure to file returns (maximum five years disqualification).
- Disqualification for unfitness. This includes:
  - Where an investigation by the Department for Business, Energy and Industrial Strategy finds the director unfit to be concerned in the management of the company.
  - Where a liquidator's report finds the director unfit to be concerned in the management of a company (minimum two years, and maximum fifteen years, disqualification).
- Other cases for disqualification. This includes:
  - participation in fraudulent or wrongful trading (maximum 15 years disqualification).
  - where an undischarged bankrupt has been acting as a director.
  - where a person acts on behalf of a disqualified director.

Breach of a disqualification order:

- This is a criminal offence, which could result in a fine and imprisonment.
- The disqualified director (or any person who acts on his instructions) is personally liable for the debts of the company while so acting.

Removal

Under s168 CA06, a company may by ordinary resolution remove a director before expiration of his period of office notwithstanding anything in:

- its articles, or
- any agreement between him and it.

Thus a director can be removed despite any provision to the contrary in his service contract, although he can sue for damages if the removal is in breach of his contract. The company must follow this procedure to remove a director:

> Special notice (28 days) is required of the resolution by persons wishing to remove a director.
>
> The company must forward a copy of the resolution to the director concerned.

> Notice of the meeting goes to the director and all members entitled to attend and vote.

> The director in question can require the company to circulate written representations to members.

> At the meeting, the director can read out representations if there was no time for prior circulation.
>
> The director must be allowed to attend the meeting and to speak.
>
> An ordinary resolution is needed to remove the director.

The power of the members to remove a director may be limited:

Bushell v Faith (1970)

Facts: A provision in the articles tripled the number of votes of shares held by directors on a resolution to remove them. Statute only required an ordinary resolution and made no provision as to how it could be obtained or defeated.

Held: The weighted voting rights provided in the articles were valid.

> ### Test your understanding 1
>
> **Which of the following states the requirements for removal of a director?**
>
> A   Special resolution with ordinary notice
>
> B   Ordinary resolution with special notice
>
> C   Ordinary resolution with ordinary notice
>
> D   Special resolution with special notice

3 Duties

General duties

Prior to the Companies Act 2006, common law rules, equitable principles and fiduciary duties made up the law on directors' duties. A fiduciary duty is a duty imposed upon certain persons because of the position of trust and confidence they are in.

These have now been replaced by the specific statutory duties provided in the Companies Act 2006 (s170). However, the old case law still has relevance in interpreting the new legislation and illustrating its application.

Duty to act within powers: s171

A director must act in accordance with the company's constitution and only use his powers for the purpose which they were given. They have a fiduciary duty to the company to exercise their powers bona fide in what they honestly consider to be the interests of the company.

If this rule is not adhered to the transaction will be void, unless it is approved by the shareholders.

Hogg v Cramphorn (1967)

Facts: The directors issued further shares and gave financial assistance for their purchase in an attempt to fight off a takeover bid, believing it to be in the best interests of the company.

Held: The directors had acted in what they believed to be the best interests of the company, but were in breach of the duty to act within their powers. Therefore, it was open to the members to ratify their actions, which they did.

Duty to promote the success of the company: s172

A director must act in good faith, in a way which promotes the success of the company and for the benefit of the members as a whole.

The Act introduced the concept of 'enlightened shareholder value' and requires the directors to have regard to:

- the likely consequences of any decision in the long term
- the interests of the company's employees

- the need to foster the company's business relationships with suppliers, customers and others

- the impact of the company's operations on the community and the environment

- the desirability of the company maintaining a reputation for high standards of business conduct and

- the need to act fairly as between members of the company.

Companies may have wider purposes than just the benefit of members such as charitable companies and community interest companies. S172(2) provides that where that is the case, then the duty of the director is to act in a way that would be most likely to achieve that purpose.

S172(3) provides that the general duty is subject to any specific enactment or rule of law requiring directors to consider or act in the interests of creditors of the company. This provision therefore formally recognises that the duty to the shareholders is displaced when the company is insolvent or heading towards insolvency (this is looked at in more detail in **Chapter 12: Fraudulent Behaviour)**.

Duty to exercise independent judgment: s173

A director of a company must exercise independent judgment.

This duty is not infringed by a director acting:

- in accordance with an agreement duly entered into by the company that restricts the future exercise of discretion by its directors, or

- in a way authorised by the company's constitution.

Duty to exercise reasonable care, skill and diligence: s174

The standard expected of a director is that of a reasonably diligent person with:

- the general knowledge, skill and experience that could reasonably be expected of a director, and

- the actual knowledge, skill and experience held by the director.

The reasonableness test therefore consists of two elements:

1　An objective test

A director in carrying out his functions, must show such care as could reasonably be expected from a competent person in that role. It is not a defence for a director to claim lack of expertise.

2　A subjective test

A director is expected to show the degree of skill which may reasonably be expected from a person of his knowledge and experience.

Re City Equitable Fire Insurance Co (1925)

Facts: The company was in liquidation and it was discovered there was a shortage of funds mainly due to the deliberate fraud of the chairman, for which he had been convicted. The liquidator brought an action against the other directors of the company for negligence on the basis that they had left the management of the company entirely in the hands of the chairman.

Held: The liquidator failed and the judge laid down the duties of care and skill to be expected of a director:

(a) A director need not exhibit in the performance of his duties a greater degree of skill than may reasonably be expected from someone of his knowledge and experience.

(b) A director is not bound to give continuous attention to the affairs of the company.

(c) Where duties may properly be left to some other official, a director is justified, in the absence of grounds for suspicion, in trusting that official to perform his duties honestly.

The low level of care shown in **Re City Equitable Fire Insurance Co (1925)** was raised in:

Dorchester Finance Co Ltd v Stebbing (1989)

Facts: The company was a money-lending company and had three directors, Parsons, Hamilton and Stebbing. All three had considerable accountancy and business experience (Parsons and Hamilton were chartered accountants). No board meetings were ever held and Parsons and Hamilton left all the affairs of the company to Stebbing. Parsons and Hamilton did, however, turn up from time to time and signed blank cheques on the company's account which they left Stebbing to deal with. Stebbing loaned the company's money without complying with statutory regulations applying to money lending, such that the loans were unenforceable.

Held: All three were liable in negligence. If a director has a special skill (e.g. as an accountant) he is expected to use it for the benefit of the company.

Duty to avoid conflicts of interest: s175

A director must avoid any situation which places him in direct conflict with the interests of the company or the performance of any other duty.

IDC v Cooley (1972)

Facts: Cooley, the managing director of IDC, had been negotiating a contract on behalf of the company, but the third party wished to award the contract to him personally and not to the company. Without disclosing his reason to the company (or its board) he resigned in order to take the contract personally.

Held: He was in breach of fiduciary duty as he had profited personally by use of an opportunity which came to him through his directorship: it made no difference that the company itself would not have obtained the contract. He was therefore accountable to the company for the benefits gained from the contract.

The IDC case also illustrates that an individual may still be subject to the duties even after he ceases to be a director.

The accountability arises from the mere fact of having made a profit, it is not a question of loss to the company.

Regal (Hastings) Ltd v Gulliver (1942)

Facts: The claimant company owned one cinema and wished to buy two others with the object of selling all three together. They formed a subsidiary to buy the cinemas but could not provide all the capital needed to finance the purchase. The directors bought some of the shares in the subsidiary to enable the purchases to be made and later sold their shares at a profit.

Held: The directors must account to the claimant company for the profit on the grounds that it was only through the knowledge and opportunity they gained as directors of that company that they were able to obtain the shares and consequently to make the profit.

Duty not to accept benefits from third parties: s176

A director must not accept any benefit from a third party which arises by reason of him being a director or performing/not performing an act as a director, unless acceptance cannot reasonably be regarded as likely to give rise to a conflict of interest.

Boston Deep Sea Fishing & Ice Co v Ansell (1888)

Facts: Ansell was managing director of the claimant company. He accepted a 'commission' (bribe) from a supplier to order goods from that supplier, on behalf of the company. When the company found out, he was dismissed.

Held: The defendant was in breach of his fiduciary duty as the agent of the company. Therefore the company could recover the commissions paid to him.

Duty to declare interest in proposed transaction or arrangement: s177

A director is required to declare the nature and extent of any interest, either direct or indirect through a connected person, that they have in relation to a proposed transaction or arrangement with the company. Even if the director is not a party to a transaction, the duty may apply if they are aware or ought reasonably to have been aware, of the interest.

This declaration can be made in writing, at a board meeting or by a general notice that he has an interest in a third party.

Aberdeen Railway v Blakie (1854)

Facts: A company bought some chairs from a firm. At the time of the contract, one of the company's directors, unknown to the company, was a partner in the firm.

Held: The company, could avoid the contract, because of this undisclosed interest in the transaction.

Breach of directors' duties

Directors owe their duties to the company as a whole, not to individual members.

Percival v Wright (1902)

Facts: A director of a company bought shares from a member at a price less than that for which the director knew that a third party had expressed interest in buying all the shares in the company. The third party interest came to nothing, but the selling member sued the director for breach of duty to the member in not disclosing the interest expressed by the third party.

Held: The purchasing director was under no obligation to disclose to the selling member the third party interest. A director's duties are owed to the company and not to individual members.

- The director may be required to make good any loss suffered by the company.

- Contracts entered into between the company and the director may be rendered voidable.

- Any property taken by the director from the company can be recovered from him if still in his possession.

- Property may be recovered directly from a third party, unless that third party acquired it for value and in good faith.

- An injunction may be an appropriate remedy where the breach has not yet occurred.

S232 CA06 provides that any provision to exempt a director from or indemnify him against any liability for breach of duty or negligence is void.

S239 CA06 states that the company can ratify a breach of duty by passing an ordinary resolution.

Test your understanding 2

Jack has acted in breach of his duty to disclose his interest in a contract as a director of JK Ltd.

Which one of the following is correct?

A   The breach cannot be ratified by the shareholders.

B   The breach may be ratified by a written or ordinary resolution.

C   The breach may be ratified by a provision in the company's articles.

D   The breach may be ratified by a resolution of the board of directors.

4   Powers

The division of power within a company

The division of power within a company is between the board of directors who manage the business on a day-to-day basis and the members who make major decisions about the running of the company's business in a general meeting.

Directors are required to exercise their powers in accordance with the company's constitution i.e. the articles, which usually authorise the directors 'to manage the company's business' and to 'exercise all the powers of the company for any purpose connected with the company's business'.

Note that the power to manage the business of the company is given to the board as a whole, not to the individual directors. Where a company's articles delegate the management of the company's business to the board, the members have no right to interfere in decisions made by the board. Directors are not agents of the members and are not subject to their instruction as to how to act.

Shaw v John Shaw (1935)

Facts: The company's board of directors resolved that the company commence litigation against two errant directors. At a subsequent member's meeting an ordinary resolution was passed that the litigation be discontinued.

Held: It was for the board to decide whether or not the company should commence litigation and therefore the ordinary resolution had no legal effect.

There are some restrictions which mean that power is placed in the hands of the members rather than the directors:

- some actions require a resolution

- a director can be removed at any time by an ordinary resolution of the members and they may see fit to exercise this right should their views be ignored

- the members can alter the articles by passing a special resolution. This power could therefore be used to restrict the directors' powers.

The control of directors

Although the directors manage the company on a day-to-day basis, a company is ultimately controlled by its members. Most decisions require a majority of over 50% (although some require 75%) therefore shareholders who are in the minority may find that their wishes are ignored.

Members can exercise their votes in their own interests. They are not required to act for the benefit of the company.

Under Model Article 4, the shareholders may, by special resolution, direct the directors to take, or refrain from taking, specified action.

Statutory control over directors

Certain matters require the approval of the members in a general meeting in order to be valid.

Directors' service contracts: s188 CA06

Directors' service contracts lasting more than two years must be approved by the members.

Substantial property transactions: s190 CA06

A substantial property transaction occurs where a director acquires from the company (or vice versa) a substantial non-cash asset.

 An asset is 'substantial' if its value either exceeds £100,000 or exceeds 10% of the company's asset value and is more than £5,000.

Failure to obtain the members' approval results in the following consequences:

- the transaction is voidable by the company, unless the members give approval within a reasonable period

- the director is liable to account to the company for any gain or indemnify it against any loss.

Loans to directors: S197 CA06

Any loans given to directors, or guarantees provided as security for loans provided to directors, must be approved by members.

Non-contractual payments to directors: S217 CA06

Any non-contractual payments to directors for loss of office must be approved by the members.

Authority of directors

At common law

Individual directors cannot bind the company without being given authority to do so. There are three ways in which this authority may be given:

Express	• Where authority is expressly given, all decisions taken are binding.
Implied	• Authority flows from a person's position. • The person appointed as the managing director has the implied authority to bind the company in the same way as the board. • The MD/CEO is assumed to have all powers usually exercised by an MD/CEO.
Apparent/ Ostensible	• Such authority arises where a director is held the other board members as having the authority to bind the company out by • If a third party acts on such a representation, the company is estopped from denying its truth: **Freeman & Lockyer v Buckhurst Park Properties (1964)** (see Chapter 5: Agency Law).

Transaction beyond the board's powers

S40 CA06 states that the power of the directors to bind the company, or to authorise another to bind the company, will not be limited by anything in the company's constitution, **provided** the other party is acting in good faith.

S40 goes on to state that even where there is **actual knowledge** of the lack of authority this is not enough to count as lack of good faith so, on the face of it, any contract entered into by the board of a company will be binding.

Where, however, the third party to the transaction is also a director of the company or a person associated with a director, the transaction becomes **voidable** at the company's instance: s41 CA06. Moreover, the third party director or associate, and any director who authorised the transaction is then liable to **compensate** the company for any profit made or to indemnify the company for any loss or damage arising, whether the company chooses to avoid the contract or not.

5   Chapter summary

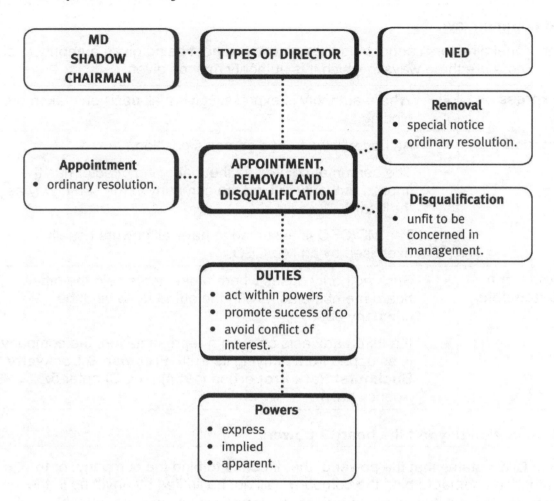

MD
SHADOW
CHAIRMAN

TYPES OF DIRECTOR

NED

Removal
- special notice
- ordinary resolution.

Appointment
- ordinary resolution.

APPOINTMENT,
REMOVAL AND
DISQUALIFICATION

Disqualification
- unfit to be concerned in management.

DUTIES
- act within powers
- promote success of co
- avoid conflict of interest.

Powers
- express
- implied
- apparent.

Test your understanding answers

Test your understanding 1

B

The removal of a director requires an ordinary resolution with special notice.

Test your understanding 2

B

S239 CA06 states that where an interest has not been disclosed, the action can be ratified by passing an ordinary resolution.

Corporate administration

Chapter learning objectives

Upon completion of this chapter you will be able to:

- discuss the appointment, duties and powers of, a company secretary

- discuss the appointment, duties and powers of, the company auditors

- distinguish between types of meetings: general meetings and annual general meetings

- explain the procedure for calling such meetings

- detail the procedure for conducting company meetings

- distinguish between types of resolutions: ordinary, special, and written.

PER

One of the PER performance objectives (PO1) is to always act in the wider public interest. You need to take into account all relevant information and use professional judgement, your personal values and scepticism to evaluate data and make decisions. You should identify right from wrong and escalate anything of concern. You also need to make sure that your skills, knowledge and behaviour are up-to-date and allow you to be effective in your role. Working though this chapter should help you understand how to demonstrate that objective.

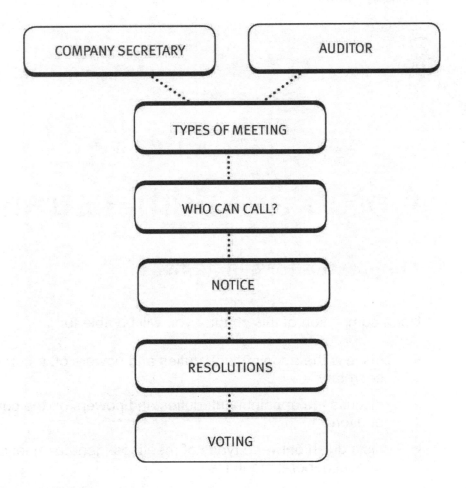

1   Company secretary

Introduction

Every public company must have a qualified company secretary. Private companies may choose to appoint a secretary, but are not obliged to do so.

The secretary is usually appointed and removed by the directors.

Qualifications

The secretary of a **public** company must be **qualified** under one of the following conditions:

- They must have held the office of company secretary in a public limited company (plc) for at least three out of the preceding five years.

- They must be a solicitor, barrister or member of ICAEW, ACCA, CIMA, ICSA, CIPFA.

- They must appear to be capable of discharging the functions by virtue of another position or qualification.

Duties

There are no statutory duties, therefore the duties will be whatever the board decides. The company secretary will typically undertake the following:

- check that documentation is in order
- make returns to the registrar
- keep registers
- give notice and keep minutes of meetings
- countersign documents to which the company seal is affixed.

Powers

The company secretary has the authority to bind the company in contract. There are two types of authority:

- express authority – this is the authority delegated by the board
- implied authority regarding contracts of an administrative nature.

Panorama Developments (Guildford) v Fidelis Furnishing Fabrics (1971)

The company secretary ordered services for his own, not the company's, use. It was held that the contract was binding on the company as the contract was of the sort that a company secretary should be able to carry out.

'He is no longer a mere clerk...He is entitled to sign contracts connected with the administrative side of a company's affairs, such as employing staff, and ordering cars, and so forth.'

However, two other cases indicate that there is a limit to the company secretary's authority:

- It does not extend to making commercial as opposed to administrative contracts: **Re Maidstone Building Provisions (1971)**.
- It does not usually carry the authority to borrow money: **Re Cleadon Trust Ltd (1938)**.

Test your understanding 1
In relation to the company secretary, which one of the following statements is correct?
A   Both a public and a private company must have a company secretary.
B   The company secretary is appointed by the members.
C   In a public company the company secretary must be qualified.
D   Company secretaries can bind companies in a contract if acting outside their actual or apparent authority.

2 The auditor

Qualifications

The auditor must be either:

- a member of recognised supervisory body (ICAEW, ICAS or ACCA) and eligible under their rules, or

- qualified by a similar overseas body and authorised by the Department for Business, Energy and Industrial Strategy.

The auditor must not be:

- an officer or employee of the company

- the partner of an officer or employee of the company.

Appointment

The auditors should generally be appointed by the shareholders by ordinary resolution. However, the directors can appoint the company's first auditor and fill casual vacancies.

A company must inform the Secretary of State if it has failed to appoint an auditor within 28 days of circulating its accounts. The Secretary of State has power to appoint an auditor in those circumstances.

Audit exemption for small companies

For financial years starting on or after 6 April 2008, to qualify for total audit exemption a company must:

- have a turnover of not more than £6.5m; and

- have gross assets not more than £3.26m.

However, these exemptions do not apply to public companies, banking or insurance companies or those subject to a statute-based regulatory regime.

Resignation

An auditor can resign at any time by giving written notice to the company: s516 CA06.

The resignation is effective from the date it is delivered to the company's registered office, or from a specified later date. To be effective it must be accompanied by the statement required by s519 (see below).

A company whose auditor resigns is required to inform the registrar: s517 CA06. Failure to do so is an offence.

Under s518 CA06, an auditor who resigns can require the directors to convene a general meeting to consider his explanation of the circumstances that led to his resignation. The directors have 21 days to send out a notice convening a meeting and it must be held within 28 days of the notice.

Removal

An auditor can be removed by ordinary resolution: s510 CA06. The resolution must be passed at a general meeting; a written resolution cannot be used to remove an auditor.

Special notice of the resolution is needed (i.e. 28 days). The company must send a copy of the resolution to the auditor and he has the right to make a statement of his case. The company then has to circulate his statement to the shareholders. However, if time does not allow for circulation, the statement can be read out at the meeting.

Notice of the resolution removing the auditor must be sent to the Registrar within 14 days.

Statement by departing auditor

Under s519 CA06, a departing auditor is required to make a statement and to deposit it with the company:

- For quoted companies, this statement must explain the circumstances surrounding his departure.

- For other public companies and all private companies, it should explain the circumstances surrounding his departure, unless the auditor thinks that there is no need for them to be brought to the attention of the shareholders or creditors. In that case, the statement should state that there are no such circumstances.

Unless there are no circumstances to be brought to the attention of shareholders and creditors, the company is obliged to circulate the statement to everyone to whom it needs to send the annual accounts. It must do this within 14 days of receiving it.

If the company does not want to circulate the statement, it can apply to the court for an order that it need not circulate the statement.

Duties

The auditor has a statutory duty to report to the members on whether the accounts:

- give a true and fair view and

- have been properly prepared in accordance with the Companies Act and the relevant financial reporting framework.

The auditor must investigate and form an opinion as to whether:

- proper books of accounting records have been kept

- proper returns adequate for their audit have been received from branches not visited by them

- the accounts are in agreement with the books of account and returns

- the information given in the directors' report is consistent with the accounts.

If the auditor is dissatisfied with the findings of his investigation he must qualify the audit report.

The report (whether qualified or unqualified) must state the name of the audit firm, or if an individual has been appointed as auditor, his name. Where the auditor is a firm, the senior statutory auditor must sign the report in his own name on behalf of the firm.

Under s507 CA06 it is a criminal offence to knowingly or recklessly cause an audit report to include anything that is misleading, false or deceptive, or to omit a required statement of a problem with the accounts or audit. The offence carries an unlimited fine.

There could also be liability under the tort of negligence for including misleading accounts (see **Chapter 3**).

Companies Act liability for auditor's report and audited accounts

s507 of the Companies Act 2006 (s507 CA06) makes it an offence for an auditor to recklessly cause an auditor's report to contain any matter that is misleading or false to a material extent. The offence is punishable by a fine.

s532 CA06 makes any provision exempting auditors from or indemnifying them against liability for negligence void in relation to providing audited accounts.

s534 CA06 provides that a company may enter into a liability limitation agreement with an auditor, limiting his liability for negligence (among other things) in the course of auditing accounts.

Powers

The auditor has the right to:

- receive notice of, attend and speak at general meetings
- access the books at all times
- require such information and explanations from the company's officers and employees as the auditor thinks fit for the performance of his duties (it is a criminal offence to fail to provide the information requested, unless it was not reasonably practicable to do so).

Test your understanding 2

If a company's auditor is to be removed before his term of office expires, what type of resolution is required and what period of notice must be given?

3   Meetings

Annual general meeting (AGM)

Timing	Public companies must hold an AGM within the six months following their financial year end: s336.
Failure to hold	The company and every officer in default can be fined if an AGM is not held.
	Any member can apply to the Department for Business, Energy and Industrial Strategy to convene the meeting.
Private companies	Private companies are not required to hold an AGM.
Notice	**21 days' notice** is required unless every member entitled to attend and vote agrees to a shorter period.
	The notice must state that the meeting is an AGM.
Business	Usual business includes:
	• consider accounts
	• appoint auditors
	• elect directors
	• declare dividends.
Resolutions	• Members holding at least 5% of the voting rights (or at least 100 members holding on average £100 paid-up capital) have the right to propose a resolution for the AGM agenda and to require the company to circulate details of the resolution to all members.
	• If the members' request is received before the financial year end, the members are not required to cover the costs of circulation. Otherwise, the members requesting the resolution must deposit a sum to cover the company's costs.

General meetings (GM)

Timing	Held **whenever required**.
	Must be held by a plc if a serious loss of capital has occurred, i.e. net assets have fallen to less than half of the called up share capital.
Notice	At least **14 days**.
Business	The person who requisitions the meeting sets the agenda.

Class meetings

Purpose	Meeting of a class of shareholders, usually to consider a variation of their class rights.
Procedure	Notice, etc. as for general meetings.
Quorum	Two persons holding or representing by proxy at least one-third in nominal value of the issued shares of the class in question.

4 Calling a meeting

Who can call a meeting?

Directors	The articles usually delegate the power to the directors.
Members	Members may require the directors to call a GM if they hold at least 5% of the paid up voting capital.
	The directors must call a meeting within 21 days of receiving a requisition.
	The meeting must take place within 28 days of the notice convening the meeting.
	If the directors do not call a meeting, the members who requested the meeting (or any members holding over 50% of the total voting rights) may themselves call a meeting to take place within three months of the initial request and recover their expenses from the company.
Resigning auditor	A resigning auditor may require the directors to convene a meeting so he can explain the reasons for his resignation.
Court	A court can call a meeting on the application of a director or member where it would otherwise be impracticable e.g. to break a deadlock.

Notice

Who must receive notice?	Every member and every director: s310.
Failure to give notice	Accidental failure to give notice to one or more persons does not invalidate the meeting: s313.
Contents of notice	Date, time and place of the meeting. The general nature of the business to be transacted. The text of any special resolutions.
Length of notice period	**AGM – 21 days** Less if every member entitled to attend and vote agrees. **GM – 14 days** Less if members holding at least 95% of shares agree. (Where company is private, can be reduced to 90%).
Special notice	Requires 28 days' notice. Required for the removal of a director or auditor.

5 Resolutions

Resolutions are the way in which companies take decisions. They are voted on by the members in person or by proxy. There are three types of resolution:

Type	% required to pass	To Registrar?	Purpose of resolution
Special	≥75%	Yes – within 15 days	• Alter name. • Wind up company. • Alter articles. • Reduce share capital.
Ordinary	>50%	Only if required by statute	Used whenever the law or the articles do not require a special resolution.
Written (private companies only)	Same majority as required in GM	Yes if a 75% majority is required	The purpose can be anything apart from resolutions requiring special notice. Members cannot revoke their agreement. The date of the resolution is the date when the necessary majority has been reached. The resolution must generally be passed within 28 days from its circulation.

Test your understanding 3

Fill in the gaps:

1   An annual general meeting requires............days' notice.

2   Members may require the directors to call a GM if they hold at least ....% of the paid up voting capital.

3   Special notice requires ....days' notice.

4   A special resolution must be filed with the Registrar within.......days.

6   Procedure at meetings

A **quorum** is the minimum number of members that needs to be present at a meeting in order to validate business. It is generally two persons who can be members or proxies: s318 CA06.

Voting is by a **show of hands** initially, unless a poll is demanded. A show of hands means one member one vote, irrespective of the number of shares held.

A **poll** may be demanded by members holding at least 10% of the total voting rights (or by not fewer than 5 members having the right to vote on the resolution). A poll means one vote per share. The result of a poll replaces the result of the previous show of hands. Quoted companies must publish the results of polls on their website: s341 CA06.

Members have a statutory right under s 324 CA06 to appoint one or more persons as their **'proxy'**. A proxy can attend meetings, vote and speak on behalf of the member for whom he is acting.

7 Chapter summary

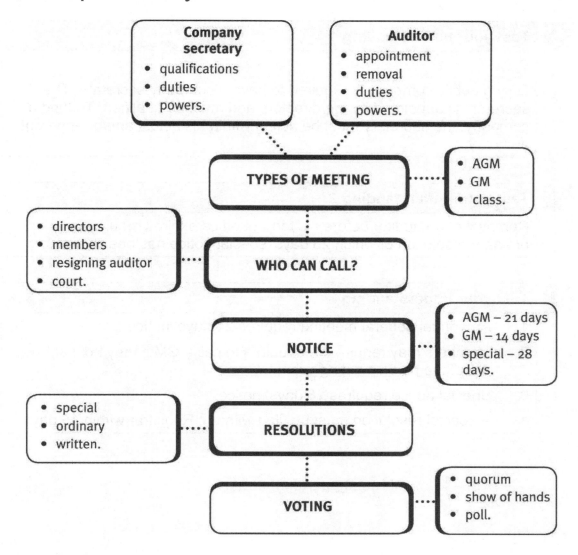

Company secretary
- qualifications
- duties
- powers.

Auditor
- appointment
- removal
- duties
- powers.

TYPES OF MEETING
- AGM
- GM
- class.

- directors
- members
- resigning auditor
- court.

WHO CAN CALL?

NOTICE
- AGM – 21 days
- GM – 14 days
- special – 28 days.

- special
- ordinary
- written.

RESOLUTIONS

VOTING
- quorum
- show of hands
- poll.

Test your understanding answers

Test your understanding 1

C

Only a public company is required to have a company secretary. The secretary is appointed by the directors and must be qualified. To bind a company, the secretary must be acting within his actual and/or apparent authority.

Test your understanding 2

Removal of an auditor before his term of office expires requires an ordinary resolution of which 28 days' special notice has been given.

Test your understanding 3

1   An annual general meeting requires **21** days' notice.

2   Members may require the directors to call a GM if they hold at least **5%** of the paid up voting capital.

3   Special notice requires **28** days' notice.

4   A special resolution must be filed with the Registrar within **15** days.

Insolvency

Chapter learning objectives

Upon completion of this chapter you will be able to:

- explain the meaning of and the procedure involved in voluntary liquidation

- explain the meaning of and the procedure involved in compulsory liquidation

- explain administration as an alternative to liquidation.

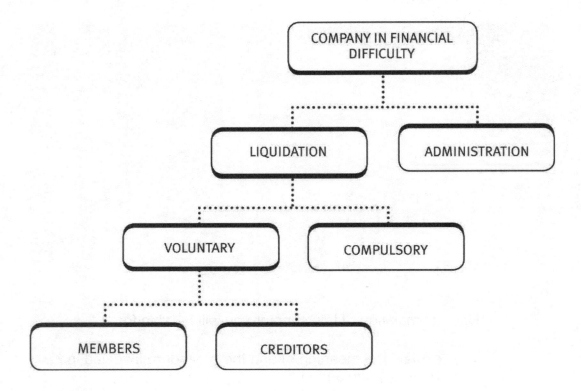

1 Introduction

If a company finds itself in financial difficulty, the two main options available to it are:

- Administration. This aims to rescue the company so that it may continue trading as a going concern.

- Liquidation. This winds up the company, thus bringing its life to an end.

2 Voluntary liquidation: s84 Insolvency Act (IA 1986)

A voluntary liquidation occurs where the members pass a resolution to go into liquidation. The type of resolution needed depends on the circumstances:

- Where the period fixed for the duration of the company expires or an event occurs upon which the articles provide that a company should be wound up, an **ordinary resolution** must be passed.

- A **special resolution** must be passed if the company is being wound up for any other reason.

There are two types of voluntary liquidation:

- A members' voluntary liquidation is used where the company is solvent.

- A creditors' voluntary liquidation is used where the company is insolvent.

Members' voluntary winding up

WINDING UP COMMENCES FROM THE PASSING OF THE APPROPRIATE RESOLUTION (S86 IA 1986).

THE DIRECTORS MAKE A **DECLARATION OF SOLVENCY** UNDER S 89 IA 1986 STATING THAT THEY ARE OF THE OPINION THAT THE COMPANY WILL BE ABLE TO PAY ITS DEBTS WITHIN 12 MONTHS. IT IS A CRIMINAL OFFENCE TO MAKE A FALSE DECLARATION.

THE MEMBERS **APPOINT A NAMED INSOLVENCY PRACTITIONER AS LIQUIDATOR** (S91 IA 1986).

THE LIQUIDATOR IS RESPONSIBLE FOR REALISING THE ASSETS AND DISTRIBUTING THE PROCEEDS.

THE LIQUIDATOR PRESENTS HIS REPORT TO A **FINAL MEETING** OF THE MEMBERS (S93 IA 1986).

THE LIQUIDATOR **INFORMS THE REGISTRAR** OF THE FINAL MEETING AND SUBMITS A COPY OF HIS REPORT (S94(3) IA 1986).

THE REGISTRAR REGISTERS THE REPORT AND THE COMPANY IS **DISSOLVED** 3 MONTHS LATER.

Creditors' voluntary winding up

WINDING UP COMMENCES FROM THE PASSING OF THE APPROPRIATE RESOLUTION (S86 IA 1986).

THE MEMBERS APPOINT A LIQUIDATOR. THE DIRECTORS MUST THEN DELIVER A NOTICE TO THE CREDITORS SEEKING THEIR DECISION ON THE LIQUIDATOR. THE DIRECTORS MUST ALSO SEND TO THE CREDITORS A **STATEMENT OF AFFAIRS** WITHIN 7 WORKING DAYS.

THE CREDITORS CAN APPROVE THE LIQUIDATOR EITHER BY VIRTUAL MEETING OR BY THE 'DEEMED CONSENT PROCESS'. UNDER THIS PROCESS, APPROVAL IS DEEMED UNLESS 10% OF THE CREDITORS OF THE COMPANY RAISE OBJECTIONS TO THE PROPOSED LIQUIDATOR. THE MEMBERS AND CREDITORS MAY APPOINT UP TO FIVE PERSONS TO SERVE ON A **LIQUIDATION COMMITTEE**.

THE LIQUIDATOR SUBMITS HIS FINAL REPORT TO THE MEMBERS AND CREDITORS

THE LIQUIDATOR SUBMITS A COPY OF HIS REPORT TO THE REGISTRAR

THE REGISTRAR REGISTERS THE REPORT AND THE COMPANY IS **DISSOLVED** 3 MONTHS LATER

Converting a members' voluntary liquidation into a creditors' voluntary liquidation

If the liquidator discovers that the company's debts will not be paid in full within the time specified in the declaration of solvency, he must convert the members' voluntary liquidation into a creditors' voluntary liquidation. This is executed by following the process for a creditors' voluntary liquidation.

Test your understanding 1

Compare and contrast the characteristics of a members' voluntary winding up and a creditors' voluntary winding up.

3 Compulsory liquidation

Grounds for winding up: s122 IA 1986

A compulsory winding up commences when a petition for a winding up order is presented to the court. The possible grounds for the petition are set out in s122 IA 1986:

- The company has passed a special resolution to be wound up by the court.

- A public company has not been issued with a trading certificate within a year of incorporation.

- The company has not commenced business within a year of being incorporated or has suspended its business for over a year.

- The company is unable to pay its debts. A company is deemed to be unable to pay its debts where a creditor who is owed at least £750 has served a written demand for payment and the company has failed to pay the sum due within three weeks.

- A dissatisfied member may petition the court for the company to be wound up on the just and equitable ground. However, the court will not make an order under this ground if some other more reasonable remedy is available.

Petitioners

The following persons may petition the court for a compulsory liquidation:

- the company itself.

- the Official Receiver, who is a civil servant in The Insolvency Service and is an officer of the Court.

- the Department for Business, Energy and Industrial Strategy.

- a contributory. This is any person who is liable to contribute to the assets of the company when it is being wound up. (The contributory must prove that the company is solvent).

- a creditor who is owed at least £750.

Effect of winding up

The winding-up petition has the following effects:

- The liquidation is deemed to have started when the petition was first presented.

- All actions for the recovery of debt against the company are stopped.

- Any floating charges crystallise.

- Any legal proceedings against the company are halted, and none may start unless leave is granted from the court.

- The company ceases to carry on business except where it is necessary to complete the winding up, e.g. to complete work-in-progress.

- The powers of the directors cease, although the directors remain in office.

- The employees are automatically made redundant, but the liquidator can re-employ them to help him complete the winding up.

Subsequent procedures

ON THE MAKING OF THE WINDING-UP ORDER, THE OFFICIAL RECEIVER BECOMES LIQUIDATOR

WITHIN THREE MONTHS, THE OFFICIAL RECEIVER WILL SUMMON MEETINGS OF THE CONTRIBUTORIES IN ORDER TO APPOINT A LICENSED INSOLVENCY PRACTITIONER TO TAKE OVER THE JOB OF LIQUIDATOR

CREDITOR APPROVAL OF THE LIQUIDATOR IS SOUGHT VIA THE 'DEEMED CONSENT' PROCESS. IF 10% OR MORE OBJECT AN ALTERNATIVE DECISION MAKING PROCEDURE SUCH AS VIRTUAL MEETING SHOULD BE USED

THE LIQUIDATOR IS RESPONSIBLE FOR REALISING THE ASSETS AND DISTRIBUTING THE PROCEEDS

THE LIQUIDATOR RETURNS TO THE COURT AND THE COURT PASSES AN ORDER DISSOLVING THE COMPANY

THE LIQUIDATOR FILES THE ORDER AND THEIR FINAL REPORT WITH THE REGISTRAR

THE REGISTRAR REGISTERS THE REPORT AND THE COMPANY IS DISSOLVED AS FROM THE DATE OF THE ORDER

Test your understanding 2

Fill in the gaps in the following sentences:

The possible grounds for a compulsory liquidation petition are set out in.....................:

A   The company has passed a............................resolution to be wound up by the court.

B   A.......................... company has not been issued with a trading certificate within...............................of incorporation.

C   A creditor who is owed at least........................has served a written demand for payment and the company has failed to pay the sum due within....................

D   It is........................to wind up the company.

Application of assets

The liquidator must repay debts in the following order:

- fixed charge-holders.

- expenses of liquidation.

- preferential creditors

    - wages or salaries due in the four months preceding the commencement of winding up (maximum £800 per employee)

    - all accrued holiday pay.

    All preferential creditors rank equally amongst themselves.

- floating charge-holders.

- unsecured creditors – rank equally amongst themselves. The Enterprise Act 2002 introduced into the Insolvency Act 1986 a ring-fencing mechanism where part of assets which are subject to a floating charge are available to unsecured creditors. The amount ring-fenced is 50% of the first £10,000, plus 20% of the rest up to a maximum ring-fenced fund of £600,000.

- post-liquidation interest.

- members – declared but unpaid dividends.

- members – return of capital (in accordance with class rights).

- any surplus to be distributed to members.

Test your understanding 3

Sharepak Ltd is being wound-up. Rank the following persons in the order in which they will be paid by the liquidator:

Preference shareholders.

Mrs Patel – an employee who is owed holiday pay of £1,000.

Barlloyd Bank – which has a charge over all the company's current assets.

Midwest Bank – which has a charge on the company's headquarters.

HMRC – which is owed corporation tax of £15,000.

Ordinary shareholders.

4 Administration

Purpose

Administration involves the appointment of an insolvency practitioner, known as an administrator, to manage the affairs, business and property of a company. It was first introduced by Schedule 16 IA 1986, but has subsequently been amended by the Enterprise Act 2002.

Administration is often used as an alternative to putting a company into liquidation, e.g. to:

- rescue a company in financial difficulty with the aim of allowing it to continue as a going concern

- achieve a better result for the creditors than would be likely if the company were to be wound up

- realise property to pay one or more secured or preferential creditors.

The administrator can only use the third option where:

- he thinks it is not reasonably practicable to rescue the company as a going concern, and

- thinks that he cannot achieve a better result for the creditors as a whole than would be likely if the company were to be wound up, and

- he does not unnecessarily harm the interests of the creditors of the company as a whole.

Who can appoint an administrator?

An administrator can be appointed by any of the following persons:

- the court in response to a petition by, e.g. a creditor, the directors or the company itself

- the holder of a qualifying floating charge over the company's assets

- the company or its directors provided that winding up has not already begun.

The court will only agree to appoint an administrator if it is satisfied that:

- the company is or is likely to become unable to pay its debts, and

- the administration order is likely to achieve its objectives.

Consequences of administration

The appointment of an administrator has the following effects:

- the rights of creditors to enforce any security over the company's assets are suspended

- there can be no enforcement of charges, retention of title clauses or hire-purchase agreements against the company

- any outstanding petition for winding up is dismissed

- no resolution may be passed to wind up the company

- the directors still continue in office, but their powers are suspended.

Carrying out the administration

The administrator has a number of tasks:

- He is the company's agent, but must act in the best interests of all the company's creditors. He can do anything necessary for the management of the company.

- He has wide powers to manage the business and property of the company, including the power to bring and defend legal proceedings, sell assets and borrow money. With regards to selling assets this includes property which is subject to both fixed and floating charges, which may be disposed of without the consent of the charge holder, although they retain first call against any money realised by the sale of the asset. In respect of assets subject to fixed charges, this will require the court's permission.

- He has the power to remove and replace directors and employees. If an employee's contract is not adopted by the administrator within 14 days, that employee is made redundant.

- He can pay out monies to secured or preferential creditors without the need to seek approval of the court. He can also pay out monies to unsecured creditors but this must be with the approval of the court.

The administrator also has a number of legal duties. As soon as is reasonably practicable after appointment:

- He must send notice of appointment to the company and publish notice of appointment.

- He must obtain a list of company creditors and send notice of appointment to each.

- Within 7 days of appointment, he must send notice of appointment to the Registrar.

- He will arrange for certain relevant people to provide a statement of affairs of the company.

- He must ensure that every business document of the company bears his identity as administrator and a statement that the company affairs and property are being managed by him.

- Based on the statement of affairs, he must draw up a statement of his proposals within eight weeks of his appointment.

- The proposals must be approved by the creditors of the company. This approval can be given by:

  - Deemed consent process

  - Virtual meeting

  - Some other reasonable method.

- The creditors have the right to form a creditors meeting of between 3 to 5 creditors. If formed the administrator must hold a meeting of the creditors within 6 weeks of its establishment.

- If the creditors do not approve the proposals, the court may dismiss the administrator or make such provisions as it sees fit.

- If the creditors approve the proposals, the administrator can carry them out.

Ending the administration

The administration will end when it is completed or when the administrator is discharged by the court:

- The administration must normally be completed within 12 months of the date on which it commenced. However, this term can be extended with the consent of the court or the secured creditors.

- The administrator may apply to the court for discharge at any time. He must make an application when the purpose of the order has been achieved. He must also notify the Registrar and all of the creditors.

5 Chapter summary

Test your understanding answers

Test your understanding 1

A voluntary winding up takes place when the company resolves by special resolution to be wound up for any cause whatsoever: S84 Insolvency Act 1986.

In both cases of voluntary winding up the passing of the resolution, which must be advertised within 14 days in the London Gazette, has the following consequences:

I   The winding up commences from the time of the passing of the resolution.

II   The company ceases to carry on business, except in so far as is necessary for its beneficial winding up.

III   All transfers of shares, except those made with the concurrence of the liquidator, are void.

In the case of a members' voluntary winding up, the directors make a declaration of solvency stating that after full inquiry into the company's affairs they are of the opinion that the company will be able to pay its debts within 12 months of the commencement of the winding up. In a creditors' voluntary winding up, such a declaration is not possible owing to the circumstances leading to the winding up. In a members' voluntary winding up, the liquidator is appointed by the members and is accountable to them. In a creditors' voluntary winding up, the members appoint a liquidator which is followed by the directors delivering notice to the creditors seeking their decision on the liquidator. The creditors can approve the liquidator either by virtual meeting or the 'deemed consent' process. Under this process approval is deemed unless 10% of the creditors of the company raise objections to the proposed liquidator. The members and creditors may appoint up to five persons to serve on a liquidation committee. Here the liquidator is primarily accountable to the creditors.

Test your understanding 2

The possible grounds for a compulsory liquidation petition are set out in s122 IA 1986:

A   The company has passed a special resolution to be wound up by the court.

B   A public company has not been issued with a trading certificate within a year of incorporation.

C   A creditor who is owed at least £750 has served a written demand for payment and the company has failed to pay the sum due within three weeks.

D   It is just and equitable to wind up the company.

Test your understanding 3

The liquidator will repay in the following order:

Midwest Bank – the charge on the company's headquarters is a fixed charge.

Mrs Patel – employees who are owed holiday pay are classed as preferential creditors.

Barlloyd Bank – the charge over all the company's current assets is a floating charge.

HMRC – the Enterprise Act 2002 removed HMRC from the category of preferential creditors. They now rank as unsecured creditors.

Preference shareholders.

Ordinary shareholders – the ordinary shareholders will share in any surplus assets.

Corporate and fraudulent behaviour

Chapter learning objectives

Upon completion of this chapter you will be able to:

- recognise the nature and legal control over insider dealing and market abuse

- recognise the nature and legal control over money laundering

- recognise the nature and legal control over bribery

- discuss potential criminal activity in the operation, management and winding up of companies

- distinguish between fraudulent and wrongful trading.

1 Insider dealing

The value of a share reflects the profitability and future prospects of a company. This type of information is usually only available to a prospective purchaser after it has been made available publicly. However, if a prospective purchaser could gain access to such information before it was made public, he could anticipate which way the price was likely to move and thereby make a profit. This is known as 'insider dealing'. Insider dealing has been made a criminal offence as it is perceived to undermine the integrity of the stock market.

Legislation

Insider dealing is a crime under part V of the Criminal Justice Act 1993.

The offences

The Criminal Justice Act 1993 sets out the three distinct offences in s52.

An individual will be guilty of insider dealing if they have information as an insider and:

- they deal in price-affected securities on the basis of that information
- they encourage another person to deal in price-affected securities in relation to that information
- they disclose the information to anyone other than in the proper performance of their employment, office or profession.

Dealing

Dealing is defined in s55 as acquiring or disposing of securities, whether as a principal or agent, or agreeing to acquire securities.

Inside information

S56 defines inside information as information which:

- relates to particular securities or to a particular issuer of securities
- is specific or precise
- has not been made public
- if made public would be likely to have a significant effect on the price.

Insider

S57 states that a person has information as an insider if they know that it is inside information and they have it from an inside source.

A person has information from an inside source if:

- he has it through being a director, employee or shareholder of an issuer of securities
- he has it through having access to information by virtue of his employment, office or profession
- the direct or indirect source of the information is a person within either of these categories.

Defences

When dealing in securities, or encouraging another to do so, a person will not be guilty of insider dealing where the individual is able to show that he did not, at the time, expect the dealing to result in a profit or in the avoidance of a loss in relation to the inside information which he knew.

It is also a defence where the insider believed on reasonable grounds that the information had been disclosed widely enough to ensure that none of those taking part in the dealing would be prejudiced by now having the information.

Where the defendant is able to show that he would have dealt with the securities in the same way or encouraged another to deal with the securities in the same way, even if he had not possessed the inside information, he will have a defence.

Consequences

On summary conviction an individual found guilty of insider dealing is liable to a fine not exceeding the statutory maximum and/or a maximum of six months imprisonment.

On indictment the penalty is an unlimited fine and/or a maximum of seven years imprisonment.

If the individual concerned is a director, he is in breach of his fiduciary duty and may be liable to account to the company for any profit made.

Test your understanding 1

1   Which statute contains the legislation on insider dealing?

2   What are the three sub-categories of the offence of insider dealing?

3   What are the three general defences to a charge of insider dealing?

2   Market abuse

Legislation

The Financial Services and Markets Act 2000 introduces concept of market abuse.

Under s118 (1) market abuse is defined as:

- behaviour in relation to any qualifying investments

- likely to be regarded by regular users of the market as falling below the standard reasonably expected of a person in that position; and

- that falls within at least one of three categories:

  1   Based on information not generally available to users of the market which, if available to a regular user, would be likely to be regarded by him as relevant in regard to the terms on which to deal in those investments.

  2   Is likely to give a regular user a false or misleading impression as to the market value of such investments.

  3   Is regarded by a regular user as likely to distort the market in such investments.

Qualifying investments are those which are traded on the UK's 'prescribed markets', as well as those traded on other European regulated markets.

The Financial Conduct Authority have also drawn up a Code of Market Conduct to detail the ways in which market abuse can occur.

There are seven types of behaviour which can amount to market abuse.

Insider dealing

As discussed above in section 1 insider dealing is when an insider deals, or tries to deal, on the basis of inside information.

Improper disclosure

This is where an insider improperly discloses inside information to another person and is also classified as insider dealing.

Illustration 1

An employee finds out that his company is about to become the target of a takeover bid. Before the information is made public, he buys shares in his company because he knows a takeover bid may be imminent. He then discloses the information to a friend.

This behaviour creates an unfair market place because the person who sold the shares to the employee might not have done so if he had known of the potential takeover. The employee's friend also has this information and could profit unfairly from it.

Misuse of information

This is any behaviour based on information that is not generally available but would affect an investor's decision about the terms on which to deal. This is also a type of insider dealing.

 Illustration 2

An employee learns that his company may lose a significant contract with its main customer. The employee then sells his shares, based on his assessment that it is reasonably certain.

This behaviour creates an unfair market place as the person buying the shares from the employee might not have done so had he been aware of the information about the potential loss of the contract.

Manipulating transactions

This is trading, or placing orders to trade, that gives a false or misleading impression of the supply of, or demand for, one or more investments, raising the price of the investment to an abnormal or artificial level.

 Illustration 3

A person buys a large number of a particular share near the end of the day, aiming to drive the stock price higher to improve the performance of their investment. The market price is pushed to an artificial level and investors get a false impression of the price of those shares and the value of any portfolio or fund that holds the stock. This could lead to people making the wrong investment decision.

Manipulating devices

This is trading, or placing orders to trade, which employs fictitious devices or any other form of deception or contrivance.

Illustration 4

A person buys shares and then spreads misleading information with a view to increasing the price. This could give investors a false impression of the price of a share and lead them to make the wrong investment decision.

Dissemination

This is the giving out of information that conveys a false or misleading impression about an investment or the issuer of an investment where the person doing this knows the information to be false or misleading.

Illustration 5

A person uses an internet bulletin board or chat room to post information about the takeover of a company. The person knows the information to be false or misleading. This could artificially raise or reduce the price of a share and lead to people making the wrong investment decisions.

Distortion and misleading behaviour

This is behaviour that gives a false or misleading impression of either the supply of, or demand for, an investment: or behaviour that otherwise distorts the market in an investment.

Illustration 6

There is movement of an empty cargo ship that is used to transport a particular commodity. This could create a false impression of changes in the supply of, or demand for, that commodity or the related futures contract. It could also artificially change the price of that commodity or the futures contract, and lead to people making the wrong investment decisions.

Consequences

Market abuse as defined in the Code can result in an unlimited fine and a public reprimand by the Financial Conduct Authority under civil law.

3 Money laundering

 Definition

Money laundering is the process by which the proceeds of crime are converted into assets which appear to have a legal rather than an illegal source. The aim of disguising the source of the property is to allow the holder to enjoy it free from suspicion as to its source.

Legislation

Money laundering is primarily regulated by the Proceeds of Crime Act 2002.

The legislation imposes some important obligations upon professionals, such as accountants, auditors and legal advisers. These obligations require such professionals to report money laundering to the authorities and to have systems in place to train staff and keep records.

The three phases

Money laundering usually comprises three distinct phases:

- placement – the initial disposal of the proceeds of criminal activity into an apparently legitimate business activity or property

- layering – the transfer of money from business to business, or place to place, in order to conceal its initial source

- integration – the culmination of the previous procedures through which the money takes on the appearance of coming from a legitimate source.

The offences

The Proceeds of Crime Act 2002 created three categories of criminal offence: laundering, failure to report, and tipping off.

Laundering

It is an offence to conceal, disguise, convert, transfer, or remove criminal property from England, Wales, Scotland or Northern Ireland: s327 Proceeds of Crime Act 2002.

Concealing or disguising criminal property includes concealing or disguising its nature, source, location, disposition, movement or ownership, or any rights connected with it.

'Criminal property' is defined as property which the alleged offender knows (or suspects) constitutes or represents benefit from any criminal conduct.

'Criminal conduct' is defined as conduct that:

- constitutes an offence in any part of the UK

- would constitute an offence in any part of the UK if it occurred there.

Failure to report

Under s330 individuals carrying on a 'relevant business' may be guilty of an offence of failing to disclose knowledge or suspicion of money laundering where they know or suspect, or have reasonable grounds for knowing or suspecting, that another person is engaged in laundering the proceeds of crime.

This offence only relates to individuals, such as accountants, who are acting in the course of business in the regulated sector.

Any individual who is covered by s330 is required to make disclosure to a nominated money laundering reporting officer within their organisation, or directly to the National Crime Agency, as soon as is practicable.

Tipping off

Section 333 states that it is an offence to make a disclosure likely to prejudice a money laundering investigation. It therefore covers the situation where an accountant informs a client that a report has been submitted to the National Crime Agency.

Penalties

The maximum penalty for the s327 offence of money laundering is 14 years' imprisonment.

Failure to report and tipping off are punishable on conviction by a maximum of five years' imprisonment and/or a fine.

Money Laundering Regulations 2017

Secondary regulation is provided by the Money Laundering Regulations 2017.

The Money Laundering Regulations 2017 implemented the EU's Fourth Money Laundering Directive.

The Regulations require firms to put preventative measures in place. They require firms to ensure that they know their customers by conducting customer identification and verification and undertake ongoing monitoring where applicable, to keep records of identity and to train their staff on the requirements of the Regulations.

At a minimum, an anti-money laundering program should incorporate:

- Money laundering and terrorist financing risk assessment.

- Implementation of systems, policies, controls and procedures that effectively manage the risk that the firm is exposed to in relation to money laundering activities and ensure compliance with the legislation.

- Compliance with customer due diligence, enhanced due diligence and simplified due diligence requirements.

- Enhanced record keeping and data protection systems, policies and procedures.

The Regulations cover most financial firms such as banks, building societies, money transmitters, bureaux de change, cheque cashers and savings and investment firms. In addition the Regulations cover legal professionals, accountants, tax advisers, auditors, insolvency practitioners, estate agents, casinos, high value dealers when dealing in goods worth over 15,000 Euro and trust or company service providers.

There are various regulators and professional bodies who have been given supervisory authority. For example, the Financial Conduct Authority supervises all financial firms covered by the Regulations and the Office of Fair Trading supervises all consumer credit firms and estate agents.

Money laundering and terrorist financing risk assessment

A written risk assessment must be carried out to identify and assess the risk of money laundering. The risk assessment must take into account information provided by the supervisory authority on risk factors in the sector. The following risk factors must also be taken into account:

- The firm's customers
- The countries or geographic where the firm operates
- The firm's products or services
- The firm's transactions, and
- The firm's delivery channels.

The risk assessment should be used to:

- Develop policies, procedures and controls to mitigate the risk of money laundering.
- Apply a risk based approach to detecting and preventing money laundering.

The firm must establish and maintain written policies, controls and procedures to effectively manage and mitigate the money laundering and terrorist financing risks identified in the risk assessment. These must be proportionate to the size and nature of the business, approved by senior management, regularly reviewed and updated and communicated internally within the firm.

Officer responsible for compliance

Firms must appoint a Money Laundering Compliance Principal (MLCP) and this person must be on the board of directors or a member of senior management. Sole practitioners with no employees are exempt from this requirement.

Firms must also appoint a nominated officer, Money Laundering Reporting Officer (MLRO), to receive internal suspicious activity reports and assess whether a suspicious activity report should be made to the appropriate regulatory body. The MLRO and MLCP may be the same person if the MLRO is sufficiently senior.

Employees

Firms must assess the skills, knowledge, conduct and integrity of employees involved in identification, preventing or detecting money laundering.

Staff training must be provided on an ongoing basis in how to recognise and handle transactions and activities which may be related to money laundering.

Customer due diligence

Accountants are required to establish that new clients are who they claim to be by obtaining satisfactory evidence of identity from the client. This is often referred to as 'customer due diligence' or 'know your customer' procedures.

Customer due diligence is an essential part of the anti-money laundering requirements. It ensures that accountants:

- know who their clients are, and

- do not unknowingly accept clients which are too high risk.

Customer due diligence must be performed as soon as is reasonably practicable after contact is first made between the two parties.

Enhanced due diligence

For higher risk clients, enhanced due diligence must be carried out. Enhanced due diligence procedures include examining the background and purpose of the transaction and increased monitoring of the business relationship.

Simplified due diligence

For clients presenting a lower risk of money laundering, simplified due diligence may be carried out.

Office for Professional Body Anti-Money Laundering Supervision

The Office for Professional Body Anti-Money Laundering Supervision (OPBAS) was established by the Government in 2018 under the OPBAS Regulations 2018. The Regulations give OPBAS duties and powers to ensure that the 22 accountancy and legal professional body anti-money laundering supervisors meet the standards required by the Money Laundering Regulations 2017 and they have powers to investigate those that do not.

Test your understanding 2
1   **Which Act contains the legislation on money laundering?**
2   **To which organisation must you report suspicions of money laundering?**
3   **Which of the three money laundering offences only applies to individuals, such as accountants, who are in business in the regulated sector?**
4   **What is meant by the term 'money laundering'?**

4 Bribery

Definition

Bribery is an act implying money or gift given that alters the behaviour of the recipient. It is the offering, giving, receiving, or soliciting of any item of value to influence the actions of an official or other person in charge of a public or legal duty.

Legislation

The Bribery Act 2010 came into force on 1 July 2011.

The Act creates four offences:

- bribing a person to induce or reward them to perform a relevant function improperly (S1)

- requesting, accepting or receiving a bribe as a reward for performing a relevant function improperly (S2)

- using a bribe to influence a foreign official to gain a business advantage (S6)

- a new form of corporate liability for failing to prevent bribery on behalf of a commercial organisation (S7).

Commercial organisation has a wide meaning and includes partnerships, limited liability partnerships and companies which carry on business.

Defence

Under S9 for a commercial organisation it is a defence to have in place 'adequate procedures' to prevent bribery. This may include implementing anti-bribery procedures. It is important that firms consider what adequate procedures are most appropriate for their firm given the risks they face and the way they run their business. The procedures should be proportionate to the risk posed.

For some firms there will be no need to put bribery prevention procedures in place as there is no risk of bribery on their behalf. Other firms may need to put in place measures in key areas, such as gifts and hospitality, as this is the area where they have identified a risk.

Penalties

The penalty for individuals is a maximum sentence of 10 years.

For commercial organisations there may be an unlimited fine.

Deferred prosecution agreement

Deferred prosecution agreements (DPA) became available to prosecutors in the UK in February 2014 under the Crime and Courts Act 2013.

A DPA allows commercial organisations to settle allegations of criminal economic activity without being prosecuted and without any formal admission of guilt.

An agreement is made between the prosecutor and the commercial organisation, under which the prosecutor will bring criminal charges but then immediately suspend the process, on the basis that the organisation has agreed to a number of conditions determined by the prosecutor such as paying a financial penalty or co-operating with the future prosecution of individuals. If the organisation does not honour the conditions, the prosecution may resume.

Test your understanding 3

A manager at a manufacturing company who has overall responsibility for the procurement of a service which is currently subject to re-tender is approached by the current supplier and offered (at the expense of the company) a day trip to London, including lunch in Harrods and a trip on the London Eye. The company says the offer is "to cement and say thank you for our longstanding business relationship".

Advise the company as to whether there are any implications of accepting the proposed hospitality.

5 Potential criminal activity in the operation, management and winding up of companies

Introduction

There are a number of criminal offences that could be undertaken by individuals concerned in the operation, management or winding up of a company. Many of these points have been covered in earlier chapters and so are only dealt with in outline here.

Failure to file accounts or annual returns

Failure to deliver accounts or annual returns on time is a criminal offence. All the directors of a company in default could be prosecuted. If convicted, a director could end up with a criminal record and a fine of up to £5,000 for each offence.

Providing misleading information to an auditor

Under s499 CA 2006, an auditor is entitled to require from the company's officers and employees such information and explanation as he thinks necessary for the performance of his duties as auditor. It is a criminal offence for an officer of the company to:

- provide misleading, false or deceptive information or explanations, or

- fail to provide information or explanations required by the auditor.

An individual can defend such as charge if he can prove that it was not reasonably practicable to provide the information or explanations required.

Business name

Under s82 Companies Act 2006 it is a criminal offence to use a business name that requires prior approval, if that approval has not been obtained.

It is also a criminal offence to fail to disclose the business details that the Act requires. These details include stating the company's corporate name and address for the service of documents.

Company Directors Disqualification Act 1986 (CDDA 1986)

Under s13 CDDA 1986, any person who acts in contravention of a disqualification order (or while an undischarged bankrupt) is guilty of an offence. The maximum penalty is:

- two years' imprisonment and/or a fine on conviction on indictment

- up to six months' imprisonment and/or a fine not exceeding the statutory maximum on a summary conviction.

S15 CDDA 1986, provides that anyone who is involved in the management of a company while disqualified, or who acts on the instructions of someone who is disqualified, shall be personally liable for the company's debts incurred during the time they acted.

Phoenix companies

S216 and s217 Insolvency Act 1986 (IA 1986) are aimed at so-called 'phoenix companies'. They apply where a person was a director or shadow director of a company at any time in the period of 12 months ending with the day before the company went into liquidation.

 The provisions apply for the five years following liquidation. They prevent the person being a director of a company with a similar name, or a name which suggests an association with the previous company, without leave of the court.

It is a criminal offence to contravene the provisions, punishable by imprisonment and/or a fine. In addition, the director will be personally liable for any debts of the new company which are incurred when he was involved in its management.

The Fraud Act 2006

The Fraud Act 2006 radically changed the law of criminal fraud.

Before the Fraud Act came into force, the statutory fraud offences under the Theft Act 1978 were based on deception. They included:

- Obtaining property by deception.

- Obtaining a money transfer by deception.

- Obtaining a pecuniary advantage by deception.

- Obtaining services by deception.

The Fraud Act swept all of the old statutory deception offences away. Instead a new offence of fraud has been defined as follows:

- The defendant must have been dishonest, and have intended to make a gain or to cause a loss to another; and

- The defendant must carry out one of these acts:

  - s2: fraud by making a false or misleading representation, this being where any person makes "any representation as to fact or law ... express or implied" which they know to be untrue or misleading.

  - s3: fraud by failing to disclose information whereby a person fails to disclose any information to a third party when they are under a legal duty to disclose such information.

  - s4: fraud by abuse of position where a person occupies a position where they are expected to safeguard the financial interests of another person, and abuses that position; this includes cases where the abuse consisted of an omission rather than an overt act.

The new offence of fraud is intended to be wide and also flexible. There is no reliance on the concept of "deception". It does not matter whether the false information actually deceives anyone, it is the misleading intention which counts.

Failure to prevent tax evasion

The Criminal Finances Act 2017 sets out the corporate offence on failure to prevent the criminal facilitation of criminal tax evasion.

The offence can make a 'relevant body' criminally liable if it fails to prevent the facilitation of UK or non-UK tax evasion by an employee or 'associated person'. The offence applies to both UK and non-UK companies as well as partnerships, as if they were corporations.

An 'associated person' can be an individual, corporate entity or an employee of a corporate associated person, carrying out services on behalf of the 'relevant body'.

A 'relevant body' is defined in the act as a company or a partnership.

The offence is of strict liability and no knowledge or intention is required. There is no requirement for the tax evader to have been prosecuted for evasion, or for the facilitator to have been prosecuted for facilitation.

The legislation focuses on the procedures that should be in place to prevent the criminal facilitation of tax evasion by an employee or associated person.

There are three stages to the offence:

- Stage one: The criminal evasion of tax.

- Stage two: The criminal facilitation of this offence by an associated person.

- Stage three: The relevant body failed to prevent the associated person from committing that facilitation.

There is a statutory defence where at the time of the offence the relevant body had reasonable prevention procedures in place to prevent tax evasion facilitation offences or where it is unreasonable to expect such procedures. The reasonable prevention procedures are judged by six guiding principles:

1   Risk assessment

2   Proportionality of risk-based prevention procedures

3   Top level commitment

4   Due diligence

5   Communication

6   Monitoring and review

The penalty is an unlimited fine for the relevant body and potential reputational damage.

6   Transactions at an undervalue and preference

A liquidator may apply to the court to set aside company transactions at an undervalue (s238 Insolvency Act 1986) or where the company gives a preference (s239 Insolvency Act 1986).

Undervalue

A company enters into a transaction at an undervalue if the company makes a gift or otherwise enters into a transaction on terms that the company receives not consideration or insufficient consideration.

The transaction would not be set aside if it was entered into in good faith on the reasonable belief that it would benefit the company.

Preferences

A company gives a preference if it does anything to put a creditor in a better position in the event of the company's insolvent liquidation than they would otherwise be.

The court will not make an order unless the company was influenced by a desire to prefer the creditor. Therefore, a payment or charge created in favour of a creditor who is threatening legal proceedings might be a defence. However, if the preference was given to a connected person it is presumed that the company was influenced by its desire to give a preference.

7 Fraudulent and wrongful trading

 Fraudulent trading

Fraudulent trading occurs where the company's business is carried on with intent to defraud creditors or for any fraudulent purpose.

Fraudulent trading can give rise to:

- civil liability under s213 Insolvency Act 1986 if the company is in the course of being wound up

- criminal liability under s993 CA06 whether or not the company is in the course of being wound up.

It is necessary to establish **dishonest intent**. In **Re William C Leith Bros (1932)** it was said that if the directors carry on the business and cause the company to incur further debts at a time when they know that there is no reasonable prospect of those debts being paid this is a proper inference of dishonesty. The court also added that if the directors honestly believed the debts would eventually be paid there would be no intent to defraud.

R v Grantham (1984)

Facts: The directors ordered a consignment of potatoes on a month's credit at a time when they knew that payment would not be forthcoming at the end of the month when it was due.

Held: The directors were convicted of fraudulent trading.

The second point required to establish liability is that the person concerned shall be **knowingly a party** to the fraudulent trading.

In **Re Maidstone Buildings (1971)** it was established that a person is not 'party' merely by reason of knowledge. They must take some active step, such as the ordering of goods.

Fraudulent trading can give rise to the following consequences:

- The court can order the individual to contribute to the company's assets.

- If a director, they may be disqualified for 15 years under CDDA86.

- If found guilty of the criminal offence, the individual can be fined and/or imprisoned for up to 10 years.

Wrongful trading

 Wrongful trading occurs where on a winding-up it appears to the court that the company has gone into insolvent liquidation and, before the start of winding up, the director knew or ought to have known that there was **no reasonable prospect that the company would avoid going into insolvent liquidation:** S214 Insolvency Act 1986.

The provision of 'wrongful trading' contained in S214 IA86 is designed to remove one of the difficult obstacles to the establishment of being party to fraudulent trading – namely proving dishonesty. **It applies only to directors and shadow directors.**

The director is expected to reach those conclusions and take such steps as a reasonably diligent person would take. The legislation also expects such a director to:

- have the general knowledge, skill and experience which may reasonably be expected of a person carrying out the same functions as were carried out by that director (i.e. this is an objective test)

- use the general knowledge, skill and experience he himself has (i.e. this is a subjective test).

When considering the director's functions, the court will have regard not only to those functions he carried out but also to those entrusted to him. This means that the director could be made liable for those actions he should have carried out but failed to.

Re Produce Marketing Consortium Ltd (No 2) (1989)

Facts: The company, after trading successfully for nine years, built up an overdraft, had a continuing trading loss and had an excess of liabilities over assets. In February 1987 the directors recognised that liquidation was inevitable but carried on trading until October 1987, arguing that this period of trading minimised the loss to creditors by allowing an orderly disposal, for value, of the company's goods.

Held: The court required them to contribute £75,000 to the assets of the company (equating to the net debts incurred during the wrongful trading period) on the grounds that:

- they would have known that liquidation was inevitable in July 1986 had the company produced timely internal accounts and this therefore marked the beginning of the period from which they should have been minimising losses to creditors

- while trading on to dispose of assets might sometimes be justifiable, the directors had done no more than dispose of assets and so had failed to take every step to minimise losses.

Wrongful trading can give rise to the following consequences:

- a liquidator may apply to the court for an order that the director should make such contribution to the company's assets as the court thinks fit, thereby increasing the assets available for distribution to the creditors

- They may be disqualified for 15 years under CDDA86.

Test your understanding 4

Explain the main differences between a director fraudulently trading and wrongfully trading.

(Your answer must not exceed 40 words.)

8 Chapter summary

Money laundering
- laundering
- failure to report
- tipping off.

Insider dealing
- dealing in price-
  affected securities
- encouraging
  another to deal
- disclosing
  information.

**Fraudulent
behaviour**

Fraudulent trading
- business carried on
  with intent to defraud
- criminal offence.

Wrongful trading
- no reasonable prospect
  of avoiding insolvent
  liquidation.

Test your understanding answers

Test your understanding 1

1   Criminal Justice Act 1993.

2   Dealing in securities.

   Encouraging another person to deal. Disclosing information.

   Did not expect the dealing to result in a profit.

3   Believed the information had been disclosed.

   Would have done what he did even without the information.

Test your understanding 2

1   The Proceeds of Crime Act 2002.

2   National Crime Agency.

3   Failure to report.

4   Money laundering is the process by which the proceeds of crime are converted into assets which appear to have a legal rather than an illegal source. The aim of disguising the source of the property is to allow the holder to enjoy it free from suspicion as to its source.

Test your understanding 3

This could be interpreted as an attempt to influence the manager actions in the current tendering and therefore be considered bribery under the Bribery Act 2010. The offer of hospitality should be refused.

Test your understanding 4

Fraudulent trading is trading with intent to defraud creditors and is a criminal offence. Wrongful trading occurs when it was known or ought to have been known that insolvency was unavoidable, and is not a criminal offence.

Questions & Answers

1   English legal system

Question 1

Which of the following identifies civil proceedings?

A   A prosecution for murder.

B   An action by a claimant for a breach of contract.

C   A prosecution by HMRC for non-payment of tax.

D   Proceedings where the accused is tried for the offence of money laundering.

Question 2

All criminal cases commence in:

A   he County Court

B   the Crown Court

C   the Court of Appeal

D   the Magistrates Court

Question 3

Which one of the following statements about the law of equity is untrue?

A   Equitable remedies may only be awarded at the discretion of the court.

B   Equity is concerned with fairness.

C   Equitable remedies include damages, injunctions and decrees of specific performance.

D   Equity will prevail in a case of conflict between it and the common law.

Question 4

Statements made obiter dicta are:

A   Binding in lower courts as they are principles of law relating to the facts of the case.

B   Binding in any court which hears a similar case.

C   Not binding unless they are made by the European Court of Justice.

D   Not binding at all.

Question 5

Which of the following describes the 'golden rule' of statutory interpretation?

A   A statute should be construed to avoid absurdity.

B   Words in a statute should be given their ordinary meaning.

C   A statute should be interpreted in such a way to give the intended legal effect.

D   Words in a statute should be interpreted in their intended context.

2   Contract law

Question 6

What is the limitation period for a contract that is made by deed?

A   5 years

B   6 years

C   12 years

D   30 years

Question 7

An offer was made by letter posted in London and delivered in Birmingham. A reply was made by facsimile machine in Manchester and received by the offeror's machine in Liverpool.

Where is the contract made?

A   Where the offer was made – in London.

B   Where the acceptance was put into the facsimile machine – in Manchester.

C   Where the acceptance was received on the facsimile machine – in Liverpool.

D   Where the letter making the offer was received – in Birmingham.

Question 8

Dee Ltd has broken one of the terms of its contract with E Ltd. If that term is a condition, which of the following is correct?

A   E Ltd is entitled to damages only.

B   E Ltd is entitled to sue for damages or to repudiate the contract.

C   E Ltd is only entitled to repudiate the contract.

D   E Ltd may repudiate the contract and sue for damages.

Question 9

Which of the following examples of performance amounts to good consideration?

(I)   The performance of an existing duty under general law.

(II)   The performance of an existing contract in return for a promise by a third party.

(III)   The performance of an act, followed by a promise to pay for that act.

A   (I) only

B   (II) only

C   (I) and (II) only

D   (III) only

Question 10

A Ltd contracts with B Ltd to supply 1 1/2 tonnes of cement each day for a 100 day period. The thirteenth delivery is defective. Which of the following is correct?

A   A fundamental term has been breached and B Ltd can treat the contract as discharged because the contract must be performed exactly.

B   Damages only will be payable because this is a minor breach in relation to the whole contract.

C   The contract is frustrated.

D   An order for specific performance is available to force another delivery.

Question 11

Where there has been anticipatory breach of contract the injured party is entitled to sue:

A   After a reasonable time.

B   Only from the moment the other party actually breaches a contractual condition.

C   From the moment the other party indicates that he does not intend to fulfil his contractual obligations.

D   From the moment that the injured party has fulfilled his obligations but the other party indicates that he does not intend to be bound.

Question 12

In an action for breach of contract, the court will not award:

A   Damages for financial loss

B   Unliquidated damages

C   Liquidated damages

D   Damages identified in a penalty clause

Question 13

In which of the following is there a presumption that legal relations are intended?

A   A promise by a father to make a gift to his son

B   A commercial transaction

C   A domestic arrangement

D   A social arrangement

Question 14

Mary cannot read. She buys a railway ticket on which is printed 'conditions – see back'. The back of the ticket stated that the ticket was subject to conditions printed in the timetable. These included an exclusion clause of liability for injury. During Mary's journey, a heavy bag fell off the racks and injured her.

What is the legal position?

A   The ticket office contained no notice of conditions of carriage and the railway could not rely on the notice given on the back of the ticket.

B   The conditions are contained in the timetable. As such, they are adequately communicated and the railway can avoid liability.

C   The railway cannot rely on Mary being able to read. The conditions should have been communicated to him verbally and the railway cannot avoid liability.

D   The railway cannot rely on the notice disclaiming liability as the contract had been made previously and the disclaimer was made too late.

Question 15

Which of the following statements best describes consideration?

A   Consideration must be adequate and sufficient.

B   Consideration must be adequate but need not be sufficient.

C   Consideration must be sufficient but need not be adequate.

D   Consideration need be neither sufficient nor adequate.

Question 16

Hilary advertised a printing press in a specialist trade journal for £15,000. Eleanor wrote to Hilary offering to buy it for £10,000. Hilary replied by return of post saying she would accept £13,000. When she heard nothing further from Eleanor, Hilary wrote again saying she would accept £10,000.

Task 1 (2 marks)

Identify whether the following statements are true or false.

	True	False
An offer cannot be made to the whole world		
The advert in the trade journal is an offer		

Task 2 (2 marks)

Identify whether the following statements are true or false.

	True	False
Eleanor's letter to Hilary is a counter-offer		
Hilary's first reply to Eleanor is a counter-offer		

Task 3 (2 marks)

Identify whether the following statements are true or false.

	True	False
The effect of a counter-offer is to bring the original offer to an end		
Hilary's second reply to Eleanor accepting £10,000 constitutes acceptance		

(Total: 6 marks)

3 The law of torts

Question 17

Which of the following does NOT need to be shown by the claimant in order to succeed in an action for negligence?

A   That the defendant owed him a duty of care.

B   That the defendant was in breach of a duty of care.

C   That the claimant suffered injury, damage or loss as a result of a breach of a duty of care.

D   That the damage was too remote.

Question 18

In an action for negligence:

Does there need to be some sort of pre-existing relationship between the claimant and defendant?

A   Yes

B   No

Does the court need to be satisfied that public policy would allow a duty of care to exist?

C   Yes

D   No

Question 19

Which of the following is NOT considered in determining whether a duty of care exists?

A   Whether it is fair that the law should impose a duty on the defendant.

B   Whether the defendant intended to cause injury to the claimant.

C   Whether it was reasonably foreseeable that the claimant might suffer damage as a result of the defendant's actions.

D   Whether there is sufficient proximity between the parties.

Question 20

In respect of audited accounts, to whom does an auditor owe a duty of care not to act negligently?

A   The shareholders only

B   The company only

C   Anyone who relies on the accounts for investment purposes

D   The company and the shareholders only

Question 21

Brad owns a property which Albert wishes to rent. Brad writes to Albert's accountant for a reference relating to Albert's financial situation. The accountant, Charles, confuses Albert with another client and does not bother to check the file properly. He replies to Brad that Albert is an excellent client with high income and capital and recommends him as a tenant.

In fact had he looked at the correct file, he would have seen that Albert was continuously in overdraft and had been in serious debt with various banks on and off for several years.

Some months later, Albert disappears having taken the flat on and run up several thousand pounds' worth of rent arrears.

Task 1 (2 marks)

Which of the following TWO statements are correct?

- **There is no need to show a loss has been made to make a claim for negligence**

- **There must have been a loss made to make a claim in negligence**

- **There must be a causal link to make a claim for negligence**

- **There is no need to show a causal link to make a claim for negligence**

Task 2 (2 marks)

Which of the following loss is normally not recoverable?

- **Loss as a result of personal injury**

- **Damage to property**

- **Financial loss directly connected to personal injury**

- **Pure financial loss**

Task 3 (2 marks)

Which of the following TWO statements are correct?

- **The accountant owes a duty of care to Brad**

- **The accountant does not owe a duty of care to Brad**

- **The accountant will be liable for the losses which Brad has suffered**

- **The accountant will not be liable for the losses which Brad has suffered**

(Total: 6 marks)

4   Employment law

Question 22

Indira works at Funky Flowers Ltd. Which ONE of the following factors is consistent with her being treated as self-employed?

A   Indira's employer deducts tax at source

B   Indira wears a Funky Flowers apron at work

C   Indira is entitled to holiday pay

D   Indira provides her own car for delivering flowers

Question 23

Within what time period must an employer provide a written statement of employment particulars to an employee following commencement of his employment (in the absence of an employment contract)?

A   14 days

B   28 days

C   2 months

D   3 months

Question 24

Which of the following does NOT constitute a duty owed by an employee towards his employer under the common law?

A   A duty not to misuse confidential information

B   A duty to provide faithful service

C   A duty to maintain trust and confidence

D   A duty to obey all orders given to him by his employer

Question 25

Joan, aged 62, had worked for Fabulous Fabrics for 25 years and the employment tribunal has ruled that she was unfairly dismissed Which of the following best illustrates the calculation of the basic award to which she will be entitled?

A   1.5 weeks' pay × 20

B   1.5 weeks' pay × 25

C   1 week's pay × 20

D   1 week's pay × 25

KAPLAN PUBLISHING

Question 26

Annika has been working at Country Sofas Ltd for 18 months but her employment contract does not specify a period in the event of termination. What is the minimum period of notice to which she is entitled under the Employment Rights Act 1996?

A   At least 5 days

B   At least a week

C   At least two weeks

D   At least a month

Question 27

Carol ran a business in London which specialised in producing computer software programmes. Diana worked for Carol for a period of three years. She was described as self-employed and paid tax as a self-employed person. Carol provided her with specialist computer equipment. Diana usually worked at home and was allowed to work on other projects. She could even arrange for her work for Carol to be done by someone else if she was too busy to do it personally.

Recently, when Carol lost her most important contract, she told Diana that there would be no more work for her.

Task 1   **(2 marks)**

Identify whether the following statements are true or false.

	True	False
An employee works under a contract for services		
An independent contractor works under a contract of service		

Task 2   **(2 marks)**

Categorise the following factors into which indicate that Diana is self-employed and which that she is an employee

	Provision of Equipment	Right of Substitution
Self-employed		
Employed		

Task 3 (2 marks)

Assuming that it was concluded that Diana was self-employed, identify which of the following she could bring a claim for?

	Claim	Not claim
Redundancy		
Wrongful dismissal		

(Total: 6 marks)

(Adapted from ACCA June 2000)

5 Agency law

Question 28

Which of the following is incorrect in relation to a contract made by an agent acting within his authority?

A   The principal can sue on the contract

B   The third party can sue on the contract

C   The agent can be sued on the contract

D   The principal can be sued on the contract

Question 29

Simon lives in Devon and one day he sees an Aston Martin parked on the beach. No one is in sight but the tide is coming in rapidly. Simon calls his neighbour and arranges for him to come and tow the Aston Martin up the beach to safety. The neighbour is happy to oblige but wants payment for what he has done. When the owner, Mike, returns, he refuses to pay because he says the action was not necessary.

Which of the following best describes the legal position?

A   An agency of necessity has arisen because Simon is unable to contact Mike.

B   An agency of necessity has arisen because there is an emergency situation and a pressing need for action.

C   No agency of necessity has arisen because the Aston Martin is not a perishable good and Simon's action was not reasonable.

D   No agency of necessity has arisen because there is no existing pre-contractual relationship between Simon and Mike.

Question 30

Preparing for her 50th birthday party, Jean went into Wine Warehouse and ordered three cases of wine, saying she was buying them in her capacity as agent for Dame Helen, a well-known celebrity who lived in the same village and was planning a summer ball in the grounds of her country house. Wine Warehouse supplied the wine and then invoiced Dame Helen.

Is there an agency by holding out or estoppel?

A   Yes

B   No

Can Wine Warehouse demand payment from Dame Helen?

C   Yes

D   No

Question 31

Andrea worked for Lady Gertrude and part of her job was to buy plants, ornaments and furniture for the gardens of her country manor house.

Andrea ordered some very expensive roses and marble statues from Lady Gertrude's main supplier and collected the goods the next day for her own garden. The invoice was delivered to Lady Gertrude.

Task 1   **(2 marks)**

With regards to an agency relationship which of the following statements is correct?

- **The contract is made between the principal and the agent**

- **The contract is made between the principal and the third party**

- **The contract is made between the agent and the third party**

- **A binding contract cannot be created**

Task 2   **(2 marks)**

In the above situation, which ONE of the following best describes the agency relationship between Andrea and Lady Gertrude?

- **There is an agency relationship by ratification**

- **There is an agency relationship by express agreement**

- **There is an agency relationship by implied agreement**

- **There is an agency relationship by necessity**

Task 3 (2 marks)

Identify which of the following statements are true or false?

	True	False
Andrea has the express authority to purchase roses and statues		
Lady Gertrude would be liable to settle the invoice for the roses and statues		

(Total: 6 marks)

6 Types of business organisation

Question 32

Are the following statements true or false?

An ordinary partnership is a separate legal entity from its partners.

A   True

B   False

The Partnership Act 1890 governs the rights and duties of partners in an ordinary partnership, in the absence of an express provision to the contrary.

C   True

D   False

Question 33

Which of the following is NOT recognised as a separate legal entity?

A   A limited liability partnership

B   A private limited company

C   A public limited company

D   A general partnership

Question 34

Sharon and Tracy formed a general partnership 5 years ago. Two years ago the partnership employed Frank as its manager. Sharon and Tracy subsequently left much of the day-to-day work to Frank who has let it be known generally that he has become a partner, although he has not. In January of this year Frank entered into a large contract with a longstanding customer, Dorian, who had dealt with the partnership for some three years.

Dorian believed Frank's claim that he was a partner in the business.

This contract has gone badly wrong leaving the partnership owing £30,000 to Dorian and unfortunately the business assets will only cover the first £15,000 of the total debt.

Task 1 (2 marks)

Which of the following TWO are not features of a general partnership?

- **The partners have unlimited liability**
- **The partners have joint and several liability**
- **There must be a partnership agreement**
- **The partnership must be registered at Companies House**

Task 2 (2 marks)

Identify whether the following statements are true or false.

	True	False
A partnership is liable for contracts made by a partner if he is acting within his express authority only		
Dorian cannot make a claim against the partnership as she entered into the contract with Frank		

Task 3 (2 marks)

Who is liable for the £15,000 shortfall of the debt?

- **Sharon and Tracy only**
- **Frank only**
- **Sharon, Tracy and Frank**
- **None of the above**

(Total: 6 marks)

7   Corporations and legal personality

Question 35

A public limited company cannot commence business or borrow money until the nominal value of the company's allotted share capital is not less than:

A   £12,500

B   £25,000

C   £40,000

D   £50,000

Question 36

Within what period of time after the year end must a company file its accounts with the Registrar?

A   Three months for a public company and six months for a private company.

B   Nine months for a public company and seven months for a private company.

C   Six months for a public company and nine months for a private company.

D   Ten months for a public company and twelve months for a private company.

Question 37

The articles of association of a company forms a contract between:

A   The shareholders and the company in all respects.

B   The shareholders and the directors in all respects.

C   The company and the directors in respect of directors' rights only.

D   The company and the shareholders in respect of shareholder rights only.

Question 38

Sarah, a promoter, is in the process of incorporating Super Ltd, and has ordered goods to be used by the company. She has signed the order form 'Sarah, for and on behalf of Super Ltd'. Who is liable if the goods are not paid for?

A   Super Ltd

B   Sarah

C   Sarah and Super Ltd jointly

D   Neither Sarah nor Super Ltd as there is no contract

Question 39

Pam was formerly employed by Dallas Ltd. Her employment contract had a covenant to the effect that she should not compete with Dallas Ltd. The covenant is reasonable and not in restraint of trade. Pam has formed a company, Pam (Services) Ltd, which has started to trade in competition with Dallas Ltd.

Will Dallas Ltd be able to get an injunction to prevent Pam (Services) Ltd from trading?

A   No, because Pam (Services) Ltd has a separate legal entity.

B   Yes, because the company has been formed as a device to hide Pam's carrying on of that trade.

C   No, because a company is not liable for the actions of its shareholders.

D   Yes, because Pam (Services) Ltd is engaging in fraudulent trading.

Question 40

Ruby sets up a new company, Super Solutions Ltd, to continue her existing business. She enters into a contract on the 15th June 20X7 on the company's behalf with Ingrid Ltd for the purchase of stock with payment to be made 30 days later.

The certificate of incorporation was issued on the 1st July 20X7, it was received by Ruby on the 8th July 20X7 and the company started trading on the 15th July 20X7.

When the payment date arrives, the newly registered company has no cash available because it has also committed large funds to taking a lease of its new premises.

Task 1 (2 marks)

Identify whether the following statements are true or false.

	True	False
Super Solutions Ltd became a legal entity capable of entering into contracts in its own name on the 8th July 20X7		
Ruby is the promoter of Super Solutions Ltd		

Task 2 (2 marks)

Identify whether the following statements are true or false.

	True	False
The company is not bound under the contract, but is able to ratify or formally adopt it by ordinary resolution afterwards		
Ruby is personally liable for the contract under common law		

Task 3 (2 marks)

Identify whether the following statements are true or false.

	True	False
Ruby could have avoided liability under the contract by delaying completion of the contract until Super Solutions Ltd was registered		
Ruby can avoid liability under the contract by insisting the original contract is discharged, and replaced with a new contract in the name of Super Solutions Ltd		

(Total: 6 marks)

8 Capital and financing

Question 41

How is authority to allot shares required to be given to the directors of a public limited company?

(I)   By ordinary resolution.

(II)   By special resolution.

(III)   By the articles of association.

A   (I) or (III) only

B   (II) or (III) only

C   (III) only

D   (II) only

Question 42

A bonus issue is the issue of additional shares, typically fully paid up, to existing shareholders in proportion to their holdings.

A   True

B   False

By making a rights issue, a company requires existing shareholders to subscribe for additional shares in proportion to their holdings.

C   True

D   False

Question 43

As a general rule, is a company able to allot shares:

At a premium?

A   Yes

B   No

At a discount?

C   Yes

D   No

Question 44

Every charge entered into by a company has to be registered. Within how many days must registration take place?

A   7 days

B   14 days

C   21 days

D   28 days

Question 45

A characteristic of a floating charge is that:

It is a charge over a class of assets present and future:

A   Yes

B   No

It is a charge over a class of assets, which, in the ordinary course of the business of the company, will change:

C   Yes

D   No

Question 46

At the start of 20X6 Crums Ltd was faced with the need to raise a large amount of capital, which it was decided to raise through the mechanism of issuing a number of secured loans. In order to raise the capital Crums Ltd entered into the following transactions:

(i)   it borrowed £50,000 from Don secured by a floating charge. The loan was given and the charge created on 1 February. The charge was registered on 15 February

(ii)   it borrowed £50,000 from Else, also secured by a floating charge. This charge was created on the morning of 1 April and it was registered on 15 April

(iii) it borrowed £100,000 from Flash Bank plc. This loan was secured by a fixed charge. It was created in the afternoon of 1 April and was registered on 20 April

(iv)   it borrowed £100,000 from High Bank plc. This loan was secured by a fixed charge. It was created on 5 April and was registered on 15 April.

Task 1   **(2 marks)**

Which of the following statements are correct?

- **A charge must be registered at Companies House within 14 days of creation**

- **A charge must be registered at Companies House within 21 days of creation**

- **A charge must be registered at Companies House within 28 days of creation**

- **A charge must be registered at Companies House within 30 days of creation**

Task 2 (4 marks)

Identify the order of the debts in order of priority.

	1st	2nd	3rd	4th
Don – floating charge of £50,000				
Else – floating charge of £50,000				
Flash Bank plc – fixed charge of £100,000				
High Bank plc – fixed charge of £100,000				

(Total: 6 marks)

9 Directors

Question 47

Which of the following is NOT one of the matters to which directors must have regard when discharging their duty to promote the success of their company?

A The impact of the company's operations on the community and the environment.

B The interests of the creditors of the company.

C The need to act fairly as between the members of the company.

D The desirability of maintaining a reputation of high standards of business conduct.

Question 48

To dismiss a director under s168 Companies Act 2006 requires:

A An ordinary resolution with 14 days' notice.

B A special resolution with 14 days' notice.

C An ordinary resolution with 28 days' notice to the company.

D A special resolution with 28 days' notice to the company.

Question 49

A disqualification order against a director of a company on the ground that his conduct makes him unfit to be concerned in the management of a company may last for:

A   A minimum of 2 years and a maximum of 5 years

B   A minimum of 2 years and a maximum of 15 years

C   A minimum of 5 years with no maximum

D   A maximum of 15 years with no minimum

Question 50

Which ONE of the following statements about the duties of directors is correct?

A   The directors have a duty to ensure that no individual shareholder suffers a financial loss as a result of purchasing the company's shares.

B   Directors owe their duties to the members and the company.

C   Directors owe their duties to the company as a whole.

D   Directors have a duty to distribute a dividend to ordinary shareholders each year.

Question 51

If a director breaches his duty, which of the following never applies?

A   The director may have to account for a secret profit if he has made one.

B   If the director holds more than 50% of the shares he can ratify his own breach of duty at an annual general meeting.

C   The director can be automatically absolved from breach of duty by the articles of association.

D   The director may be liable in tort.

Question 52

Len is a director of Mod plc, but he also owns a majority interest in Nim Ltd.

Last year Mod plc entered into a contract to buy new machinery from Nim Ltd. Len attended the board meeting that approved the contract and voted in favour of it, without revealing any link with Nim Ltd.

At the same meeting the board of Mod plc decided not to pursue the development of a new product that had been offered to them by its inventor. Len, however, liked the new product and arranged for it to be produced by Nim Ltd. It has proved to be a great success and Nim Ltd has made a great deal of money from its production.

Task 1 **(2 marks)**

What of the following TWO statutory duties has Len most likely to have breached as a director of Mod plc?

- **S.172 – Duty to promote the success of the company**
- **S.173 – Duty to exercise independent judgement**
- **S.175 – Duty to avoid conflicts of interest**
- **S.177 – Duty to declare an interest in a proposed transaction or arrangement**

Task 2 **(2 marks)**

Identify whether the following statements are true or false.

	True	False
Len should have declared the full extent of his relationship with Nim Ltd		
Len should have waited at least twelve months before taking on the production of the inventor's product		

Task 3 **(2 marks)**

What remedy is Mod plc most likely to seek in relation to Len's breaches?

- **Damages for loss suffered**
- **An account of any profits made by Len on both contracts**
- **Rescission of contract between Mod plc and Nim Ltd**
- **Compulsory winding up of Nim Ltd**

(Total: 6 marks)

(Adapted from ACCA June 2000 examination)

10   Corporate administration

Question 53

Under which circumstances must the directors of a plc convene a general meeting?

A   If the company makes a trading loss.

B   If the company's net assets fall to half or less of its issued share capital.

C   If the company secretary resigns.

D   If the company's net assets fall to half or less of its called-up share capital.

Question 54

What is the quorum for a general meeting of a public limited company?

A   Two persons being members or proxies for members

B   Five persons being members or proxies for members

C   Two persons being members

D   Five persons being members

Question 55

Which of the following resolutions cannot be made by a public company?

A   Special resolutions

B   Written resolutions

C   Ordinary resolutions

D   Ordinary resolutions with special notice

Question 56

What is the minimum period of notice for an AGM?

A   7 days

B   14 days

C   21 days

D   28 days

11 Insolvency

Question 57

Which ONE of the following statements is incorrect?

A   A members' voluntary liquidation is used where the company is solvent.

B   A members' voluntary liquidation is usually commenced by the passing of a special resolution.

C   A creditors' voluntary liquidation is where the company is insolvent.

D   A creditors' voluntary liquidation is commenced by creditors.

Question 58

In a liquidation, how many months after the liquidator files his final report with the Registrar will a company be dissolved?

A   One month

B   Three months

C   Six months

D   Twelve months

Question 59

Which of the following is not an unsecured debt when a company goes into liquidation?

A   Arrears of holiday pay due to employees.

B   Money owed to HMRC for PAYE deductions.

C   Money owed to gas and electricity suppliers.

D   Money owed to an engineer for repairs carried out on company machinery.

Question 60

Which of the following is NOT a ground for compulsory winding up under the Insolvency Act 1986?

A   A public company has not been issued with a trading certificate within a year of incorporation.

B   The company has not paid a dividend during the last two years.

C   It is just and equitable to wind up the company.

D   The company has passed a special resolution to be wound up by the court.

12 Corporate and fraudulent behaviour

Question 61

Insider dealing is the offence of dealing in:

A   Shares

B   Securities

C   Cash

D   Property

Question 62

Which of the following Act covers market abuse?

A   Criminal Justice Act 1993

B   Proceeds of Crime Act 2002

C   Financial Services and Markets Act 2000

D   Company Director Disqualification Act 1986

Question 63

Which of the following is a money laundering offence?

A   Alerting client

B   Flagging up

C   Tipping off

D   Failure to detect

Question 64

Which of the following is a corporate bribery offence?

A   Bribing an individual

B   Receiving a bribe

C   Bribing a public foreign official

D   Failure to prevent bribery

Question 65

Nelly and Tim are directors of Bouncy Castles Ltd. Tim is not involved in the running of the business as he is too busy with other business ventures. Three months ago Nelly was told by the company's accountant that the company is facing mounting debts and that its assets and projected income is not sufficient to pay them. In spite of knowing this Nelly orders another 10 bouncy castles. Three months later, the company goes into compulsory liquidation.

Task 1 (2 marks)

Which TWO of the following statements are correct?

- **Fraudulent trading can only be a civil action**
- **Fraudulent trading can be a civil action and a criminal action**
- **Wrongful trading can only be a civil action**
- **Wrongful trading can be a civil action and a criminal action**

Task 2 (2 marks)

Which TWO of the following statements are correct?

- **Fraudulent trading applies only to directors and shadow directors**
- **Fraudulent trading must include dishonest intent**
- **Nelly is liable for fraudulent trading**
- **Tim is liable for fraudulent trading**

Task 3 (2 marks)

Which TWO of the following statements are correct?

- **Tim is not liable for wrongful trading**
- **Tim is liable for wrongful trading**
- **Wrongful trading applies only to directors and shadow directors**
- **Wrongful trading must include dishonest intent**

(Total: 6 marks)

Test your understanding answers

Question 1

B

The terms used ('action', 'claimant', 'damages') make it clear that these are civil proceedings.

Question 2

D

Question 3

C

Equitable remedies do not include damages.

Question 4

D

Obiter dicta has persuasive authority.

Question 5

A

The other options describe alternative rules of statutory interpretation.

Question 6

C

The limitation period for a contract made by deed (a specialty contract) is 12 years. All other contracts (simple contracts) have a limitation period of 6 years.

Question 7

C

A fax is treated in the same way as a telephone conversation. The message must be received for the acceptance to be communicated.

Question 8

D

A condition is a major term, going to the root of the contract. When breached, the injured party can repudiate the contract and claim damages. In contrast, when a warranty has been breached the injured party can only claim damages.

Question 9

B

(I) is not good consideration as it is no more than one would be expected to do in the circumstances. (III) is past consideration.

Question 10

B

This is a minor breach in relation to the whole contract, therefore the remedy is damages.

Question 11

C

The injured party is entitled to sue immediately: Hochster v De La Tour.

Question 12

D

Penalty clauses are void in contract law.

Question 13

B

Legal relations are presumed in commercial transactions.

Question 14

B

The facts are very similar to that of Thompson v LMS Railway.

Question 15

C

Consideration must have some identifiable value ('sufficient') but does not need be equal in value to the consideration received in return ('adequate').

Question 16

Task 1

	True	False
An offer cannot be made to the whole world		X
The advert in the trade journal is an offer		X

Task 2

	True	False
Eleanor's letter to Hilary is a counter-offer		X
Hilary's first reply to Eleanor is a counter-offer	X	

Task 3

	True	False
The effect of a counter-offer is to bring the original offer to an end	X	
Hilary's second reply to Eleanor accepting £10,000 constitutes acceptance		X

Question 17

D

This is a matter for the court to decide in assessing damages once negligence has been shown (i.e. once the claimant has proved A, B and C satisfactorily).

Question 18

B

There does not need to be any relationship at all.

C

The question of public policy is one of several tests applied, but if public policy dictates that no duty should exist, then none shall exist.

Question 19

B

This may be relevant when assessing damages but is not relevant to whether a duty of care exists at all.

Question 20

B

Since the Caparo case, it is clear that the auditor's duty of care not to act negligently is owed to the company only.

Question 21

Task 1

- There must have been a loss made to make a claim in negligence
- There must be a causal link to make a claim for negligence

Task 2

- Pure financial loss

Task 3

- The accountant owes a duty of care to Brad
- The accountant will be liable for the losses which Brad has suffered

Question 22

D

This suggests that Indira is a contractor but in itself is not conclusive.

Question 23

C

In accordance with Employment Rights Act 1996.

Question 24

D

An employee is only under an obligation to obey orders which are lawful and reasonable.

Question 25

A

An employee is entitled to 1.5 week's pay for each year of service from the age of 41 plus up to a maximum of 20 years.

Question 26

B

An employee who has continuous employment of between one month and 24 months is entitled to at least one week's notice.

Question 27

Task 1

	True	False
An employee works under a contract for services		X
An independent contractor works under a contract of service		X

Task 2

	Provision of Equipment	Right of Substitution
Self-employed		X
Employed	X	

Task 3

	Claim	Not claim
Redundancy		X
Wrongful dismissal	X	

Question 28

C

Question 29

D

Although Simon acted in good faith and possibly reasonably, the law is unlikely to say that an agency of necessity has arisen, because it is not inclined to allow a person to be bound by the act of a complete stranger.

Question 30

B

It is the conduct of the principal that might give rise to an agency by estoppel, not the conduct of the 'agent'.

D

The contract can only be enforced against Jean personally.

Question 31

Task 1

- The contract is made between the principal and the third party

Task 2

- There is an agency relationship by express agreement

Task 3

	True	False
Andrea has the express authority to purchase roses and statues		X
Lady Gertrude would be liable to settle the invoice for the roses and statues	X	

Question 32

B

This is true of a limited liability partnership but not an ordinary partnership.

C

Question 33

D

A, B, and C all have a separate legal personality.

Question 34

Task 1

- There must be a partnership agreement
- The partnership must be registered at Companies House

Task 2

	True	False
A partnership is liable for contracts made by a partner if he is acting within his express authority only		X
Dorian cannot make a claim against the partnership as she entered into the contract with Frank		X

Task 3

- Sharon, Tracy and Frank

Question 35

D

Question 36

C

Question 37

D

The Eley case illustrates that the statutory rules only apply to rights as a shareholder.

Question 38

B

A company cannot be liable on a pre-incorporation contract as the company does not exist at the time the contract is made.

Question 39

B

This is very similar to the facts of Gilford Motor Co Ltd v Horne.

Question 40

Task 1

	True	False
Super Solutions Ltd became a legal entity capable of entering into contracts in its own name on the 8th July 20X7		X
Ruby is the promoter of Super Solutions Ltd	X	

Task 2

	True	False
The company is not bound under the contract, but is able to ratify or formally adopt it by ordinary resolution afterwards		X
Ruby is personally liable for the contract under common law	X	

Task 3

	True	False
Ruby could have avoided liability under the contract by delaying completion of the contract until Super Solutions Ltd was registered	X	
Ruby can avoid liability under the contract by insisting the original contract is discharged, and replaced with a new contract in the name of Super Solutions Ltd		X

Question 41

A

Question 42

A

D

There is no obligation on the members to take additional shares.

Question 43

A

A sum equal to the premium on each share must be transferred to a share premium account.

D

Shares cannot be issued at a discount on nominal value.

Question 44

C

Question 45

A

A floating charge is typically over a class of assets of a company, present and future, with which the company may continue to deal prior to crystallisation of the charge.

C

A floating charge typically covers assets that change in the ordinary course of business and only fixes to those assets at the time of crystallisation.

Question 46

Task 1

- A charge must be registered at Companies House within 21 days of creation

Task 2

	1st	2nd	3rd	4th
Don – floating charge of £50,000			X	
Else – floating charge of £50,000				X
Flash Bank plc – fixed charge of £100,000	X			
High Bank plc – fixed charge of £100,000		X		

KAPLAN PUBLISHING

Question 47

B

This is not one of the six matters listed.

Question 48

C

Question 49

B

Question 50

C

Question 51

C

The articles cannot exempt directors from liability.

Question 52

Task 1

- S.175 – Duty to avoid conflicts of interest
- S.177 – Duty to declare an interest in a proposed transaction or arrangement

Task 2

	True	False
Len should have declared the full extent of his relationship with Nim Ltd	X	
Len should have waited at least twelve months before taking on the production of the inventor's product		X

Task 3

- An account of any profits made by Len on both contracts

Question 53

D

Question 54

A

Question 55

B

Only private companies can pass a written resolution.

Question 56

C

For an AGM 21 days notice is required, for a GM 14 days notice is required.

Question 57

D

A creditors' voluntary liquidation is usually commenced by the passing of a special resolution.

Question 58

B

Question 59

A

This would rank as a preferential creditor.

Question 60

B

Question 61

B

Question 62

C

Question 63

C

Question 64

D

Question 65

Task 1

- Fraudulent trading can be a civil action and a criminal action
- Wrongful trading can only be a civil action

Task 2

- Fraudulent trading must include dishonest intent
- Nelly is liable for fraudulent trading

Task 3

- Tim is liable for wrongful trading
- Wrongful trading applies only to directors and shadow directors